The Podcast Handbook

The Podcast Handbook

Create It, Market It, Make It Great

Jacqueline N. Parke

Foreword by David S. Weinstein

McFarland & Company, Inc., Publishers
Jefferson, North Carolina

ISBN (print) 978-1-4766-8193-1
ISBN (ebook) 978-1-4766-4453-0

Library of Congress and British Library
cataloguing data are available

Library of Congress Control Number 2022004089

Front cover image: The author retooled her sports webzine into a successful podcast (author's collection)

Printed in the United States of America

McFarland & Company, Inc., Publishers
Box 611, Jefferson, North Carolina 28640
www.mcfarlandpub.com

This book is dedicated to my loving and supportive parents,
Gloria H. McDonnough-Parke (1940–2005)
and Keith "Sticky" Parke (1936–2017).

Table of Contents

Acknowledgments

To my first podcast hosts, my brother Maurice "Mo" Parke and his good friend Jason "J-Lee" Lee. I started it all with both of you and I'm forever grateful. Special thanks to Alison Preece, my little bookworm, actress, friend and motivator. You encouraged me to believe in myself and have supported me from day one. The proposal and subsequent book could not have happened without your incredible insight, writing and editing. To my sounding board, editor, writer and friend, and also *HWTP*'s first guest and host, the incomparable sportswriter and biographer Bill Gutman: I could not have done any of this without you. Your guidance has been immeasurable.

This book is a culmination of *Huddlin' with the Pros* throughout the years, from the time it first launched as an online sports magazine in 1996 until its reinvention in 2014 as a podcast. It is only fitting to thank the people who were there from the beginning, such as five-time Super Bowl Champion and NFL assistant coach, Thomas "Pepper" Johnson. I appreciate your friendship and support with all my crazy ventures. You never say no and I'm proud to call you a friend. Then there is former beat writer and news bureau chief Sandra Frederick, who brought credibility to our editorial content. Thank you for that and, most importantly, thank you for your friendship. And also Rori Brown-Pitt, my first business partner, who kept me organized at *Huddlin'*, and who also shared my love of food.

HWTP Sports Talk had some great hosts in the beginning and without them the show would not have been possible. Madison Carter, fellow Cuse alum, now a local NBC News anchor for WKBW Buffalo, New York, I'm so proud of you. Other hosts who helped build the show were Champ Jordan, LeAna Masiello and David Starr. My appreciation to all the terrific interns from over the years—I am forever grateful for your talents and dedication.

David S. Weinstein, what can I say? You have brought enormous credibility to *Huddlin'* and I cannot believe how lucky I am to have found you. Francine Weinstein, thanks for keeping us in check and sharing your husband with us on Wednesday evenings.

Two great educators who provided priceless guidance and feedback to this book are Amrika Maikoo-Mann and my cousin Lunie Campbell. Tresa Sanders (love you, girl) and Luther "Uncle Luke" Campbell, thank you both for giving me the opportunity to produce and edit *The Luke Show*. It was challenging to say the least, but I am thankful for the invaluable experience I gained.

To my ride-or-dies, Wendy Fahey, as well as author and life coach Marion Franklin: thank you both for always showing up when I needed you the most. When I'm down you lift me up, and I love that my enemies become yours without question. That type of loyalty is rare. I love you ladies.

I am also blessed to have the support of my family, Jillian and Billy Gallagher Sr., my nephews William Jr., Jordan and Keith Parke II, and my beautiful niece who is wise beyond her years, Britney Gallagher. My two little schnookums, Zayn and Isabella Gallagher, AKA the mischievous twins, AKA the devilish twins who have brought so much light during a very dark time. Nana and Sticky would have adored you both. My dearest friends who are my family, Shelley and Dwayne Wiggins, the beautiful Dickerson family, Shirley, Gregg and Sherrill—thank you all for always making me feel special, for the unconditional support and, most importantly, for your love. To my extended family, Suzette "Snoozie" Williams, Dr. Maxine and Stanley LeeFatt, Faye and Mario Smith, Simone and Patrick Greenwood and Stephaney Thomas-Musson: thank you for your unconditional love and caring for my family and me, and for making sure that we were all right during the dark times. You all are very special and I love you dearly. To my cousin and composer extraordinaire, Craig Deleon, thank you for the great jingle for *HWTP Sports Talk*. To my sweetest cousin, Melanie Smith-Lewandowski, thank you for your support after I lost my father in 2017. Your love and kindness have been immeasurable. I love you, kiddo.

I'm a proud graduate of the S.I. Newhouse School of Public Communications at Syracuse University, a great program with incredible professors. You challenged me beyond belief and I'm blessed to have been one of the first graduates of the S. I. Newhouse School of Public Communications at Syracuse University online master's degree program. It was worth every penny. Special thanks to four terrific Syracuse University educators for all your support and contributions to my book proposal. You did not hesitate. I'm truly grateful to Lee Buttolph, Clay Crocker, Christine Rushton, and Leah Rachel Stacy.

Last but not least, to my incredible parents. My mom, Gloria "Sweet G" McDonnough-Parke, and my dad, Keith "Sticky" Parke, your love and support were immeasurable. I was inspired by my dad and in awe of my mom. She was my first investor. Céline Dion's song "Because You Loved Me" is dear to me because the lyrics encompass exactly how I felt about my mom and what she meant to me. Mom, "I'm everything I am because you loved me."

Foreword

by David S. Weinstein

Caricature of author and David S. Weinstein (author's collection).

What is a podcast? If you are reading this book, you probably already know the answer to that question and are eager to learn how you, too, can have a successful podcast.

I initially met Jackie through an email about six years ago. She was producing *HWTP Sports Talk* and was the driving force behind the program. I had been interviewed by a reporter who was writing a story about the Drug Enforcement Agency's investigation of the National Football League and Jackie was asking me to speak about that story on her podcast, which they called *Huddlin'* for short. That was the start of my relationship with the world of podcasting, Jackie, and the *Huddlin'* family. Over the years, we have developed a personal and professional relationship and eventually, despite the significant geographical distance between us, had a chance to meet each other in person. Jackie has a passion for broadcasting, one that comes to her both genetically and naturally. Her dad, "Sticky," would be proud of what she has accomplished.

Jackie has an all-in personality and work ethic. Whatever task she undertakes, she does it with a one-hundred-percent commitment. *The Podcast Handbook* is another example of that commitment. Jackie knows that in order to understand a topic, you have to examine the topic and then learn from the history of that topic. *The Podcast Handbook* takes you back to the early roots of radio, then moves forward through the evolution of radio broadcasting, the Internet, and finally podcasting. It is more than a how-to book, it is also a "how-can" book, one that enables you to learn good habits, as well as avoid the bad habits and mistakes you can make along the way.

At *HWTP Sports Talk*, where I went from being a guest to a host, we are known for our "no holds barred good questions" by former NBA player Adonal Foyle, and for having "informed conversations" by Linda Robertson, columnist for the *Miami Herald*. That did not just come from me. Jackie and I have never been afraid to seek out any guest, no matter how big or small he or she might be, nor any topic connected in some small way to the world of sports. *HWTP Sports Talk* was never meant to be about the X's and O's. It is about stimulating conversation and bringing social issues into the world of sports. With this philosophy, we have been able to talk with sports legends like Tommy John and Evander Holyfield. But we have also spoken with sports reporting legends like Melissa Ludtke, the first female sports journalist to be allowed into an MLB locker room, and Laura Okmin, an NFL sideline reporter who has founded Galvanize, a program training young women entering the sports world on and off camera. We have also addressed topics like racism, discrimination, sexual assault, sexual orientation and gender identity. To accomplish this, Jackie had to develop the skills necessary to create, market, promote, produce, edit, and push out the podcast.

Podcasting is our generation's version of the town crier. Long before there were newspapers, radio or television, people roamed around the towns and cities screaming out the news of the day. This method of distributing the news slowly evolved to print, then to radio, then television, the Internet and then podcasting. But like all of its predecessors, knowing how to use your method of delivery is as important as the product itself.

The Podcast Handbook will become your bible and roadmap for turning your idea into an actual podcast. What platform should you use, should it be live or taped, one host or two? When, if ever, is it the right time to add video? If your mission is to advance the goals of your company, how will you get the backing you need to push the project forward? More importantly, how will you keep the podcast fresh and interesting every week? *The Podcast Handbook* also looks to the future, both of podcasting technology and the potential regulatory efforts from the Federal Communications Commission (FCC).

So why read this book instead of any other guide to podcasting? The answer is simple: because Jackie has been through the process and while she has made a few mistakes (we all do—that is why they are called mistakes), she has had more success than failure. She will help you avoid some common errors and save you time, as well as frustration. Plus, Jackie is a risk-taker, so she has already exposed the process to the extremes, meaning that you do not have to.

The Podcast Handbook is a road trip on a journey that has covered a lot of miles and has many more miles to go. I'm thrilled to have been a passenger on Jackie's journey, and I look forward to putting in more miles with someone who has taught me a lot and has made me a part of her podcasting family.

I hope that your copy of *The Podcast Handbook* becomes dog-eared and tabbed frequently as you embark on your own journey to deliver your message, whatever that might be.

There is an age-old proverb, "The tongue can paint what the eyes cannot see." *The Podcast Handbook* will provide you with a palette to create a masterpiece from your thoughts and ideas that everyone will want to admire.

David S. Weinstein is a partner at Jones Walker LLP. He has decades of experience as a criminal defense attorney and also as a federal and state prosecutor. He has also appeared as a legal analyst in print media as well as on a number of national, international, and local television news programs for networks that include ABC, CBS, NBC, PBS, CNBC, MSNBC, CNN, FOX, CTV, and the BBC World News.

Preface

The Podcast Handbook: Create It, Market It, Make It Great is really a culmination of all the journalistic and entrepreneurial steps I have climbed throughout my life. I was born in Kingston, Jamaica, the daughter of hard-working parents, Gloria McDonnough-Parke and Keith "Sticky" Parke. From them I learned the value of education and the importance of hard work. As the youngest of three children, I was the most outspoken and the one who ultimately developed an entrepreneurial bent. I was also closest to our father. Do not get me wrong—he loved his children equally, but I always had a special connection to him.

I wasn't intimidated by his large stature and voice, and I grew to idolize him. I always wanted to listen to music with him, watch what he was watching and accompany him whenever I could. We connected through music and sports, and I loved sitting at the table with him and his friends listening to them discuss politics over their many glasses of rum. I enjoyed hearing his stories about how he was Bob Marley's engineer and how he also recorded Jamaica's first million-record single, "My Boy Lollipop," by Millie Small.

My dad and I came to America first, in 1968 when I was three. We settled in Corona, Queens, in New York City, living right around the corner from the great trumpeter Louis Armstrong. Shortly afterward, my mom followed, as did my sister a few years later. My brother came to live with us after we had moved to New City, a New York City suburb. In 1977, at the age of 15, I was sworn in with my parents and siblings as United States citizens, one of the proudest days of my life.

My father worked at CBS for over 25 years as a senior radio technician before retiring. I would often sit in awe watching him edit audio reels. One of the shows he would edit was CBS Radio's *World Tonight*, which aired on AM 880 in New York. The show was a 15-minute round up of world news—old-fashioned radio. I remember the distinctive sound the tape would make when it was rewound or fast-forwarded. Dad would stop and rewind, stop and rewind, and then cut the tape. He kept doing that throughout the reel. Then when airtime rolled around, the anchor would discuss the news and then stop so my father could play whatever it was he was editing. I could not believe what I was hearing. It was seamless and just flowed with the show. Once the reel played, the anchor would move onto the next story.

CBS Radio was located at 524 West 57th Street in New York City, and I felt as though I grew up in the halls of that building. It was a great experience watching my dad work and also seeing soap opera stars, celebrities and newscasters roaming the halls or simply leaving the building. My dad took me to meet the great Walter Cronkite. While I did not know then that I was meeting a legendary newscaster, Mr. Cronkite was kind and greeted me with a big smile. Since I grew up in that atmosphere, I have always had a fascination with journalism and celebrities. I also think that I acquired my natural editing skills from watching my father work.

In the late 1980s, I created a magazine called *A Sign of the Times*. I was obsessed with Prince and named it after his song, "Sign O' the Times." I remember going to my mom and asking her for $2,500 so that I could create a color print markup of the magazine. She agreed to give me the money, and the markup turned out great. I then sent it out to Hudson News, one of the leading magazine and newspaper distributors in New York, and also to various record labels. One by one, the record companies contacted me to say they would support it. The most valuable response was from Hudson News, because they agreed to distribute it. At the age of 22, I had absolutely no clue as to what I was doing. I could not even fully grasp or seize the opportunity that was being presented. Unfortunately, I let the opportunity fall by the wayside because I had no mentor or guidance.

In 1990, I was offered my dream job as a marketing assistant at Jive-RCA Records. Needless to say, I was really excited about working there. While at Jive, I met a young hip-hop manager named Tony Rahsaan, who was a part of the original Boogie Down Productions rap group, and we soon became good friends. He was smart and, like me, a natural entrepreneur with great ideas. He went on to manage some great rap artists through 40th Street Black Music & Management, a company he formed with former rapper Derrick "D-Nice" Jones. When I left Jive, Tony and I stayed in touch. I remember receiving a call from him in the summer of 1994. He told me he was starting a hip-hop trade magazine and needed my help. He explained the concept, and I thought, "Wow, that is really innovative."

The magazine was to be the *Billboard* of hip-hop music. *Billboard* is a trade publication that lists all the top selling albums and singles by genre. At that time, however, the one genre it would ignore was hip-hop, and Tony wanted to fill that void with *The Four One One*. It was a publication that looked similar to the entertainment trade publication *The Hollywood Reporter* but included hip-hop music news and sales charts. The magazine created buzz within the industry, with artists embracing the "no-fluff" rule in our articles. In fact, *Vibe Magazine*, a publication created by legendary record producer and musician Quincy Jones, offered to purchase *The Four One One*. The publication, including my article ("Rappers appear on female charity compilation," Parke & Rahsaan, 1995), is stored on Cornell University Library's Digital Collections in the Adler Hip Hop Archive. The archive was created by Bill Adler, a noted journalist, legendary publicist and founding Vice President of Publicity at Def Jam Recordings. The articles and publications in this archive offer an unprecedented view into hip-hop's history.

One of my proudest moments at the trade magazine was when Fredro Starr, one of the founding members of the rap group Oynx, read my article out loud in front of his band and me. He praised it because I wrote about its newly released album at the time, *All We Got Iz Us* (1995), and did not criticize the album, just stated the facts. That was one thing Tony instilled in us, "no-fluff, just the facts," and it worked. I began making a name for myself among the artists and music executives, made many friends and learned a great deal about the business.

Using *The Four One One* as a model, I produced my online sports magazine, and later my podcasts following that same formula. While researching story ideas for *The Four One One*, I read that Shaquille O'Neal was releasing a hip-hop album. His music publicist at the time was a big fan of *The Four One One*, so I reached out to her and asked if Shaq would do an interview for the magazine. He agreed. It was during that interview when I first realized that many athletes have off-court, off-field dreams and businesses.

Through *The Four One One*, I also met Tresa Sanders, the publicist for Def Jam under Adler's tutelage. She became, and still is, one of my dearest friends. I remember telling her that I wanted to start a sports entertainment magazine that focused on the off-court and off-field activities of top athletes. She thought it was a great idea and I asked her to be my business partner. We tried to come up with a name for the publication and she suggested *Huddlin' with the Pros*. I loved the name, and it stuck. As a top publicist in the business, Tresa was very busy and constantly being pulled in several directions at once. So, she gracefully bowed out and told me to keep the name, which I did.

I launched *Huddlin' with the Pros* in the late 1990s, which I promoted as the first behind-the-scenes, online sports magazine that focused on the off-field aspects of sports. Athletes and others in the sports industry became immediate supporters. In 1998, the *Rockland Journal News* described *Huddlin' with the Pros* as "a mix of *Sports Illustrated*'s flair with words [and] *ESPN The Magazine*'s love of photos" (Havsy, 1998).

Huddlin' conducted one of the last interviews with stunt legend Evel

Knievel before his death in 2007. The article was quoted by the Associated Press in 1999 (Gallagher, 1999) and also picked up by other media outlets. The *New York Beacon* cover story called us "one of the liveliest online sports entertainment magazines to hit the Internet" (Bernard, 2000). The magazine was also included in a college marketing book, *Sports Marketing: A Strategic Perspective, Second Edition* by Mathew D. Shank (Pearson/Prentice Hall College Division, 2002).

Unfortunately, *Huddlin' with the Pros* folded in 2002 because of a lack of marketing. Editorially we were strong, but as one EA sports marketer said to me in 1999, "Wow, how come I have never heard of you?" I had focused fully on the editorial aspects of the publication and completely ignored the marketing. I thought if we were strong editorially the ads would find us, but I was still somewhat naive and inexperienced. Advertisers just do not find you without the proper marketing.

I could not let *Huddlin'* go and, in 2013, I decided I wanted to relaunch the webzine. I reached out to Sandra Bush, who was one of the original writers for *Huddlin'* and one of the major reasons why *Huddlin'* was so strong editorially. At the time, she was writing for the *Daytona Beach News Journal* in Daytona Beach, Florida, as a NASCAR beat writer. Whenever Sandra would interview a driver like Tony Stewart for the *Journal*, she would structure some of the questions to meet the editorial format of *Huddlin'*. This was how we learned that Tony Stewart bred greyhound racing dogs. She did the same kind of research with Jeff Gordon and other NASCAR greats. It legitimized us and we caught the eye of publicists, athletes, and the various sports leagues.

When we spoke in 2013, I asked her if she would be interested in restarting *Huddlin'*. She was more than excited, so we reached out to everyone and even had a conference call with Jeff Gordon's father and manager John Bickford. He loved the name but said he did not think it would work. The problem was, what was so unique in the 1990s was now widespread. We were met with this same answer everywhere. Almost every program and publication had learned to use human-interest, narrative storytelling to enhance their featured profiles and sports news stories. Not to mention, athletes now had their own social media pages.

I was disheartened and remember even crying at my desk. One of my co-workers at the law firm where I work talked to her sister, who was a publicist. She put me in touch with a friend who owned a marketing company. When I explained *Huddlin'*, like the others he quickly stated that it was nothing new. He then said, "Jackie, do yourself a favor and create a podcast version of your magazine." I had never heard that concept before; it was foreign and sounded daunting. He explained it and told me to try using Blog Talk Radio, a popular podcasting platform that hosts and records your podcast. I started out with the free subscription, which I eventually upgraded and relaunched *Huddlin' with the Pros* as a podcast with the same core format of off-field/off-court discussions, mixing sports with politics and social issues. My dad suggested I make the name call letters, so I called it *HWTP Sports Talk*. It all worked. My podcasting career had begun.

In 2017, I founded Sweet G. Communications, a marketing and podcast production firm. Sweet G. Communications is named in honor of my mother Gloria. Sweet G. was the nickname given to her by my father. Under the Sweet G. Communications banner, I am now the executive producer of *HWTP Sports Talk with David Weinstein*, a podcast that discusses social and political issues with a sports focus, and a show that has seen an audience growth of 500% in the past three years. I also produce *The Luke Show*, a podcast that discusses pop culture, sports, and politics, hosted by hip-hop pioneer and producer Luther "Uncle Luke" Campbell, and I am planning an upcoming sports podcast with former NFL player, five-time Super Bowl champion and former New England Patriots coach Pepper Johnson called *Pep Talk with Pepper Johnson*.

In addition to my producing and marketing work, giving back to the community is extremely important to me. I founded Bowl for Life, a 501(c)(3) non-profit organization that benefits the National Marrow Donor Program's "Be the Match" initiative. Through bowling events, the organization focused on helping people of color, because I was passionate about assisting with the national crisis of securing donations for people in that demographic. Bowl for Life sought out African Americans, Asians, Native Americans and Hispanics, registering more than 200 people of color to the national registry. Out of those 200-plus people, two were lifesaving matches.

I now have over 25 years of marketing, business development and communications experience at a top tier law firm, as well as in the sports and entertainment industries. In addition, as an adjunct professor at a local college, I designed a course called "Podcast: Creation and Strategy." I'm also a consultant teaching podcasts to executives and attorneys.

I received a Master of Science degree in Communications from S.I. Newhouse School of Public Communications at Syracuse University and a Bachelor of Science degree in Communications-Public Relations from Mercy College. All of this has helped prepare me for writing *The Podcast Handbook: Create It, Market It, Make It Great*.

Introduction

The Podcast Handbook: Create It, Market It, Make It Great is an overview of the industry, from its roots in radio to the proliferation of genres, topics, and styles in today's podcasts, both individual and corporate. This book will present a thorough examination of the rise and enduring popularity of podcasts, dissecting trends, audience demographics and game-changing podcast series. *The Podcast Handbook* will cover programming, platform options, advertising and sponsorships, as well as evolving regulations from the Federal Communications Commission, helping the reader navigate the many available structures of a podcast. In addition, the book will provide exercises for the reader, which can double as class discussion topics. The structure of the book is conducive to a lesson plan on the topic of podcasting.

Obviously, the text will draw heavily on my extensive experience as a podcast producer and marketer, as well as my time as a Business Development and Communications student, while turning over every relevant stone in the podcasting realm. There are case studies placed throughout the book from experts in the field, which will enable the reader to draw conclusions based on relevant real-life experiences.

I will share lessons and anecdotes from my work as a producer of three podcasts: *HWTP Sports Talk with David Weinstein* featuring five-time Super Bowl champion Pepper Johnson and *The Luke Show* with hip-hop pioneer Luther "Uncle Luke" Campbell. My own experience will serve as my strongest point of reference.

To give students a better idea of the evolution of podcasting, there will be a look back at America's Golden Age of Radio, drawing a parallel with the popularity of podcasts today in order to provide insight into this enduring audio medium. It will include the rise of radio through the Golden Age of the 1930s and '40s, the advent of television and the Internet, and radio's evolution into satellite radio and finally podcasts. The growth of radio from its inception had a major impact on Americans during the decades of the 1930s and 1940s, which was a time of economic struggle during the Great

Depression and World War II. Americans gathered around their radios for news about the war as well as much-needed entertainment during those difficult times.

This section will include the current state of media in the digital age, which has led to vast changes in how we receive our information and communicate with each other. In the midst of this fast-paced digital age, the rise of podcasts is something of a unique phenomenon, partly because the form actually brings back aspects of the Golden Age of Radio, especially in the personal way it reaches its audience.

As with all new and innovative forms of communication, there are key moments in the history of podcasting that serve as markers in the medium's upward trajectory. As examples, I will highlight podcasts such as *Serial*, an award-winning investigative journalism podcast hosted by journalist Sarah Koenig. The podcast investigates the 1999 murder of Hae Min Lee, an 18-year-old Baltimore County high school student. Her ex-boyfriend, Adnan Syed, was convicted of killing her. The popularity of this podcast gained global attention and has given rise to an HBO special called *The Case Against Adnan Syed*. This was a turning point in the popularity of podcasts, with the numbers of both broadcasts and listeners skyrocketing in the months and years after *Serial* debuted.

Highlighting *Serial* and other popular podcasts will enable an exploration of the elements that make certain podcasts successful, and how the big players have brought the medium into the communications mainstream.

We will examine podcasting trends, both historic and current, as well as projections for the future. Statistics on podcast listenership will be used to show the growth of the medium while providing insight on audience demographics as well as the popularity of various genres, tones and subjects. Data on advertising dollars and the growth of in-house company podcasts will prompt a discussion of the use and popularity of podcasts across various industries.

Additionally, there are a number of things the neophyte podcaster must consider before beginning his or her podcasting quest. *The Podcast Handbook* will outline the practical steps needed for an individual to create a podcast. The first step is to identify the motivation behind the endeavor. Just blindly starting a podcast is a recipe for disaster. In my experience, most podcasts fail because the creator has no direction. I'll detail the ways to outline production goals and then determine the kind of content to be shared with listeners, as well as how to determine the ideal audience. This book includes exercises to create hands-on experience through research, much of which will come from my personal experience in creating my podcasts.

The many factors that go into deciding whether to broadcast live or to pre-tape a show will also be examined. Broadcasting live comes with its own set of challenges that will be described in detail, along with ways to overcome them. Also important are the types of skills that are required for a live broadcast, such as developing the talent for good verbal communication and the ability to think quickly on your feet. Then there are the methods for preparing a live show, including detailed blueprints for organizational tools such as show outlines and talking points, as well as other tips for producing a smooth-running show. Readers will also gain an understanding of the benefits and pitfalls of both broadcasting live and pre-recording, making it easier for them to choose the best way to go.

Choosing the appropriate podcasting platform is extremely important. There are not many platforms that will provide seamless live broadcasting. In fact, there is only one that does this well—Blog Talk Radio. There are many more options for podcasting hosting platforms for pre-recorded shows, such as Libsyn and Podomatic. Chapter 6, "Choosing Your Podcasting Platform," will examine the differences between the various platforms so that readers will be able to make an informed decision as to which platforms are suitable for their podcasting needs. It will also provide them with a framework for evaluating future platforms that may enter the market.

Editing your podcast is one of the most important tasks a podcaster will have to master. It is also the most daunting. *The Podcast Handbook* will provide a detailed roadmap to a successful self-editing process. It will include an evaluation of the different tools on the market, from free platforms to more sophisticated programs such as Adobe Premiere. Various scenarios that can occur during both a live broadcast and a pre-taped show will be discussed in order to help new podcasters decide whether they should work to learn this skill or simply outsource it.

Also important are the roles and expectations for a host, co-host, and producer. You must first decide whether you are going to be your own host. To help with this decision, there will be interesting tips and a fun interactive exercise akin to a personality test. Readers will learn that since podcasts are an audio medium, hosting requires special skills. Keeping a captive audience can be difficult if you have a dry or reticent personality, or if you cannot think quickly on your feet. These are some of the skills you need to self-evaluate before deciding whether you feel you can host your own show or if you need to enlist others. There will also be an examination of the pros and cons for each position so you can put together the best podcast possible.

The "Podcasting for Business" chapter is geared towards serious podcasters—specifically, the marketing and communications professionals who want to help a company or cause growth. While doing my research, I realized that not many businesses understand what a viable marketing tool a podcast can be. Hillary Nappi, an attorney in New York City, spoke to the importance of podcasts when she told me, "This guide is essential for lawyers who are novices at marketing. Podcasts are our generation's radio, and for any lawyer who knows how to be persuasive, this book will provide the groundwork one needs to break into a new area of marketing."

The legal sector, along with other industries such as financial services, have special needs when it comes to using podcasts properly. These are addressed in the "Podcasting for Business" chapter, giving readers valuable business development insights to include in their arsenal. The chapter shows ways in which both young and established professionals can use podcasting as a viable marketing tool, and how marketing and communications departments are using podcasts in the digital age. It includes a contributing column by an attorney on how to leverage podcasts to build connections and career opportunities in a professional services firm.

Readers will learn how to implement a podcast for their company through both research and their knowledge of the company's mission and goals. They will also learn how to create a solid podcast proposal to present to their company, which will help them get the green light to proceed.

The "Podcasting for Business" chapter will also provide an overview of podcasts and the role played by the Federal Communications Commission, as well as insight into the agency's current work in the field. As of this time, podcasts are not regulated, but there will be discussions on if and why there may be future regulations.

The Podcast Handbook will also provide hands-on experience for new podcasters. Educators, as well as individual readers, will be able to use the tools provided to assist in helping both themselves and others to create and record their podcast. Most podcasting platforms offer a free level that is somewhat limited, but the readers will still be able to learn how to create their own podcast through hands-on experience. The "Let's Create Your Podcast" section will provide exercises and class discussions that will encourage students to create their own show. The exercises will also be helpful to individual readers. It will teach readers how to create an organized outline for their show, as well as a production schedule, scripts and a plan for show topics. They will learn the value of research and the use of evergreen stories—stories that have a long shelf life—along with handling breaking news for podcasters who tape their shows. Finally, the chapter will show ways of securing guests through research and the creation of pitch letters.

"Perception is reality" is the motto I live by when it comes to marketing. Readers who would like to have a career in podcasting, be it as a host or producer, will learn how to develop a very solid marketing concept. When I started *HWTP Sports Talk*, I wanted my podcast to be seen as professional and worthy, so as to attract interesting guests. Over the years, I have teamed up with professional hosts, such as Bill Gutman and David S.

Weinstein, invested in the creation of a logo, developed an online presence and honed a strong pitch letter. I knew exactly what my podcast content would be—social issues with a sports focus. It was worth the hard work, because we have had impressive guests from the world of sports, as well as award-winning journalists.

Not everyone, however, will have the means to hire an artist or web developer to create their brand. Therefore, *The Podcast Handbook* will show readers how to create professional-looking content and designs through inexpensive and free platforms such as SquareSpace and WordPress. They will also learn about the various podcasting platforms such as Podbean and Podomatic, which can provide attractive artwork for their podcast page on their website. There are also platforms that create inexpensive jingles for your show's intros, breaks and outros. All will be explained.

In addition, *The Podcast Handbook* will show new podcasters various ways to market their shows, including on and offline marketing through grassroots efforts. It will also explain how transcripts of your shows can promote Search Engine Optimization, which will increase your number of listeners. Then there is the power of hashtags, something that should not be underestimated.

Podcasting doesn't come without issues. Readers will learn about the various issues that often arise during a live or pre-taped show and how to deal with them, such as the common problem of guests talking over each other, as well as communication between the host, producer and guests. Ways to handle these potential problems will be illustrated by free video platforms. Other issues that may occur are no-show guests, guests cursing (cursing may not fit your format), offensive listener call-ins or unmuting the wrong line. As a producer or host, you have to be prepared for anything.

Throughout the book, you will see editorial pieces called *Insights*. These essays were written by professionals in various industries, and they provide valuable information and tips to enhance your podcasting experience.

Finally, I will discuss in detail how video platforms can be used as a visual aid for the host, guest and producer. Having a video component is a great way to diminish the issue of guests talking over each other, and promotes better communication between host and producer, as well as between host and guest.

This may seem like a great deal of material to absorb, but producing a great podcast is not easy. There is much to learn, much to implement, and much work to do. *The Podcast Handbook* will lay it all out, one step at a time. Not only will it serve as a "how to" for students, but also as a reference book that podcasters can return to as often as needed after their program is up, running and flourishing.

Part I

Industry Overview: The Golden Age to the Digital Age

CHAPTER 1

The Golden Age to the Digital Age

In a sense, radio was the earliest form of social media, the first means created to reach masses of people, and a medium that endures today, but in a very different way from its beginnings. Early radio was a far cry from podcasting, but it can accurately be called its great-grandfather. While the principles of radio, or wireless communication, began late in the nineteenth century, it was in the first half of the twentieth that radio grew and thrived as a medium the public came to love. The decades of the 1930s and 1940s are generally referred to as the Golden Age of Radio, a time when families would gather around the radio to hear a variety of programs from news, entertainment and sports. It began to change again in the 1950s with the widespread advances in television. And, of course, the technological age has led to many innovations, including podcasting, which has again changed the shape of traditional radio.

The Beginning of Wireless Communication

Without getting too technical, here is how it all started. In the mid–1800s, scientists began to theorize about the relationship between electricity and magnetism. Those experiments led to the development of the telegraph, which became the first way to communicate instantly from one place to another. The transmissions, of course, had to be sent over a wire in a series of dots and dashes developed by Samuel Morse (and appropriately called Morse code). But there was no way to transmit the human voice at that time.

The first attempts at wireless communication came as early as 1865 when James Maxwell, incorporating the experiments of Michael Faraday, developed a unified theory of electromagnetism. During the following decades, several scientists, including Thomas Edison, actually patented methods of sending and receiving wireless transmissions, but none developed a system that worked. Things began evolving more quickly in the latter 1880s. By 1887, Heinrich Hertz developed a system that enabled him to send wireless signals to a wireless receiver. Hertz did not create a real working system, but his research helped those that followed move to the next step.

That step was taken by a Serbian-Croatian immigrant named Nikola Tesla. Tesla was the first to create a radio transmitter and receiver in 1892 and, in that sense, was the man who invented radio. By 1895, Tesla was getting ready to demonstrate his radio transmission system over a distance of 50 miles when a fire in his laboratory caused the demonstration to be canceled. Tesla ended up demonstrating the first radio controlled boat in 1898 and subsequently filed a number of patents for radio in the early 1900s.

So who officially invented radio? Many give that honor to an Italian, Guglielmo Marconi, who, in 1894, came up with a device that would ring a bell first from about 30 feet away, then across the distance of a mile. When there was little interest in Italy, Marconi went to England, where, in 1896, he demonstrated his technology to the English Post Office, and they immediately secured his services. By 1901, Marconi had transmitted the first broadcast signal across the Atlantic Ocean from Europe to America. That feat alone led to an acceleration of efforts to develop radio broadcasting that would reach the masses.

At first, the new radio technology was used aboard ships, enabling them to communicate with nearby vessels or the shore. The first radios on ships communicated through the use of Morse code, as did the Titanic when calling for help in 1912. Early versions of radio were also used in aviation after a demonstration in 1910 proved that it would work. A Canadian-American named Reginald Fessenden redesigned Marconi's technology with the belief that it could eventually lead to audio broadcasts, and he proved it before 1910 by broadcasting himself playing a violin and then reading from the Bible.

It was Fessenden who developed what is called amplitude modulation (AM for short) that allowed for multiple transmitters to broadcast on different frequencies and thus share the airwaves. He demonstrated his work in 1910 at the Metropolitan Opera House in New York, where the great Enrico Caruso was singing. The broadcast was heard some 20 miles away on a cargo ship heading to New York. After that, the use of radio and new technologies began advancing more rapidly.

One of the early uses of radio was by the military. Radios were first put on naval ships and then were used extensively to contact troops and track their movements during World War I. At the end of the war, President Woodrow Wilson was able to speak to Germany about its surrender through radio, and there was yet another 1918 broadcast from a radio station in Arlington, Virginia, to the Eiffel Tower in France. In 1921, radios were installed in public safety vehicles in Detroit at the order of the police commissioner. By this time, it was apparent that the potential of radio was unlimited, and before long big business began getting into the act.

The Birth of Modern Radio

Radio's period of rapid growth began in 1919 when a Westinghouse engineer named Frank Conrad began broadcasting music in Pittsburgh. Most of the listeners used rudimentary crystal sets, which were made with a tuning coil and a crystal detector, and required the use of headphones. The advantage was that these early receivers did not need a battery or electric source. The broadcasts quickly became extremely popular, leading to Westinghouse creating radio station KDKA in November of 1920. By 1921, KDKA began broadcasting boxing matches as well as major league baseball games. The first baseball broadcast was on August 5, 1921, with a man named Harold Arlin making the call.

That really opened the floodgates. By the end of 1921, there were stations in New York; Boston; Detroit; Philadelphia; Stockton, California; Los Angeles; and San Francisco. By the end of the following year, there were more than 100 stations all over the country. It was time for big business to become involved.

As early as 1922, AT&T planned for the start of advertisement-supported broadcasting, introducing plans to develop the first radio network. The idea was to develop a chain of thirty-eight stations linked together by the company's telephone lines and to simultaneously transmit commercially sponsored programming. With the main studios located at AT&T-owned WEAF in New York City, the network became known as the WEAF chain. To broadcast successfully, special lines had to be used to connect the stations. The first link between WEAF and WMAF in South Dartmouth, Massachusetts, went on line in the summer of 1923.

It did not take long for others to jump in. RCA was next, creating a smaller network, partly because it did not have as good a means to link the stations. In the fall of 1926, its chain had just four core stations in the Mid-Atlantic states, while the WEAF network had stretched out to seventeen cities from Maine to Kansas. That is when AT&T decided to leave the broadcasting business, selling to a group headed by RCA that soon became the National Broadcasting Company (NBC).

In 1927, the Columbia Broadcasting System (CBS) began competing and grew more rapidly when William S. Paley became company president. While NBC saw itself as mainly a public service organization whose goal was to break even financially, CBS under Paley saw the potential for big profits in its radio network. The CBS business model was to provide network programming to affiliate stations at a nominal cost, which led to a much wider distribution for both programming and advertising. With advertisers as their primary clients, CBS was also able to charge more for ad time. The affiliate stations had to carry network programming for part of their broadcast day and would receive a portion of the advertising revenues for being part of the package. Radio was now going big time and rapidly becoming part of the fabric of the country.

To understand how quickly radio spread, one has to look no further than the heavyweight championship fight between former champ Jack Dempsey and titleholder Gene Tunney on September 22, 1927. Billed as the "Fight of the Century," the bout was held before some 100,000 fans at Soldier Field in Chicago. NBC broadcast the bout, which became known as the long-count fight, with Graham McNamee doing the call. It was estimated that 50 million people worldwide heard the fight. That number might have been exaggerated. The *Chicago Tribune* reported that 74 stations carried the fight in the United States with a potential audience of 15 million people. Either way, it was apparent that radio had become the world's number one vehicle to bring entertainment and information to the masses.

During this period, about one-quarter of the radio stations were owned by manufacturers, retailers and other business enterprises. Even newspapers owned stations. Their purpose was to publicize their products or simply to increase business. Other stations were owned by educational institutions, churches, civic groups, and radio-related firms. Having a radio station was also a great way to sell more radios: in its first three years of selling radios, RCA brought in more than $83.5 million. By 1930, nine out of ten radio stations were selling advertising time. Radio had hit the big time, but the best was yet to come.

The Golden Age of Radio

During the 1930s and 1940s, radio began to play a major role in American life. It was the perfect technology for communicating and entertaining in two difficult periods—the Great Depression of the 1930s, followed by the devastating years of World War II. During these years, which brought both tragedy and hardship to so many, radio helped not only to entertain but also to bring the latest news to people throughout the country. Listening to the radio was now a major part of daily life in America. In the days before television, families gathered around their radios in the evenings to both escape their daily travails and to hear the latest news, both good and bad.

Much of the programming during this period was controlled by advertising agencies. They often created the shows and hired talent, technicians and staff, while leasing airtime and studio space from the radio networks. Many programs were aired in fifteen and thirty-minute segments with a variety of formats. There was news, live music, comedy programs, variety shows and full dramas, often utilizing the biggest stars of the day, most of whom welcomed this new medium to bring their talents to more people, as well as to make more money for themselves.

Back then, most people did not listen to small radios, and certainly not miniature radios with an earphone as not to bother anyone else. No, the radios of the day were built into large cabinets that were often more like elaborate pieces of furniture. They had to be that size since they contained large vacuum tubes before the days of transistors and integrated circuits. They also contained large speakers with a rich bass sound and loops of wire wrapped around a drum inside an adjustable cabinet so that the radio might capture distant stations. In a sense, they were like the large, flat screen televisions today, something families could proudly gather around and enjoy programming together. By 1935, there were 22 million homes in the country with radios, and soon they began to appear in the new automobiles as well.

Beginning in the 1930s, radio programs were geared for all family members. There were news and sports broadcasts, as well as children's shows such as *Little Orphan Annie*. There were also many comedies, including *Amos 'n' Andy*, *The Jack Benny Program*, *Burns and Allen* and *The Edgar Bergen and Charlie McCarthy Show*. Crime shows were also popular, with programs like *The Shadow* and *Yours Truly, Johnny Dollar* enjoying large audiences, as did westerns like *Gunsmoke* and *The Lone Ranger*. For the housewives, there were soap operas such as *The Guiding Light*, *Ma Perkins*, *Our Gal Sunday* and *The Second Mrs. Burton*. Most of these shows began as 15-minute serials that continued with their various storylines.

In addition, there were also dramas such as *The Lux Radio Theatre* and the *Academy Award Theater*. These shows often featured the top movie stars of the day, sometimes performing live versions of their prominent movie roles. Top stars also took part in the original dramas. The National Broadcasting Company put together its own symphony orchestra, with outstanding musicians conducted by the well-known Italian maestro Arturo Toscanini. And to tap into the popularity of the Big Band or Swing Era of the 1930s, radio often broadcast "remotes," which featured the live music from bands led by Benny Goodman, Glenn Miller, Duke Ellington, Tommy Dorsey and Artie Shaw performing at various venues.

The entertainment portion of radio was well covered and suited a variety of tastes, and if some of the radio programs sound familiar, it is because they later transitioned to television. *Gunsmoke*, *The Lone Ranger*, *Burns and Allen* and *The Jack Benny Program* are examples of this, as is the long-running soap opera, *The Guiding Light*. But perhaps the greatest example of the power of radio during this period occurred on October 30, 1938.

On that night, the iconic actor and director Orson Welles and his Mercury Theater presented an adaptation of H.G. Wells's science fiction thriller, *The War of the Worlds*. The book and subsequent radio show depicted a Martian invasion of Earth. Welles shaped the show in documentary style, having "newscasters" describing the invasion and resulting carnage. The invasion was supposedly beginning in New Jersey and spreading elsewhere, and though there was a quick disclaimer at the beginning telling the audience it was a fictional presentation, many people missed that. To them, the broadcast sounded so real that they believed it was an actual alien invasion with supposedly regular programming interrupted by increasing frantic "news" bulletins about the invasion.

Police departments and other government offices were deluged with phone calls from listeners who wanted to know if the invasion was real. Some people even panicked, fled their homes and took to the roads to get away from the murderous Martians. While the panic was relatively short-lived, the Welles broadcast showed how powerful radio had become, and how it was a believable source of instant news.

The entertainment facet of radio continued into the 1940s, when the war years made radio even more valuable and important. The big networks had young reporters overseas in the war zones reporting directly to the American public. Perhaps the most noteworthy war correspondent was Edward R. Murrow, who would later transition to television. Murrow had a deep, resonant voice, wrote his own copy, and really brought the war into the living rooms of millions. He even broadcast a live report from London as German planes dropped bombs overhead. The sounds behind his broadcast were not being produced in a studio. They were the real deal, and the result was quite dramatic—something only radio could produce in those days.

Radio also gave a platform to President Franklin D. Roosevelt during the war years. His weekly "fireside chats," given in an informal manner rather than sounding like a speech, were geared to boost the morale of the American public. People gathered around their radios felt that the president was speaking directly to them, almost on a one-to-one basis. Not only did the broadcasts increase the president's popularly, but they gave the public confidence that the war would ultimately be won.

The Golden Age of Radio had something for everyone. Familiar voices came into homes on a daily basis like old friends. It was the perfect vehicle for the times. People did not have to leave their homes or pay to hear plays, concerts or other public performances. Radio could make you laugh or cry, bring world events into your home, and made people feel less isolated. It began to change in the 1950s, when television added another dimension to mass communication. The new kid on the block began to captivate people the way radio had two decades earlier. Radio would survive, but it would change, and continue to change as new technologies began arriving.

The Road to Podcasting

One of the first advances beyond traditional AM radio programming was the development of FM radio. Edwin Armstrong, an American engineer, invented it way back in 1933. He developed it, in part, due to some of the problems with AM, such as static, interference caused by lightning, and the fact that AM radio signals would "drift" at night, causing listeners in New York, for example, to partially or completely lose their local stations for faraway stations on the same frequency. Listening to AM radio at night, New Yorkers could find themselves picking up signals from Baltimore, Charlotte, Chicago, Boston, St. Louis, and other cities.

Early on, the AM radio magnates, such as David Sarnoff, looked at FM radio as a threat to their financial empires, especially after Armstrong showed just how clear the FM sound could be. Sarnoff and the others lobbied the Federal Communications Commission (FCC) to make changes that would put off any public reaction and keep FM from gaining a strong threshold. The plan worked, and it wasn't until after the end of World War II that the FM band was moved from 42–50 MHz to 88–106 MHz, and a year or so later to its present 88–108 MHz.

The band was moved up in part because radio signals below 54 MHz also tended to skip or drift, with faraway stations interfering with local broadcasts. It almost never happened with the new FM frequency allocations. Yet from the 1940s to the early 1960s, FM radio was nicknamed the "Forgotten Medium," not only because of the band change but because the cost of the new FM radios was very high and not very many people were willing to invest the money when they already had a variety of AM programs to hear. AM remained the primary radio band until the early 1970s.

It was the development of stereo FM in 1961 that slowly began changing the radio dynamic. Once the FM stations adopted the stereo sound, more people began listening. The same people who owned the AM stations then owned most of the FM stations, and they began simulcasting some of their programs on their FM stations. But in 1966, the regulations were changed and simulcasting was stopped. That's when more original FM programs began to be created.

Throughout the 1970s and into the early 1980s, the dominant FM form of programming was music, first called "beautiful music" and later "easy listening." The shift in programming continued as FM drew more listeners. Music was still the primary form of entertainment on FM, with a wide variety from classical to country, to top 40 rock 'n' roll, to jazz. At the same time, there was more talk radio on the AM dial, including all-news stations, as well as music and sports. And the modern radio—whether it be a small transistor radio, larger console, a stereo tuner or car radio—now had both AM and FM frequencies available to the listener. Radio had come full circle, but the technology was also beginning to move in new directions.

The advent of the Internet and World Wide Web in the 1980s once again changed everything, since both music and even talk-related software were now available to radio stations in a digital format.

New formats led to the development of programs for wider distribution. Networks like the Mbone began operating. Mbone was a Multicast Network that distributed both audio and video files over the Internet, though at that time it was used mostly by educational and research institutes for audio talk programs. By the mid–1990s, jukeboxes and websites had a way to sort and select music or audio files of different digital formats. There were even a few websites that began providing audio subscription services.

Internet radio was in its infancy by 1993 when Carl Malamud launched *Internet Talk Radio*, considered the first computer-radio talk show, which featured a weekly interview with a computer expert. It was distributed "as audio files that computer users fetch one by one." According to Malamud, listeners could pause and restart the audio files whenever they desired, and could also skip content they did not want to hear.

It wasn't long before some websites enabled users to download audio shows. In 1996, for example, AOL.com produced a comedy show called *The Don and Scott Show*, which was made available to its subscribers. Downloaded music did not become widely available until the launch of Napster in 1999, then a free service that allowed the downloading and sharing of music. The company was shut down two years later by court order over copyright infringement, but the Napster name was later revived as a subscription service. At any rate, legal or illegal, music was now available for download on the Internet.

With the technology advancing quickly, the audio blog soon came into play. In September of 2003, a former *New York Times* reporter named Christopher Lydon, who was at the time a Boston TV news anchor and National Public Radio (NPR) talk show host, conducted in-depth interviews with bloggers and political figures from a portable recording studio and posted the MP3 files on the internet as part of his Harvard blog. They were released gradually after Lydon had done about 25 interviews.

That October, developer Dave Winer helped organize the first BloggerCon conference to demonstrate the potential of high-quality MP3 content and show how it could be marketed and delivered. A few months later, in May 2004, Eric Rise and Randy Dryburgh introduced a service called Audioblog.com, which became the first commercial podcasting hosting service. It became Hipcast.com in June 2006, and has hosted hundreds of thousands of podcasts since. The podcasting era had begun and, in a sense, radio had once again come full circle.

Technology journalist Ben Hammersley first suggested the term "podcasting" in 2004, as more and more people and platforms entered the rapidly growing field. To illustrate the growth, blogger and technology columnist Doc Searls began keeping track of the number of results Google found for the word "podcast." In the early autumn of 2004, the hits on Google's search engine for the word "podcasts" began increasing rapidly, sometimes doubling every few days and moving into the thousands. There was little doubt the interest and popularity of podcasts was now growing quickly. By that time, there were also more online "how to" articles appearing, showing people how to create, send and receive podcasts. More podcasts began to appear with different topics and tones. There was no doubt that the format was here to stay.

It wasn't long before some people began producing video podcasts, so they could be seen as well as heard. And like talk radio of earlier years, listeners could often call into podcasts and speak with the hosts. The advent of YouTube also made it possible for more people to see these video podcasts whenever they had the time. Now, of course, podcasts can be seen and heard on all devices—computers, smartphones, and tablets—at any time and in any place where an Internet connection is available.

Traditional radio, of course, will never die, and people can still use the original medium to hear news, music, sports and a variety of talk shows on both the AM and FM dials. From the old crystal sets and large console radios, to transistors and now the Internet, radio has been part of the fabric of American life for a full century. And it will certainly continue into the future, with podcasting leading the way.

Chapter Review

The early technology of wireless communication led to the invention of the radio in the 1890s, which became a very popular entertainment and news medium for the American public. Radio transmissions were first used on ships and in the military, and by the 1920s broadcasts of music and sporting events were being sent to the general public. These broadcasts proved so popular that companies started to develop widespread radio networks with a variety of programming, backed by advertisers and transmitted to major cities free for anyone with a radio to listen.

The 1930s and 1940s are known as the Golden Age of Radio. Through the Great Depression and World War II, Americans tuned in both for entertainment and for the dissemination of news during those tumultuous times. Radios became ubiquitous in American homes and cars. While advances in technology brought about television, then the Internet, audio-only media persisted. In the 1990s, computer-radio programs were invented, which listeners could download, pause, and fast-forward as they pleased. The stage was set for podcasts to enter the scene, which they did in 2003, slowly at first, then rapidly gaining popularity.

Next, we'll take a look at the early and enduring podcasts that shaped the medium and led to the widespread popularity of this form of news and entertainment.

Exercises and Discussion Questions

a. Why do you think radio was so important in the 1930s and 1940s?
b. What is the value of traditional radio in this digital age?
c. What motivated the advertising industry to create and promote content for radio?
d. What challenges did the FM band have in reaching a broad audience? Can you imagine similar hurdles with new technologies entering the market today?

Resource

Hipcast.com: https://www.hipcast.com/

Chapter 2

Game-changing Podcasts

Middle aged women talking about their sex lives. Moms discussing diapers. Grumpy men complaining about what's wrong with the world. Reporters sifting through old evidence against serial killers. These topics may or may not be your personal cup of tea, but each one of them was at the heart of a podcast that represented a significant shift in the industry.

Podcasts originally developed as an extension of blogging when the Internet was first becoming widespread. Blogging was very popular at the turn of the twenty-first century, as people enjoyed new ways to dispense information. Bloggers were free from the gatekeepers of traditional media, such as networks, publishers and advertisers, all of which played a hand in the content that made it to the air. Media personalities found great freedom in being able to express their opinions on world events directly to the reader or listener, and to get direct feedback.

Other people were just enjoying the ability to post their thoughts online—about recipes or sports or cat outfits—for anyone to consume. One early popular podcast (although they did not use that term) that served to shape the nascent medium was *In Bed with Susie Bright*, launched in 2000 on the audio content platform Audible. Susie Bright is a writer and activist with a focus on sexual politics, and her weekly audio program addressed everything from sex trafficking and abortion to the latest erotic novels, as well as how to achieve better orgasms. The content of the show was much racier than most traditional media at the time, due both to regulatory restrictions and the perceived appetite for this sort of content by consumers.

Large, institutional media organizations are often controlled by decision makers who, in turn, are trying to keep advertisers happy. This creates a bureaucracy that often prevents radical new works from making it to air, since the big producers are generally concerned with attracting as broad an audience as possible.

Individual podcasters like Susie Bright were free from all such restrictions. Without the pressure to please everyone, they could concentrate on topics that were important to them personally and get direct feedback from listeners, which they then used to further shape their shows. A feature of Bright's program was that anyone could email her with their most private sex questions, similar to the radio call-in format, except more anonymous and with no topic taboo. Later, she was able to patch them in on her studio phone.

This program was an important milestone in the early podcast world, as it proved to developers that there were markets for more specialized programming that did not yet have a place in mainstream entertainment. *In Bed with Susie Bright* did well with its initial niche of listeners and grew steadily to be recognized by the established press and advertisers. The popular program is still being recorded and released weekly on Audible nearly 22 years later. And Audible, which took a chance on this risqué program, sold to Amazon for $300 million in early 2008.

But the term "podcast" wasn't yet in use when Bright's program first aired. In a 2004 article for the *Guardian* on the rise of online radio, Ben Hammersley first coined the term "podcasting." The word came from the widespread use of Apple's product, the iPod, a device used solely for consuming audio content. Other MP3 or digital audio players existed, but Apple was the main player in terms of market share and consumer recognition.

While Apple did not invent the podcast, it is somewhat fitting that the name should be tied to the technology behemoth, because it often helped the medium grow. Podcasts were first made available in the iTunes store as early as 2005. Then, starting in 2012, Apple began including a stand-alone app for podcasts on every iPhone. This accessibility made it easier for consumers to integrate podcasts into their entertainment options, since they did not have to seek out a new platform in order to listen.

The Technology Evolves

Dave Winer and Adam Curry are credited with developing the technology for the first podcasts, which were originally called audio blogs. The technology evolved slowly but steadily in the first years, as various web developers began working to improve the growing medium. Basically, they figured out how to add audio files to an RSS feed and, later, how to have that file automatically download to a listener's device.

Podcasting technology has remained essentially the same since those early days. But what has changed—at first slowly and then at high speed—is the popularity, breadth of topics and market viability. Market viability in this instance means advertising money, because even with the growth in subscription-based, ad-free podcasts, free shows with ads will always have a starring role in the podcast world. Advertising often makes the difference for successful long-term podcasts.

Businesses were slow to put their money in podcasts at first, but as more data came out it became clear that podcast listeners were a smart bet for advertisers. Podcast listeners tend to be well educated and more successful financially. Because the ads are read by the host, they're seen as less obtrusive, which means people are more likely to sit through them. Having the host read the ads also leads to trust, which may be responsible for the high click-through rate that podcast advertisers enjoy. Listeners are more likely to learn more about and even purchase what's being sold on a podcast in comparison to other mediums.

Perhaps the biggest upside for advertisers is the clear, built-in target audience of podcasts. Rarely is a podcast aimed at a broad, general audience. An early milestone for podcast advertising arrived with *MommyCast*, the popular weekly "Mom" podcast that featured two mothers, Paige Heninger and Gretchen Vogelzang. *MommyCast* discussed the day-to-day running of a house and family, from choosing the best paper towel to what to do when your child gets bullied at school. The industry took notice when the show inked a $100,000 advertising deal in 2005 with Dixie Consumer Products.

The deal was historic in several ways. Because it was the first six-figure ad deal with a podcast, marking a turning point in the industry, it showed established companies' value in the form. It was also an "aha" moment for the industry as Dixie, a major consumer brand, recognized that their main customers—mothers—would be more likely to see their products in a favorable light when they're being recommended directly by other busy mothers like themselves. Dixie also must have recognized the value in the personal aspect of the podcast host-listener relationship, as Heninger and Vogelzang built a trusting bond with their audience, one mother to another. Professional-sounding hosts with good content will always build trust in their listeners.

Still, it would be nearly another decade before podcasts properly enjoyed a slice of the mammoth pie that is ad funding in mainstream entertainment. And there is yet room for much growth.

While financial interest grew slowly, podcasts continued to find their footing in terms of content. The most successful programs were those that took advantage of the medium's uniqueness. Marc Maron's podcast, *WTF with Marc Maron*, is often seen as helping define the genre and even, as the *Boston Globe* put it, "[aiding in] establishing the viability of the form."

Maron was a comedian struggling with his career when his fourth radio show with Air America—a short-lived, progressive talk-radio network—was canceled in 2009. With the help of a producer, Maron then started the *WTF* podcast after-hours in the Air America studios before moving to record it in his private residence.

Maron's approach has always been personal conversations with his guests, who are often comedians, actors, and others in the entertainment industry. Maron is famous for recording most episodes in his home garage and often bringing friends on the show with whom he already has an established rapport, and his interviews are popular in large part because of their intimate nature. Many of his guests are celebrities and other high-profile people, but when sitting in a garage with Maron, they are more open and forthcoming than they might be when appearing on more traditional platforms.

A recent conversation on his podcast with John Cleese, co-founder of the hit comedy troupe Monty Python, illustrates the intimate nature of the medium:

> **Marc Maron:** Nowadays people are so isolated, they may not come out to the theater but with a podcast they can sit there and feel like they have a relationship with you, and not feel like they're alone in their dark hole.
> **John Cleese:** A relationship they would not have if we were on television.... I just love radio.... I have always felt there is a kind of intimacy—you and I, we're talking now and it is easy because it is eyeball to eyeball, we're picking up each other's nonverbal signals, which is what keeps a conversation flowing. Television, we'd be sitting *next* to each other looking *out* at an audience...
> **MM:** Doing lines.
> **JC:** Doing lines! In television everything's prepared, people come in and remove lint from your jacket... (Maron 2018).

Maron and his guests enjoy free-flowing conversation, and the listeners feel like they're eavesdropping on a private conversation that seems less polished and more authentic than what is often seen in other mediums. Even the title ("WTF" being a popular abbreviation for "what the fuck") illustrates what is possible when creators produce content without the restrictions and red tape that often come with established media networks.

Maron's approach has certainly paid off, as he interviewed then-U.S. president Barack Obama in 2015, another watershed moment for podcasts. Ten years after it started, *WTF* continues to be one of the top performing podcasts in terms of listenership and advertising money, and Maron continues to speak with guests one-on-one in his home garage.

Another major turning point in podcasting resulted from the popular radio show, *This American Life*. The show began on radio in 1995 and existed in various digital forms before its current set-up, which is a weekly radio broadcast that is released as a podcast a couple days after each airing. While the show began (and remains) on radio, its popularity as a podcast illustrates two related benefits of the medium. It proves that listeners have an appetite for long-form, nonfiction narrative, as well as a desire to conveniently access these shows on demand.

Despite cries that "video killed the radio star," Americans never lost their love affair with radio, even though lifestyles are very different than in radio's heyday. In the modern world, most people aren't able to schedule their days or weeks around their favorite programs. Instead, they need their shows to be available whenever they can listen, along with the ability to pause a program and come back to it, particularly longer-form pieces.

This American Life always had a variety of programming, but one show in particular—*Serial*—was a major breakout hit, often credited with establishing podcasting as a viable entertainment medium. *Serial*, established in 2014, is an investigative journalism podcast that dives into one true crime story per season. The host, journalist Sarah Koenig, interviews witnesses and pores over police reports and other documents to piece together what did and did not happen. A typical episode is 30 to 60 minutes long, and there are 10 to 12 episodes per season.

Serial tapped into America's appetite for true crime, mixing robust reporting with compelling storytelling. It was exciting to listeners, advertisers and industry professionals alike, as the numbers of listeners skyrocketed beyond previous podcast numbers. The news and entertainment industry took notice when the show earned a Peabody Award, the first podcast to win this benchmark of excellence in the world of electronic media.

The popularity of the series had a larger impact on the industry, as more and more people began talking about podcasts and tuning in, not just to *Serial* but across the board. In the five years before *Serial* debuted in 2014, the number of monthly podcast listeners across the medium grew by about 35 percent. According to Edison Research, in the five years after *Serial*, that same metric rose by a dramatic 130 percent, from 39 million to 90 million. Not surprisingly, all this consumer attention began attracting more advertisers. The Interactive Advertising Bureau noted that ad revenue for podcasts increased from $314 million in 2017 to $479 million in 2018, and is projected to hit $1 billion by 2021.

The groundswell that began with *Serial* also helped podcasting make the leap across the Atlantic. Podcasts have had a harder time breaking into the European market, at least in part because of a difference in technology usage. Apple's iPhone has included a podcast app in the standard interface since 2012, which has helped make it easy for iPhone users (a large proportion of the U.S. market) to access podcasts. However, iPhone usage is less widespread in Europe, which may be one reason podcasts haven't caught on as readily.

However, once the appetite for deep-dive journalism in the form of podcasts was proven with *Serial*, established news organizations such as the *New*

York Times and the *Washington Post* started focusing on their own podcasts. They saw the need in the market, and they were well positioned to adapt their reporting to the medium. This in turn encouraged European media organizations to take the plunge as well, and the results have been positive.

A turning point in podcasts across the pond was the establishment in 2018 of *Dobré Ráno* (*Good Morning*), a daily news podcast produced by Slovakia's largest news website, SME.sk. The program, modeled after the *New York Times*' podcast *The Daily*, was popular immediately, with 100,000 listens in the first month.

And media organizations were not the only ones taking note. In the years following the debut—and explosive success—of *Serial*, a wide variety of industries began hopping on the podcast bandwagon. Perhaps most notable was the embrace of podcasts by the banking industry.

The financial sector was initially wary of podcasting because banking is a heavily regulated industry, and insight on markets is a premium service. Releasing a weekly podcast seemed like a risky endeavor. While there were some early efforts, such as *Exchanges at Goldman Sachs*, which started in 2014, by 2019 nearly every major financial institution had at least one podcast. Some have several, such as JP Morgan Chase's three: *Market Insights with David Kelly*, *Eye on the Market with Michael Cembalest*, and *My Next Move with Michael Liersch*.

Banking podcasts focus on presenting their market research in an accessible and engaging way. They also serve as a marketing platform, as the banks build trust with their listeners who, in turn, are building significant loyalty with a brand that may have otherwise seemed not only mammoth, but faceless as well.

Through all these turning points, podcasts have officially moved from the fringe to being more firmly entrenched in the established entertainment industry. As of mid-2019, there were over 700,000 podcasts in production, with more than 60 million Americans tuning in at least weekly. As the numbers continue to grow, is it not time for you to get on the bandwagon?

Chapter Review

Early podcasts had an emphasis on the individual. Unlike other forms of media at the turn of this century that were backed by large corporations and influenced by advertisers and other stakeholders, podcasts were often created by "regular" people speaking, sometimes very casually, about a topic of personal interest. This niche programming fed into the intimate nature of the host-listener relationship, as podcasts were free to explore topics eschewed by the more entrenched entertainment mediums.

As podcasts on different topics proved popular, major businesses started to invest in advertisements. Companies appreciated the niche nature of the programs because it made it easier for them to target their potential customers, and they capitalized on the sense of trust and familiarity between listener and host. A major turning point in the industry was the true crime podcast *Serial*, which was explosively popular and encouraged major media organizations, and in turn major companies, to start developing their own podcasts. It was also the first podcast to win a Peabody Award, establishing the medium as a viable and respectable media format.

In the next chapter, we'll examine the trends and statistics in the podcast industry to gain a better understanding of how the medium operates and where it might be headed.

Exercises and Discussion Questions

a. What were podcasts originally developed as?
b. What was the first six-figure advertising deal for a podcast, and why was this relevant?
c. What were the circumstances in the media industry in the early 2000s that fed into the development of personalized podcasts on a wide range of niche topics?
d. Why was *Serial* such a game-changer for the podcast industry?
e. Find your podcast. Do some research and find a podcast that appeals to you. You can even listen to a podcast mentioned in this chapter. The podcast could be on sports, music, or anything that you find interesting.
f. Listen to a couple of episodes and explain why you picked the podcast.
g. Did the podcast meet your expectations as far as sound quality and content? Explain why or why not.

Resources

WTF with Marc Maron: http://www.wtfpod.com/
Serial: https://serialpodcast.org
New York Times' The Daily: https://www.nytimes.com/column/the-daily
Washington Post podcasts: https://www.washingtonpost.com/podcasts/

Chapter 3

Industry Trends and Statistics

Podcasting may be a relatively young industry, but there are a number of metrics that are worth examining. They can be helpful to the beginner podcaster, as well as those already on the air who are looking to increase their audience and hone the direction of their show. Looking at the trends can also provide insight into where this industry is going and how you can best become a part of it.

An Industry on the Rise: An Overview

In less than two decades, podcasting has gone from an arcane curiosity of the Internet to a highly popular news and entertainment medium. Early listenership tended to be college-educated, relatively affluent white males. Over time, audiences expanded as producers began tapping into niche audiences and embracing the unique storytelling aspects of the form.

These days, podcasts hold a comfortable place in the American media landscape, with most industry experts forecasting a continuation of the growing popularity. From small-scale, niche businesses to multinational Fortune 500 corporations, companies are leveraging the intimate nature of podcasts to encourage brand loyalty and recognition.

Podcasting's entry into the mainstream was accelerated by the wildly popular true crime investigative series *Serial*, which secured the medium as both a respectable source of news and journalism as well as a compelling storytelling platform.

Following *Serial*, there was a proliferation of shows from all manner of genres, both fiction and nonfiction, including subcategories of history, comedy, sports, health, politics, business, hobbies, technology, culture and more. One clear facet of this burgeoning industry when it comes to genres is that the more niche your topic, the better chance you have of standing out, attracting a loyal audience, and ultimately monetizing your work.

Production values have risen along with popularity. While it is still possible for the proverbial "guy in his garage" to create and distribute a podcast for a relatively modest sum, companies like MasterCard and Microsoft are making six-figure investments in their podcasts.

At the same time, software and equipment options at all price points have improved. Popular hosting platforms such as Spreaker and SoundCloud offer free options and can scale up to a professional level. Audacity is a free editing software popular with podcasters.

Web-based recording platforms for podcasts, such as Zencastr, are further democratizing the process of creating a podcast. These platforms offer studio-quality sound recording over the Internet, and many of them are adding a video component. This enables podcast hosts to have guests on the show from any location around the globe (as long as they have decent WiFi), and the video (which allows the hosts, guests, and producers to see each other, but which is not for audience consumption) makes for smoother conversations and more seamless shows.

Ultimately, the medium will likely start to use more one-stop virtual studios, with recording features, video components, and even avenues for distribution and monetization from a single platform or setup.

Podcast advertising is another area of growth, despite the sluggish start. The unique form of podcasts—audio-only, often consumed solo, frequently niche programming, and a built-in skip-ahead feature that makes it easy to bypass ads—has caused hurdles for advertisers, and some experts doubt the viability of podcast ad revenue moving forward. However, the current trend is upwards, with PwC's IAB Podcast Advertising Revenue Report reporting $1 billion in podcast ad revenue for 2020. The current trend, which is likely to continue, is towards native ads, where the host mentions the product or service in a way that fits the tone and format of the show, so as to be less intrusive and therefore more effective.

Podcasts are also emerging as ripe ground for new television productions, often acting as a proof of concept for an episodic story and increasingly living as a companion piece to the show. At the same time, the medium is being embraced more and more for its unique storytelling potential, with creative teams, sometimes including A-list actors and directors, making robust fiction podcasts that harken back to the radio plays of the pre-television era.

Trends and Statistics

Podcasting is generally understood to have begun in 2004. Fifteen years later, there were more than 700,000 active podcasts for consumers to choose from (Whitner, April 2021). In 2006, a mere 22 percent of

Americans were familiar with podcasts. By 2010, that number had ballooned to 45 percent, but then the growth slowed and seemed to almost level off over the next five years. It began rising again in 2016 and, by 2017, 60 percent of Americans were familiar with podcasts. By 2019, that number had risen to 70 percent (Edison Research, 2019).

But how many people were actually listening to podcasts? Interestingly, the number of listeners has outpaced the number of people simply aware of podcasts. In 2010, about half the people who were familiar with podcasts were tuning in, which remained roughly true through the early years. But the gap started to close in 2014. By 2016, 65 percent of the people who were aware of podcasts were listening to them, with the number rising to 73 percent by 2019 (Edison Research, 2019). The big takeaway from these numbers is that podcasts were no mere blip in the media landscape. They had captured America's attention.

Who Is Listening?

According to Edison Research, men have historically outpaced women as podcast listeners. By 2019, 36 percent of men had listened to a podcast in the last month, while only 29 percent of women had done the same, a gap that has pretty much remained constant. When it comes to age groups, the variance in listenership becomes even more pronounced. In 2019, while 32 percent of Americans had listened to a podcast in a single month, that number rises to 39 percent when you look at listeners ages 25 to 54, and 40 percent in the 12 to 24 age group. In the age 55-plus category, only 17 percent were listening to podcasts in a single month.

Another notable difference is income level, with 41 percent of podcasts listeners having household incomes of $75,000 or more, compared to the national average of 29 percent. Similarly, 25 percent of podcast listeners have a four-year college degree, and 28 percent have some grad school or another advanced degree, as opposed to the national averages of 19 and 20 percent respectively.

There are also statistically significant racial differences among podcast listeners. According to Nielsen's Audio Today 2019 Report, 67 percent of podcast listeners over the age of 18 are White, while 15 percent are Hispanic and just 9 percent are Black. Compare this to the general U.S. population, which is 76.5 percent White, 18.3 percent Hispanic and 13.4 percent Black, and it becomes clear that there is room for significant potential listener growth in the African American demographic.

There are several different approaches to making use of these statistics. One approach is for producers and hosts to lean into the current demographics, focusing their content (and advertising) on topics of interest to educated, affluent young white men, since that is the direction in which the market seems to be moving. The other approach is to create programming that can take advantage of the gaps in listenership, targeting niche audiences, such as women of color over age 55, in order to draw more of that potential audience into the podcasting fold.

If you choose the latter approach, it is helpful to consider why certain demographics seem less inclined to listen to podcasts, in order to determine how you might bridge the gap.

Untapped Audience

Edison Research recently conducted an interesting survey of people who were aware of podcasts, but have never listened to them. Some 75 percent of respondents said simply that podcasts aren't for them. But if they've never tried it, how would they know?

Other answers uncover a fundamental lack of understanding about the medium, with 40 percent saying podcasts are too long (someone should introduce them to the *Thirty Seconds or Less* podcast), and 38 percent thinking you have to pay to subscribe to podcasts (most remain free, with ads). About 35 percent of respondents admit they do not know how to find a podcast, while 33 percent report that they are not sure how to listen to a podcast. Another 32 percent say the amount of choices is overwhelming. At the same time, 16 percent say most podcasts are for educational purposes, and 16 percent lament that there are no podcasts that include music or discussions about music (Edison Research, 2019).

This is truly an exciting area of growth for podcasts, as much of the aversion to the medium is based on incorrect information, or simply a lack of knowledge. Because podcasts are all about niche topics and audiences, entrepreneurial individuals and companies that are looking to corner the market on, for example, female Baby Boomers, simply need to spend a little more time on research and education.

A particularly encouraging statistic when considering the untapped podcast audience is the number of Americans listening to radio. As of 2018, a full 93 percent of Americans ages 18 and older were listening to radio at least once a week, which outpaces any other medium, including television and smartphones. While there are certainly differences in the mediums, both radio and podcasts are pure audio media and can therefore be consumed in similar ways. Many long-standing radio broadcasters, such as those on National Public Radio (NPR), take advantage of the similarity in formatting by offering their radio programs as podcasts shortly after the initial broadcast. This provides a level of convenience to radio listeners, who can then listen to their favorite radio programs at their leisure on a device of their choosing. In this way, podcasts and radio stations do not need to be competing for an audience, but instead can both benefit from the popularity of audio-only listening.

How, Where, and When We Listen

Part of the reason podcasts have proliferated so rapidly in America is due to the accessibility of the medium. Apple began including a built-in Podcast app on its iPhone back in 2012 when the podcast industry was still relatively new. Even before that, podcasts were included as a category within the Music app. A full 65 percent of United States listeners tune into podcasts via their smartphones or tablets, and 80 percent of Americans have access to a smartphone, with about 45 percent of those being iPhones (Statista, 2021). Thanks to the technology, podcasts became available to listeners wherever they were, as long as there was Internet service.

As technology evolved with new ways to make audio programming even more accessible, listenership also increased. Sales of smart speakers (such as Amazon Alexa or Google Home) have taken off in recent years, with 7 percent of the U.S. population over the age of 12 owning one in 2017, and 23 percent in 2019 (Edison Research, 2019). These home speakers can be connected to a smartphone, giving Americans another convenient way to hear podcasts.

Another common way for people to listen to podcasts is in their automobiles, with 52 percent of listeners saying they tune in while driving (Edison Research, 2019). Americans spend a lot of time in their cars, commuting and sitting in traffic. Radios are installed in every car, so it is a natural time and place to enjoy audio media, and bridge technologies are making it easier for people to hook their smartphones to their car radios and tune into podcasts while on the go. This, in turn, is attracting more advertisers to the podcasts, since drivers are closer to the point of purchase (as opposed to being at home), and individuals in their cars are a captive and engaged audience.

Indeed, most podcast listeners overall tend to be quite engaged, making the podcast attractive to advertisers. Some 70 percent of listeners often tune in to podcasts without doing anything else at all, while many others listen during an activity that is physical in nature, such as exercising, doing housework, cooking or walking. This level of focus contributes to the intimate nature of podcasts. Further, people who listen, listen often: the majority of individuals who reported listening to a podcast during any given week did not just listen to one, but listened to an average of seven podcasts per week.

The Rise of the Super Listener

Producers and advertisers have recently begun to focus on what is being called a "Super Listener," someone who habitually listens to more than five hours of podcasts per week. These voracious listeners provide valuable insight into the efficacy of podcast advertising, according to a recent study by Edison Research and PodcastOne, the Los Angeles–based podcasting platform.

Most Americans feel inundated with advertisements, making it difficult for companies to reach their target customers amid all the noise. According to this study, while 50 percent of these Super Listeners work to avoid ads across all platforms, 44 percent are more attentive to ads on a podcast, with 70 percent saying they have actively considered a new product or service after hearing it advertised on a podcast. The Super Listeners also agreed (at a rate of 41 percent) that podcast advertising was the most likely to be relevant to their interests. By comparison, the study participants found only 31 percent of magazine ads to be relevant to them, and a mere 23 percent of TV and radio ads.

Much of this comes back to the trust and intimacy inherent in the medium, as well as the targeted topics and tones of successful podcasts. While consumers' reactions to advertisements in this age of constant information can range from disinterest to downright hostility, 60 percent of podcast listeners appreciate that the advertisers are supporting their favorite programming. Money simply cannot buy that kind of positive goodwill towards ads.

Podcasting Trends in Business

Not surprisingly, the rise of podcasts has attracted the interest of established companies, both large and small. The initial interest took the form of advertising, an area that continues to grow. In recent years, more and more companies have started to develop their own podcasts, some of which have become very successful. In terms of advertising, it actually took some time for companies to start investing in podcast ads. In 2015, podcast ad revenue was a modest $105 million; by 2019, that number had ballooned to $679 million, and was expected to surpass $1 billion by 2012 (IAB, 2019).

Part of the reason for this timid start is also one of the big draws for advertisers: the podcast audience tends to be niche. As opposed to television or radio, where a company can expect to hit a much broader demographic, podcasts are often targeted to audiences with specific interests or leanings. For example, the long-running weekly podcast *The Pen Addict* is dedicated to all things stationary and has a loyal following. This highly rated program is eight years running, and counting. The advertising opportunities are clear, as this is an audience that is self-identifying as super interested in things like pens, pencils, paper, ink, etc.

Niche programs such as *The Pen Addict* also offer a particularly good advertising opportunity for small to mid-sized businesses. Another attraction is that podcasts with smaller audiences provide a budget-friendly option for advertisers. With their audience as a specific target, companies need not worry that they are wasting advertising dollars on individuals with no interest in their products.

There are a few ways to advertise in a podcast, including traditional ads, embedded (host-read) ads and product placements. The majority (about 67 percent) of podcast ads are read directly by the host throughout the program. This is found to be the most effective, in large part because of the perceived bond that a listener tends to feel with their favorite podcast host(s). The voice of the host is like listening to an interesting friend, and so product plugs feel less like advertising and more like a friendly recommendation from someone the listener knows and trusts.

Advertising revenue is concentrated in a few genres, with 65 percent coming from programs focused on news, politics, current events, comedy, business, education, and arts and entertainment. Interestingly, there are discrepancies between these numbers and the genres that hold the most interest for people. While it is true that the most popular topics include music (with 39 percent of listeners interested in this topic), news (36 percent) and entertainment (32 percent), there are many other areas of interest that are not far off, with 31 percent of podcast listeners interested in shows about history, as well as sports, and 30 percent interested in food topics. These numbers point to the large potential for niche and targeted marketing in the podcasting arena.

As with any advertising opportunity, companies are interested in investing where they are likely to connect with their customers. As podcasts grow in popularity, this naturally increases competition and, therefore, the quality of the shows being produced. This, in turn, attracts more listeners, which results in more advertising dollars.

Branded Podcasts

Another approach that is becoming more and more common is for companies to produce podcasts in-house, with subject matter that is fundamentally tied into their products or services. For example, Johnson & Johnson, a multinational corporation in the healthcare industry, created a podcast in 2017 called the *J&J Innovation Podcast*. The company's products range from staple consumer goods like shampoo and Band-Aids, to complex medical devices and new pharmaceuticals. Its brand is all about innovation as a means to making the world healthier, and the podcast was developed to deliver this message.

With episodes like "Hijacking Fat Cells to Throttle Disease-Causing Proteins" and "The Science 'Rebel' Who's Teaching Microbes to be More Productive," the J&J podcast seeks to engage its audience by positioning itself on the cutting edge of health innovation. This, in turn, encourages familiarity, loyalty and trust from the listener who, of course, is also their customer or potential customer.

This approach is proving to be effective. In a study conducted by BBC's branded content division, BBC StoryWorks, along with neuroscience researchers at Neuro-Insight, the rate of engagement and brand awareness was shown to be higher in podcasts than in other mediums. The study focused on individuals who actively avoid advertisements and found that their positive associations around brand mentions in podcasts were greater than that in television ads by at least 22 percent. The study also points to the effectiveness of podcasts in terms of breeding familiarity, loyalty, and trust between brand and listener in the following statement:

> Listeners create subconscious associations with the brand, based on words they hear in the podcast. In the *J&J Innovation Podcast*, the word "innovative" was mentioned 12 times during the podcast. Listeners were later more likely to call the sponsor innovative, showing that they instinctively associate the brand with the message.

Some companies are taking an even more direct approach, creating podcasts that discuss and celebrate their products. This approach can work as long as the main thrust of the program is always based on information that will be of value or interest to the listener. One of the longest-running branded podcasts is *Keeping You Organized* by Smead, a company that mainly sells file folders and related products. In each episode, the host interviews a professional organizer on best tips for removing clutter and organizing different areas of the home and workplace. The podcast has ads throughout the program for Smead products and services. However, the programming is distanced from the ads by eliminating the popular host-read, embedded ad in favor of stand-alone spots that are surrounded by musical interludes. It also plugs the company at the beginning and end of the program, but otherwise focuses on the guest and his or her organizing tips. This deliberate separation between content and ads serves to legitimize the programming, while still always coming back to the brand in a way that feels respectful to the listener.

Another successful branded podcast, and one which indicated a moment of change in the industry, was the McDonald's podcast *The Sauce*. This three-episode podcast was released in 2018 in response to a shortage of certain sauce packets across the fast-food chain restaurants that had led to fights breaking out at several locations, and a resulting stream of negative press coverage. The company produced the podcast as a spoof on the popular true crime podcast *Serial*, hoping to bring levity to the situation while apologizing for the company's miscalculation surrounding the demand for the sauce. The program proved popular, breaking into the top 100 podcasts on iTunes a day after its release. This approach enabled McDonald's to control the message of its apology and turn a PR nightmare into an opportunity to connect with customers.

Branded podcasts can also be a particularly effective platform for Business to Business companies (also known as B2B), which are companies that do business with each other. An example of a B2B would be a wholesale company doing business with a retail company. According to market research firm Bredin, executives at more than one third (39 percent) of all small to medium businesses were listening to podcasts in 2018. Targeting this demographic via a branded podcast is a valuable way to develop brand awareness and loyalty with decision makers at these companies.

Podcasts Join the Mainstream Media Arena

A clear indication of the rise of podcasts can be found in the proliferation of events related to the medium, including conferences, festivals and awards nights. Podcast Movement, an annual conference that began in 2014, has become the largest such event in the industry, with 3,000 attendees expected to attend in 2020.

There are also conferences dedicated to podcast editing (Podcast Editors Conference), podcasting for businesses (RAIN Podcast Business Summit), and independent or beginner podcasters (Pitfalls of Podcasting by Queer Podcasters Network). As with any industry conference, these events serve as informational and networking hubs, a place for professionals to gather and learn. Advertisers and sponsors are responding to the popularity of these events, making them sustainable.

Several festivals in celebration of podcasts have also sprung up in recent years, including Brooklyn Podcast Festival, Philadelphia Podcast Festival, and Adelaide Podcast Festival, to name just a few. At these events, listeners gather at local venues to hear live recordings of their favorite podcasts, often for free. These are also attractive events for sponsors and advertisers.

Broadcasting awards are another area where we can mark the entrance of podcasts into the entertainment mainstream. There are awards dedicated solely to podcasts, the most established of which is the People's Choice Podcast Awards, or simply the Podcast Awards. This event was first established in 2005 and currently has twenty categories tied to podcast genres such as "Kids and Family," "Games and Hobbies," and "Religion and Spirituality."

Perhaps more significant in terms of mainstream recognition is the inclusion of podcasts in more traditional media awards. The Webby Awards is a pioneer in online media recognition, having been established in 1996—very early days for the Internet. In 2006, they began including podcasts, and they now have 18 podcast categories, including Best Mini Series and Best Original Music/Sound Design. In a watershed moment for the industry in 2015, the breakout podcast *Serial* was the first podcast to win a Peabody Award, the highly respected award for excellence in broadcasting established in 1941.

Many of these events and awards take place on or around September 30, which was declared National Podcast Day in 2014, and later expanded to become International Podcast Day.

It is clear that the popularity and mainstream acceptance of podcasts is on the rise. One of the main features of podcasts—and what makes them so attractive to both listeners and advertisers—is their intimate nature. Many people listen to podcasts alone or perhaps with a friend, such as during a long drive. On the other end, the host is most often in a closed studio with a single producer and the guest(s). Furthermore, the topics and tones of the podcasts tend to be niche and targeted. All this adds up to a sort of best friend relationship between host and listener, which in turn breeds loyalty and trust.

The most successful podcasts, whether hosted by individuals or managed by international corporations, are leaning toward this intimacy in order to take advantage of this increasingly profitable sector.

Insights: Podcasting Trends in Europe

Rachel Stern

Rachel Stern is a Berlin-based journalist and editor (updated December 2019).

Rachel Stern.

Two years ago, "podcast" was a concept that was completely new to most people in Slovakia. That is why Bratislava-based journalist Dávid Tvrdoň received skeptical comments when he suggested producing one himself.

Yet with the help of his colleagues at Slovakia's largest news website, SME.sk, Tvrdoň assembled a lively daily news podcast inspired by the *New York Times' The Daily*. By the end of its first month of production, *Dobré Ráno* (or "Good Morning" in Slovak) already counted 100,000 listens.

Now the podcast is one of nearly 200 Slovak language podcasts, up from a mere seven when Tvrdoň launched his podcast at the beginning of 2018. A recent survey shows that .6 percent of the Central European country listens to his show on a daily basis. By comparison, .8 percent of the U.S. listens to *The Daily* every day.

"There were other podcasts operating before too, but they were so small that we know each other," says Tvrdoň. "They were really happy that we were doing this podcast because it is getting podcasts mainstream."

A U.S. Phenomenon Crosses Continents

In Europe, podcasts are still a relatively new phenomenon due to differences in technology use and media culture, but have been growing exponentially over the past few years.

An increasing number of not only European journalists, but also lately TV and radio personalities and YouTubers, have begun utilizing the popular platform.

Podcasting has grown exponentially in Europe for the past four years, according to London-based digital consultant Izabela Russell, who co-founded the broadcasting company New Media Europe with her husband, Mike, a long-time radio journalist.

In 2013, the two visited the U.S. for a digital media conference and were inspired by all of the podcasters they met. Russell said, "We thought, 'There is nothing like this in the UK, so why don't we create an event for podcasters here?'"

Soon their "UK Podcasters" event expanded to encompass 200 podcasters "from all corners of Europe," said Russell. In 2017, the British Podcast

Awards were established to crown the country's best podcasts, and by 2019 two other major UK events devoted to the up-and-coming medium followed: the Edtech Podcast Festival and London Podcast Festival.

Podcast penetration of the market can be largely traced to listening devices, says Russell. Europe is largely Android-based, with only 25 percent of people using an Apple iPhone (10 percent in Russell's native Poland), which has a built-in automatic podcast app. The Google Play Music app, built into the Android, does not yet have a built-in podcast application, though users can download an app like Stitcher to listen to them.

Major radio broadcasters in the UK, such as the BBC, now have podcasts to accompany their traditional programs. "Quite often on the show you will hear 'download our podcast app' or 'listen to our app,'" said Russell. "Radio stations have created this wave of podcasting."

Thirty-six percent of podcast listeners in the UK now get their podcasts after being directed from a media company, such as the BBC, according to the Reuters Institute for the Study of Journalism.

In the past year, Russell has also been contacted by an increasing number of companies and nonprofits, such as the World Health Organization, who are creating podcasts around a specific topic. Professors and researchers from European universities are also using them "to create a really compelling [program] for students," she said.

They include Chris Smith, a Cambridge University virologist who hosts *The Naked Scientist*, the first BBC regional program to be published as a podcast.

"I was a scientist and a researcher, but did not know a lot about media," said Smith, who now uses the format to help students communicate their research in specialized segments.

There are also a number of alternative ways that podcasters are attracting new listeners. Tvrdoň mainly reaches his audience through SoundCloud, and recently begun placing new episodes on Spotify.

It is also becoming increasingly easy to produce a podcast, especially with free tools such as Anchor, which *The Verge* in May 2019 dubbed as "the YouTube of podcasts."

A study by an independent podcaster in Slovakia found that 50 percent of the country's podcasters use Anchor, which was acquired by Spotify in February 2019.

"Anyone can make a podcast; the tools are there, available and inexpensive," said Ángel Rodríguez Lozano, a former radio journalist with Spain's Radio Nacional de España (RNE) who now hosts his own science podcast.

In Spain, "virtually all radio stations now have podcasts for their programs, something that did not happen before," said Lozano.

Embracing the Trend

Many journalists feel podcasts are working their way into mainstream media vocabulary. In 2016, for the first time PRIX EUROPA, the European Broadcasting Festival, launched a digital audio category.

"In 2017 we decided to focus more strictly on innovative approaches and creative presentations of audio in this category," said online manager Marta Medvešek. "Independent productions do not need to have a connection to a broadcaster any longer. Now it is enough if they 'broadcast' themselves on the Internet."

This is exactly what several journalists throughout Europe are doing, whether in Slovenia, where independent investigative journalist Taja Topolovec co-founded a weekly podcast detailing her research results, or in Poland, where Jakub Gornicki launched a global affairs podcast linked to his multimedia storytelling company Outriders.

Russell also has noticed an upswing in interest in Italian, French, and Spanish podcasts—the latter of which formed an expanding web network, Podium Podcast, for news and entertainment podcasts from Spain and Latin America in June 2016.

According to a recent Reuters' Institute Digital News Report, 39 percent of people in Spain reported listening to a podcast in the past month—even higher than the 35 percent in the U.S. and Sweden. In Germany, the Netherlands, and the UK, 21 percent reported listening to one in the last month.

As a whole, 42 percent of the population in Slovakia listens to podcasts regularly, and about 38 percent in Spain.

Working with Cultural Differences

In the U.S., there has long been a bottom-up approach to broadcasting, with a large number of college radio stations and smaller affiliate stations, observes radio and podcast journalist Jill Beytin. A native Californian who has worked with major media outlets in both the U.S. and Germany, Beytin founded Bear Radio to help encourage the podcasting scene in Berlin.

"In the US people have been into talk shows since Johnny Carson," says Beytin. "Here the media landscape is more insular and very much top down, and people are more risk-averse."

Yet Beytin is optimistic: unlike with radio, each podcast targets a niche audience, making them more attractive to advertisers and enabling small productions to find support. Even large radio stations, while streaming great content, have to aim for as large a group as possible in the content they create, she says.

Podcasting does not just present a new medium for listening to content, but a new, more intimate manner of storytelling.

British-American journalist Clare Richardson co-founded an explanatory podcast of European affairs, *Europe to Date*, in the summer of 2017 to break down the topics she often reported on in her day job at Deutsche Welle. "I think [podcasting] leaves more room for talking things out," she says, "in a manner where the audience can see your thought process."

Chapter Review

A close look at the metrics of podcast listenership and awareness makes it easy to track the rising popularity of the medium, which often coincided with the immense popularity of individual programs. We can also see the breakdown of listenership by gender, age, race, and other demographics, which can be helpful in the development of new programs and in the ever-growing distribution of advertising dollars. Podcast listeners tend to be young, educated, and affluent, which makes this an attractive group for advertisers. It also opens up the possibility for niche programming aimed at other demographics, as research shows that non-listeners, such as older people or racial minorities, are often averse to the medium simply because of a lack of understanding or familiarity.

The accessibility of podcasts also helps to explain their growing popularity in the U.S., where about a third of the population owns an iPhone, which comes with a built-in podcast app, and where car culture (with built-in radios) continues to exist in abundance.

Tracing the dollars being spent on podcast advertisements also shows a clear rise in the medium's popularity and indicates a shift in thinking when it comes to targeted ads. In another clear metric of podcasts going mainstream, companies started to develop in-house podcasts, working to connect directly with consumers, hawk their products, and build trust in their brand. Walking through the history of branded podcasts shows a clear learning curve for companies that continues today.

In the next chapter, we will explore the various reasons an individual may want to start his or her own podcast, and how to go about putting it in motion.

Exercises and Discussion Questions

a. What is the importance of learning about trends and statistics in podcasting?
b. In the "Who is Listening?" section of this chapter, what did you learn about the demographics of podcast listeners? Analyze and explain what stood out to you.
c. What is the percentage of Americans 18 and older who listen to podcasts once a week?
d. Define what it means to be a Super Listener.
e. There has been a slow rise of businesses using podcasts as a marketing tool. Research one brand that has a podcast and listen to two of its episodes. Provide an honest description of what you thought of the podcast.

Resources

Edison Research: https://www.edisonresearch.com/
NPR: https://www.npr.org/
Apple Podcast: https://itunesconnect.apple.com/login
PodcastOne: https://www.podcastone.com/
BBC StoryWorks: http://www.bbc.com/storyworks#Storyworks
Neuro-Insight: https://www.neuro-insight.com
Podcast Editors Conference: https://podcasteditorsconference.com/
RAIN: Podcast Business Summit: https://rainnews.com/tag/podcast-business-summit/

Part II

Podcasting Platforms

CHAPTER 4

What Is Your Podcasting Goal?

"A goal without a plan is just a wish."
—Antoine de Saint-Exupéry

Why do you want to start a podcast? Like most new endeavors, understanding your goal is crucial to success. Success doesn't always mean a large number of listeners. Yes, that is certainly a satisfying thing to achieve, but perhaps you are more interested in meeting new people in your industry, or building trust with a small but loyal customer base. Maybe you are just very passionate about your hobby and spend a lot of time talking about it with friends and family. So why not get it on "air"?

Fully understanding your motivation before you begin will help you build a podcast that is successful on your terms. Starting one blindly is a recipe for disaster. In my experience, most podcasts fail because the creator has no direction and underestimates what it takes to create a successful show. Whatever your motivation, make sure your podcast is one you will truly enjoy. After all, if you are not enjoying it, no one else will.

Start by asking yourself some questions. Is this a casual podcast, a hobby where you can just get your voice heard and maybe blow off some steam? Maybe you want to market your business and make money? Or do you want to meet interesting people who have the same or similar interests? You may even have another reason. In any case, you have to know what it is, because that is your motivation.

Knowing your ultimate objective will determine how you approach your podcast. If you are a hobbyist and not particularly interested in profiting from a podcast, you can take a more casual approach, work on your own timeline, experiment with content, and not worry about the bells and whistles.

On the other hand, if you are a podcaster who wants to attract an audience, draw customers and/or get advertisers, then your approach to podcasting will be quite different. You will want to develop a clear theme, make it professional, and be very well organized. You will also want to present consistent content, set a timeline, and stick to it—that is, broadcast when you say you are going to broadcast. Bottom line: you will want to produce and market a polished, consistent and appealing show.

The information you are being given here will help you achieve your goals, no matter what they are. But it all starts with motivation.

Before we get into the specific details of podcasting, let us address some terms. Many people assume podcasts are audio only and, traditionally, that is true, but there are options from which to choose. One example is a video form of podcasting called Vodcast. There is also some confusion about the different platforms, even within the industry, so let us go over the key terms: Audio, Vlog, or Video Podcast (AKA "Vodcast").

Audio: As mentioned earlier, podcasts are traditionally audio only, and most are pre-recorded, but there are some podcasts that are streamed live. Podcasts that stream live can be compared to Internet radio, which is always aired live on a specific day and time.

Vlog: People often get vlogs mixed up with vodcasts/video podcasts. However, vlogs are not truly considered podcasts. They are more accurately defined as blogs with a video component. Videos are included to enhance the written content, which remains the focus.

Video Podcasts: Video podcasts are also known as vodcasts. Vodcasts are a fairly new format, and there are not many statistics yet available for them. Like audio podcasts, vodcasts contain more in-depth programming, usually with commentary and, from time to time, guests. They do not typically have breaking news like you find being streamed on social media platforms, because the programming schedule tends to be more static.

In a nutshell, vodcasts are podcasts with video. Instead of just listening to hosts and guests talk, you can also watch them. It's basically the same concept as audio podcasts, but in video form, recorded in a home format or studio. Vodcasts can be more expensive, depending on the degree of video quality you want to achieve, and generally more complicated both logistically and technically. You also risk losing some of the intimacy with audiences and forthrightness of guests that make audio podcasts so appealing. As a general rule, I would not suggest starting a vodcast until you have built a solid audience with your podcast.

What Type of Content?

Once you have determined your podcasting goal(s), you have to focus on your content. Remember, it is important to push out consistent content, which will be much easier if you truly enjoy your topics.

If you are creating a podcast for your business, your customer or client base should determine your content. If you are working as an individual, the sky's the limit in terms of content. If you are unsure about what to discuss, consider the following questions: When you are with family and friends, what do you most enjoy talking about? What sort of websites or social media accounts do you follow? What kinds of books do you read, and what do you watch on television? Are you most interested in sports, politics, science, pop culture, or something else? These are questions you should answer before you begin planning your podcast.

My main areas of interest are sports, politics, and social issues, so I created a podcast that combines all three. *HWTP Sports Talk with David Weinstein* featuring five-time Super Bowl champion Pepper Johnson blends sports with politics and social issues. I have never regretted following my interests, because it has kept me engaged and motivated to keep working, and has led to some of the most satisfying moments of my career. Sometimes David and Pepper will insert a discussion about an actual game, and I tend to become bored. So be sure to stick to what really interest you.

One particular highlight was an episode we did with a sports columnist from the *Miami Herald*, Linda Robertson. The discussion related to the Obama administration's decision to allow Cuban baseball players to join Major League Baseball without having to make the dangerous and sometimes expensive decision to break Cuban law and defect. Two years later with the Trump administration in place, we did a follow-up story with Linda on the same subject.

This was a topic that absolutely fascinated both my host and me, and the audience feedback reflected that same level of interest. Listeners were enthralled with the story, and we really delved into the details, taking the in-depth yet conversational approach that works so well in the podcast medium. I learned a great deal about the topic, which was personally satisfying, and our listeners did as well, which was a professional boon.

If you find content that you truly enjoy, your podcast will thrive as you grow a community of listeners who are just as interested in the topic as you are.

Once you have decided upon the broad strokes of your intended content, it is time to plan out the details. When I decided to marry sports, politics and social issues in podcast form, I did some research on my competition. While it may be disconcerting to discover just how many people are producing podcasts about your chosen topic, this can actually be a good thing.

There will always be naysayers who will tell you that your idea is not unique. I heard that reaction from many directions and almost gave up before I started. But in truth, if there are already a good number of shows focused on your chosen topic, it means there is a huge audience for your platform. Yes, everything has a saturation point, but there is always a new angle or approach that will make your podcast different and unique. You just have to find it.

This is why market research and competitive analysis are so important. Properly conducted, these efforts will lead to good decision making and, depending on your research, could be the difference between starting and not starting your podcast. Or it can be as simple as getting the right guests for your show. Careful and thoughtful research is a crucial step that I cannot recommend highly enough. In my case, I found five podcasts that I perceived were similar to mine and listened to each of them for about a month. I took extensive notes, marking down the ways in which they differed from and were similar to the podcast I was planning. Then I looked at what I liked and what I did not like in terms of content, layout, tone and length, particularly focusing on areas that I thought needed improvement. I also did research on the demographics of podcast listeners.

One of the main things I discovered was how much the news industry had changed since the late 1990s when I launched an early version of what would ultimately become my first podcast, an online magazine called *Huddlin' with the Pros.* Back then, not many media outlets were focused on the storytelling aspects of sports, so I knew I could stand out by creating the first behind-the-scenes sports entertainment magazine on the web.

The magazine was focused on the off-field and off-court activities of professional athletes, with an emphasis on the human interest side of sports. Our writers shared stories about athletes giving back to their communities, with features on people such as NASCAR champion Tony Stewart, who bred greyhound dogs. The magazine blazed a new trail and was embraced by the sports industry, including athletes, fans, and media outlets. *Huddlin' with the Pros* was voted into the Top Ten Links in the Sports Magazine category of *Yahoo!* from 1996 to 2000, alongside such long-standing and popular outlets as *The Sporting News* and *ESPN, the Magazine.*

Fast forward to 2014 when I decided to relaunch *Huddlin'*. What was a ground-breaking approach to news back then was now par for the course, as storytelling had become an integral part of news reporting. So it was back to the old question: how do I stand out? What I noticed was that while there were television programs focusing on the human interest side of sports, like ESPN's *30 for 30* and HBO's *Real Sports with Bryant Gumbel*, there was nothing of that nature in the podcasting realm.

Bingo! I had found my niche: a show that ties in sports with politics and social issues, done in podcast form for added intimacy and audience loyalty. I also wanted my podcast to be intelligent and thought provoking, and wanted my listeners to learn and engage with the content, as I knew this would really help the show stand out from the rest.

I was excited about diving into this new industry, but I also knew I would be happier behind the scenes, so I sought out hosts with the same level of interest in my subject matter and who were outgoing and had engaging on-air personalities. Blending all these elements together, I was able to build a podcast that had some similarities to the successful podcasts on the market with the same cross section of topics, yet was different enough to stand out.

Separating ourselves with unique and relevant content from the very start has made a huge difference over the years. We regularly receive positive feedback from both our guests and listeners. Linda Robertson of the *Miami Herald* called us "more intelligent than most sports shows ... very multidimensional." Ken Belson, a sports writer for the *New York Times*, told me, "You guys do it right. Good questions, informed conversation." And Super Bowl champion Pepper Johnson summed it up nicely: "Unlike so many sports talk shows, *HWTP Sports Talk* doesn't ask the usual questions. The hosts go right to the meat and potatoes of an issue and make you think."

This feedback is in line with our listener numbers, which have shown a growth of 500 percent in the past five years. This is proof that it pays to take your time and create a format with content that excites. It will build your audience and make you proud of the job you did.

Naming Your Podcast and Using Taglines

Naming your podcast is a very important step. It can be as simple as using your own name or as complicated as coming up with something more clever or complex. But whatever you decide, make sure it is a name that satisfies you, since you may have it for a very long time.

Always keep this in mind: your podcast is your brand and, by building it, you will create brand identity with both existing and future consumers. Branding is created through a combination of your podcast name, tagline and logo. This is how consumers will know you. If you are a serious podcaster, brand identity will develop into listener loyalty, which, in turn, could get you advertisers. Podcast branding is the same marketing concept as consumer product branding. Examples of effective consumer product branding can be found with technology companies Apple and Android. Both companies have cult-like followings. In fact, there is a rivalry between the users, and humorous memes have popped up perpetuating this friendly feud. This is some very clever marketing. Effective branding creates shared community and a family sense, making it very important for the podcaster.

You may be feeling a bit nervous or anxious about choosing a name or tagline for your podcast because you do not think you are creative enough.

Don't be. Just do your research. I find the best way for finding your own name and tagline is to look at popular podcasts and see what types of names and taglines they are using. By researching other podcasts, you will learn that the name of your show and your tagline should be concise, clear and memorable. I've had a few different names for my podcasts. *Huddlin' with the Pros Sports Talk*, then *HWTP Sports Talk*, and finally *HWTP Sports Talk with David Weinstein* featuring five-time Super Bowl champion Pepper Johnson. HWTP stands for *Huddlin' with the Pros*, a name that was created as a way to let our audience know that we have firsthand, inside scoops from our guests. In other words, with each athlete who comes on our show, we are able to go with them inside the "huddle," which is a sports term for when teammates gather together to strategize. When you listen to what we say or read what we report, you know that it is from inside the huddle—firsthand knowledge from the pros.

As I discussed previously, *Huddlin' with the Pros* started off as a webzine. Because the name was a bit of a tongue twister, some people had a hard time pronouncing it. Most people would pronounce it "Huddling with the Pros," as opposed to pronouncing it with more of a "street" sound by dropping the g, *Huddlin'*. In addition, my father, who was a senior engineer at CBS radio, told me I should use an acronym and call it *HWTP*. Be sure to pick a name that is not hard to pronounce or spell, because that would make it difficult for people to find your podcast. The tagline for *Huddlin'* was "the first behind-the-scenes magazine on the web," and that is what we were at the time.

When trying to come up with a name and tagline for my podcast, I asked myself the following: What do I want to convey to my potential listeners? Who is my ideal audience and why? How is my show different than the other podcasts out there? I literally grabbed a piece of paper and answered my own questions.

What do I want to convey to listeners? It is not your regular sports talk show discussing only the X's and O's.

Who is my audience and why? Millennials. Millennials listen to podcasts more than any other group. They were known at the time (and probably still are) for sharing content and causing it to go viral, and they love engaging on social media. I also read that Millennials like listening to podcasts because they are able to listen whenever and wherever they want. Thus, podcasts suit their lifestyles.

What makes my show different than the rest? We talk about off-field, off-court activities of professional athletes by discussing social issues but with a sports focus. Voilà, my tagline: "Discussing Social Issues with a Sports Focus."

Hip Hop pioneer and producer Luther "Uncle Luke" Campbell named his podcast *The Luke Show* and has the tagline, "Unfiltered. Uncut. Unapologetic." Proudly, I came up with this tagline. People who are familiar with Uncle Luke's personality and his music will quickly realize that this tagline fits Luke perfectly. It's him in a nutshell. He is unapologetically himself; he is bold, and has a tendency of being crass.

When Luke's manager first approached me about starting a podcast, I was somewhat a fan of his music, and mostly admired the fight he took on in the 1990s for freedom of speech, for recording artists not to be censored. Yet I still had to do my research.

I listened to some of his old podcasts that were recorded informally. When I say informally, I mean he recorded from his cellphone and from his home, not in a recording studio. On one recording, you could actually hear his dog snoring in the background. I also noticed that these podcasts were sporadically released, not consistent. Surprisingly, the quality of the recordings from his cell phone was actually pretty good. Listening to the podcasts was helpful, because it enabled me to examine the tone and content of his episodes, as well as his views on politics and sports—the two subjects he most frequently discussed. My view of Luke's podcast after listening to each and every one was that he was raw and unfiltered, offensive at times, and he did not seem to care what anyone thought. All of this research helped me develop his tagline. It encompassed his personality.

In reality, you do not have to be an incredibly creative person to come up with a catchy, successful tagline. You can often find the name of your show or your tagline in your content or your personality.

Insights: Motivation to Start a Podcast Comes in Many Forms

Alexandra Ferrara

Alex Ferrara and Tina Scariano are the creators of the podcast Obsessed with the Best with Alex & Tina. *The podcast is produced by DimlyWit Productions (November 9, 2020).*

My partner-in-crime Tina Scariano and I actually didn't even set out to start a podcast! We are both based in NYC, and we're friends, colleagues, and also kind of career twins. We're what I'd call "multi-hyphenates"—actresses, singers, models, makeup artists, and producers, and we might have a different job depending on the week. Because of the nature of our ever-changing and unpredictable careers, we naturally come into contact with new people, products, and recommendations every day. Tina and I decided to chat over a weekly Instagram Live to share whatever it was that week that made our lives better, easier, and more fun, or helped us to stay healthy, happy, and informed. For a few months, these weekly IG Live check-ins were purely a source of joy for ourselves and a way for us to share insider tips with each other and our close friends and family. A production company happened to see one of our IG Live shows and asked if we'd be interested in turning it into a podcast! We loved the idea and were excited about getting to let our conversations continue to evolve.

Question: What Type of Advice Would You Give Podcasters Starting Up?

You have to love who you work with, and live and breathe your podcast theme/concept/common thread, etc. It's so much more work than you think, so you've got to be passionate about the information you're putting out there and WHY you're putting it out there. Get very clear on your WHY and stay clear on it. How are you providing value to your listeners? Always bring it back to WHO is your audience and what are you GIVING them. If you're going to sit down and talk for an hour, you must be talking about something that you can't WAIT to dive into, something you're so excited or curious about that the words just tumble out of your mouth, so that preparing is never a chore. Learn as much about social media and marketing as you can. And LISTEN to your podcast each week. Always keep a running list of how it can improve, down to the little things, like not interrupting people, and limiting your "buts," "ums," and "likes," which is harder than it sounds.

Question: How Did You Come Up with Your Podcast Name?

We wanted to keep it simple and straightforward, while also somehow being specific and all-encompassing at the same time! *Obsessed with the Best with Alex & Tina* lets the listener know exactly what they're getting, and it doesn't limit our conversation at all. We always say we ONLY share "the best of the best" with our audience, and that can mean a product, book, workout, film, artist, cocktail, or interview. We include anything at all that truly inspires us and makes our lives better, because we know a documentary or thought provoking conversation can sometimes add just as much value to your day as a jade roller or an eye mask.

Chapter Review

It is important to know why you want to start a podcast. It is more than just wanting large listener numbers, because you will have to earn that. Determine whether you would like to produce a professional show that will eventually result in advertisers, or a show that is more fun and relaxed. Remember, understanding your motivation before you begin will help you build a podcast that is successful on your terms.

Another key step is determining the type of content you would like to produce and the importance of pushing out consistent topics that you will enjoy discussing. Think about what you enjoy discussing and build your podcast around that. Do your market research and competitive analysis. You do not have to be a creative genius to come up with a name and tagline for your podcast. Have fun and do not get caught up with the complexity of it, and keep it simple.

The next chapter will go over defining your audience, which will build on everything you've learned so far.

Exercises and Discussion Questions

a. Let's get creative: come up with a name for your podcast.
b. If you are feeling adventurous, try to come up with a tagline.
c. Name three topics that you love to discuss.
d. Research and list at least three podcasts that you perceive to be similar to the three topics you would love to discuss.
e. Describe each of the podcasts, including similarities and differences to your idea; include a pros and cons list.
f. If possible, take note of their listenership—that is, the number of subscribers and/or listeners per episode as well as their demographic information.
g. Write an essay about how you would make your podcast stand out based on your answers to the above.

CHAPTER 5

Defining Your Audience

Knowing your audience is the key to marketing your show and understanding the behaviors and habits of potential listeners. You will want to be sure of this from the very start so you can direct your content and format to that audience. It will also be a big help once it is time to start looking for advertisers. When I was creating my podcast, one of the first things I did was visit the website of the Pew Research Center at www.PewResearch.org. Pew is a reputable organization that offers informative statistics on all sorts of consumer trends, such as politics, entertainment, social issues and more. It has been tracking podcast usage and views since 2005, just a year after the term "podcast" was coined. The website is easy to use and accessible, and the staff is helpful if you need clarification on any of the information. Best of all, it's free. Companies may choose to hire a market research firm for more in-depth analysis of past trends and forecasting, but Pew is an excellent starting point.

Pew told me that more men listened to podcasts than women, and that the majority of listeners were from the Millennial generation (born between 1981 and 1996). I was excited to learn these facts, because they told me that my thought-provoking sports show would easily fit into this demographic.

As mentioned previously, I was reinventing *Huddlin'* as a podcast, and it was facing new challenges in this storytelling world of journalism. It no longer had its once strong fan base, and the marketing and advertising landscape had completely changed. In addition, it had to reintroduce itself to the sports industry and rebuild the trust and interest that it once had. A daunting task.

Initially, my podcast attracted an older segment, Generation X (born 1965 to 1980) and Baby Boomers (1946 to 1964). The reason for the older demographics was because both Generation X (my age group) and Baby Boomers are the generations of my friends and family. When you first launch your podcast, you will find that your biggest supporters will be friends and family, especially those that follow you on social media platforms. Knowing this, we needed to expand our audience and target market to include Millennials. In this new age of marketing and social media content sharing, Pew Research told us that Millennials are extremely important because they are a generation that regularly shares content. Shared content equals more exposure. As reported by the American Marketing Association, "Millennials define themselves by their social media use and are eager to share content, so long as it is relevant." The next step for *HWTP Sports Talk* was to make its content relevant to this market segment without losing its mission of discussing social issues with a sports focus, and without turning off our current audience of Generation X and Baby Boomers.

Additional research told me that Millennials are the most socially conscious group. They use social media platforms to engage and effect change, and they enjoy podcasts because they give them the freedom to tune in wherever and whenever they choose. Podcasts suit their lifestyle and, of crucial importance, advertisers love them. Advertisers are attracted to Millennials because of their influence, brand loyalty and enormous buying power, which generates billions of dollars annually. Due to this kind of information, Millennials have changed the face of marketing. Here are the questions that guided my research:

- When it comes to media consumption, what resonates with Millennials?
- Where do they get their news and information?
- How do Millennials consume sports content? Via streaming? Podcasts, YouTube? Legacy media (radio/TV)?
- What types of social issues are currently resonating with Millennials?
- How can *HWTP Sports Talk* be positioned to appeal to the Millennial sports/social issues audience?
- What attitudes and behaviors inspire Millennials to feel brand loyalty to a podcast?

According to MediaPost, an integrated publishing and conference company whose mission is to provide a complete array of resources for media, marketing and advertising professionals, Millennials are consuming sports everywhere, "24 hours a day, 7 days a week. And the screens are no longer just a family's television, but have gotten smaller and are in each individual's hands, oftentimes more than one at a time" (Urban, 2016). In a 2016 article, MediaPost also revealed that Millennial sports fans crave digital platforms, sports content and sports-focused social influencers.

In that same 2016 MediaPost article, 1,298 people between the ages of 13 and 24 were surveyed. The survey revealed that this generation "favored watching their favorite social media influencers over their favorite professional athletes across five different sports," and "eighty-seven percent of 13–24 year olds use social media to regularly consume sports-related content. This is nearly twice as much as the 13–24 year olds who consume sports content regularly through mainstream sports media websites or apps." Knowledge is power, and reviewing these statistics was a crucial step in my decision-making process. This research also empowered me because it enabled me to not only keep my Generation X and Baby Boomers market, but also expand my audience to attract the all-important Millennials.

Obviously, you can interchange Millennials with Generation X, or whatever your potential audience may be. Be as specific as necessary. If you are planning a podcast on quilting, figure out not only who quilts (in terms of gender, age, socio-economic background, education, race, etc.) and why they quilt, but also how they listen to their media (what time of day, where, on what device), whether they are attracted to "short and sweet" or more in-depth programs, and what other things hold their interest.

Statistics like these are also incredibly helpful in tailoring content for your show. For example, according to Twitter, *HWTP Sports Talk*'s listeners have the following interests: 97 percent go to music festivals and concerts, 93 percent read sports news and 93 percent go to sporting events. Knowing this information, we decided to work in some music-related content that was related to sports, such as the halftime show at the Super Bowl and other major sporting events, and we also created the Hit List segment for the 93 percent of our listeners who regularly read factual sports news—that is, who won last night's game, who's injured and which teams are heading into the finals. Our focus was still off-court and off-field activities of athletes, but we wanted to also give our listeners the quick sports facts they were craving.

While doing additional audience research, I discovered it was equally important to choose a podcasting platform that enabled easy access via mobile devices. Smartphones had been considered the "second screen" and, according to Nielsen, "Millennials have officially become the mobile-first generation." So I learned where my audience was listening and made sure to meet them there.

While doing the bulk of the planning up front is smart, even essential, it is also important to monitor your listenership as it grows and develops. That way you can keep yourself attuned to its specific interests and listening habits, and tailor your show accordingly. Once we launched the podcast, I immediately started tracking our audience demographics. There were definitely some surprises, such as learning that the gender of our listeners varied by social media platforms in the following way:

Statistics in 2014

Facebook:	46% Female
	54% Male
Twitter:	38% Female
	62% Male
Instagram:	46% Female
	54% Male
Blog Talk Radio:	52% Female
	48% Male

As you can see, we were attracting more women than men at Blog Talk Radio, our podcasting platform, which is not what we were expecting based on the Pew statistics. So, it is important to stay flexible and expect to be surprised.

It is important to note that some social media platforms offer more in-depth analytics than others. Twitter used to offer a very useful audience insight page in its analytics, but removed it on January 30, 2020. It is unclear why it removed this feature (it may be moving to a paid service), but perhaps it will offer a similar free alternative by the time this book is published. Facebook's insight is not as in-depth as Twitter's used to offer, but it is effective. Through Facebook's analytics, not only will you see the percentage of page followers by gender, but also by age group. Facebook also provides the country and state your followers are from, which I found very interesting. When you have various social media platforms, compare the demographics to your actual listeners and see where they match up. Also, most podcasting platforms have their own analytics page, which is helpful because you can also see where your listeners are finding your podcast from—for example, via organic search, Twitter, Facebook, etc. This will also determine which social media platforms produce the most listeners for your podcast. We found that Twitter and Facebook were the two most important social media platforms for the podcast. It showed that our hashtags worked because we were receiving more listeners than were actually following our social media pages.

All this targeting will help you develop a show that will resonate with your desired demographic and help you build a real community of listeners who are excited and engaged by your programming. Of course, knowing the demographics of your audience is also incredibly helpful when it comes to seeking advertisers.

Another useful website is offered by the Small Business Administration, a government agency that assists prospective and small business owners in growing their companies. I worked with SBA many years ago, and it has a useful website along with great mentors who will help you achieve your goal. They encourage you to gather demographic information so that you will better understand the pros and cons of gaining customers, as well as analyzing your competitors, which I have done. Their service is also free.

Below are questions inspired by ones that appear on the Small Business Administration website that provide a great starting point. I tweaked the questions a little to fit podcasts. Conduct a preliminary search and try to answer these questions.

- **Demand:** Is there a desired audience for your podcast? If so, explain why.
- **Market size:** How many people would be interested in your podcast content?
- **Economic indicators:** What is the income range and employment rate of your potential listeners?
- **Location:** Where do your listeners live? Will you have a problem reaching them?
- **Market saturation:** How many similar podcasts are already available to your potential listeners?

Depending on your time and financial resources, there are other research methods that you could try, such as surveys and focus groups.

Surveys: This method is less time-consuming and more cost-friendly. There are many survey companies out there, such as SurveyMonkey and Mailchimp, that could assist you in creating effective and simple surveys that you could measure through their analytics. I found both companies to be user-friendly. I used SurveyMonkey in school for a podcasting idea, and I posted it on both Twitter and Facebook using the hashtags #Survey and #Podcast. Although I did not receive as many responses as I hoped, it was enough for me to make an informed decision. In addition, Twitter offers a survey option. When you compose a tweet, there is an icon that looks like sidebars. Click on that icon and just follow the prompts; it is so easy to use. See image below.

From author's Twitter account to show how to start a survey.

On an unrelated note, another reason to use polls is that they can be a great way to get media exposure for your podcast and/or social media pages. Oftentimes reporters look to Twitter polls to enhance their articles. Here's an example: A pretty gross, but funny video went viral involving Michigan University Wolverines football coach Jim Harbaugh, who happens to be the brother of John Harbaugh, a head coach in the National Football League. Jim was caught on camera picking his nose and snacking on it. Many news outlets picked up the story, and there was a debate about whether or not he ate his boogers. In fact, the incident was labeled "BoogerGate." To our surprise, the Annapolis, Maryland *Patch* wrote about BoogerGate and included our poll (Belt, 2016). As you can see in the image below, only 12 people participated in our poll, but it just goes to show you never know who will see your content. Earned media is hard to come by, so be sure to seize every opportunity.

And a poll may settle the question for fans.

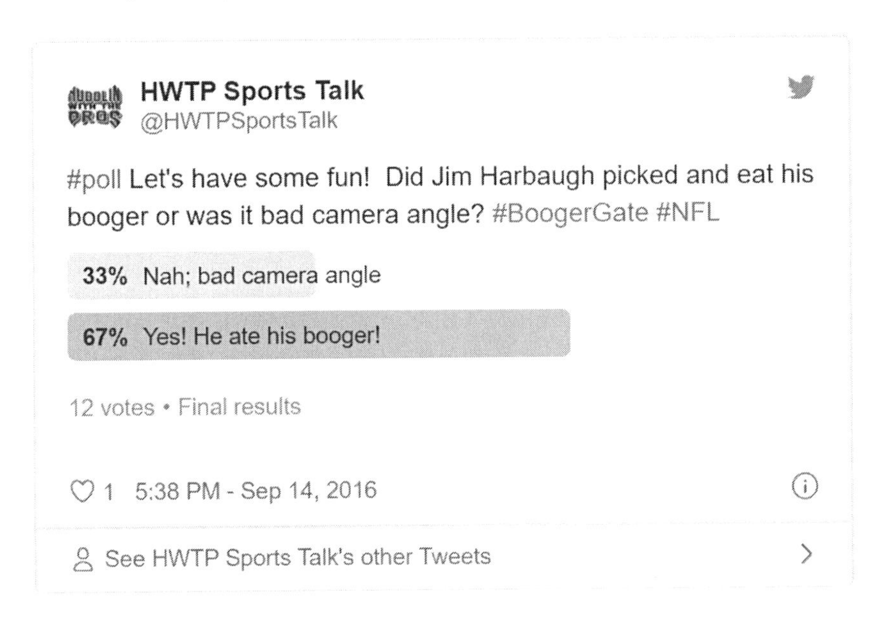

From author's Twitter account, showing the results of the survey on BoogerGate.

Focus Groups: Focus groups can be costly, but they are very effective and will provide you with detailed information. Your focus group should be demographically diverse and promote open discussion. Not always ideal, but you can create an informal focus group starting with friends and family. You can also arrange a formal focus group and hire a company, or rent out a conference room and invite a targeted group akin to the interest of your podcast content. This method is effective, but costly.

Defining your audience takes research, which is a crucial step to making sound decisions as to how you approach and attract your potential market. In this ever-changing world of media, we need to be knowledgeable about current and future trends. This will assist in making projections and assessments about podcasts' growth (or lack thereof) in this digital age. It will also assist in improving your content and determining how it is being received, both now and in the future.

Knowledge is power! The Small Business Administration sums it up succinctly: "Market research helps you find customers for your business; competitive analysis helps you make your business unique. Combine them to find a competitive advantage for your small business." Use the available tools out there that can help assist you in research and analysis such as Pew, MediaPost and social media platforms, and also conduct your own research. Use the Resources section of this chapter as a guide.

Chapter Review

Knowledge is power! You learned in this chapter why defining your audience is so important. After all, how can you market to an audience you do not know anything about? Knowing your audience and understanding the behaviors and habits of potential listeners is the key to marketing your show. There are many tools out there, such as Pew Research, MediaPost and the Small Business Administration, that will help you answer those questions. Remember to think about your potential audience's media consumption and what resonates with them, even how they get their news. Research is extremely important and will be mentioned often throughout this book.

This chapter, along with the previous ones, has led you to the next chapter, "Choose Your Podcasting Platform." But before you can choose your podcasting platform, you will need to understand your audience. Look at the chapter discussion questions and exercises to assist you.

Exercises and Discussion Questions

a. Which generation is your ideal audience? Why? Provide three solid sources that you used for your research.

- **Baby Boomers**: Born 1946–1964
- **Generation X**: Born 1965–1980
- **Millennials**: Born 1981–1996
- **Generation Z**: Born 1997–2012

b. What type of podcast content are your potential audiences listening to? Provide at least three examples and explain the content.
c. What other media is your potential audience consuming? For example, YouTube, Facebook, etc.
d. What else holds your audience's interest?
e. How might you incorporate those other interests into your show?

Resources

The Small Business Administration: www.SBA.gov
Pew Research Center: www.PewResearch.org
MediaPost: www.mediapost.com
SurveyMonkey: www.SurveyMonkey.com
Mailchimp: https://mailchimp.com

CHAPTER 6

Choosing Your Podcasting Platform

To Be or Not to Be (Live)—That Is the Question

As mentioned before, knowing your personality and knowing whether or not you can think quickly is essential to knowing whether you should host the podcast yourself or enlist the talents of another. This mindset should also be present when thinking about whether to pre-tape your podcast, the most common method in podcasting, or broadcast live, which is often compared to live stream radio and is rare, but which some podcasters like to produce. In addition, there are many podcasting platforms available, and it is important to pick the platform that will meet your recording needs. Also, keep in mind what you learned in chapter 5, Defining Your Audience. Knowing your audience will also determine the platform you choose. Millennials like the freedom to listen to podcasts whenever and wherever, so streaming your show live might not be an efficient way to go if you are trying to attract this audience. So you will have to make sure to catalog your episodes effectively.

After much thought, I decided to produce a live show. Knowing that I was completely new to all of this, you are probably thinking that I was either crazy or simply naive. People who know me best thought the former, but I was actually that naive. What I did not know then is that going live is not easy, especially when you don't have a clear plan. It requires organization and talking points, among other things.

Taping your podcast, as mentioned, is the traditional method to podcasting. It enables you to go back and edit mistakes or clean up dead air, the "ums," "ahs" and the dreaded talking over each other—something that occurs quite frequently. Broadcasting live, especially if you are a novice, is risky, because you really have to be well prepared. A live audience can be turned off quickly by mistakes, inadvertent dead air and noises. Another important point to keep in mind is that there are only a few podcasting platforms that offer seamless live streams.

When I first started my podcast, one of my hosts had a habit of saying, "You know what I mean" after almost every point. Another issue we had was the platform; although the "studio" was web-based, we would use a designated telephone number for both host and guests, and the host would often forget he was not on a call talking to a friend. He would often provide reinforcement after each point the guest was making by saying "uh huh" and "mmm-umms." This became problematic because there was a 30-second delay and the guest would think the host was interjecting with a point when he was just reinforcing what the guest said. The guest would then pause or ask, "Did you say something?" At times the whole thing would sound chaotic. Although I would tell the host not to do it, he would forget and do the same thing again. Why? Because most podcasters are not trained broadcast journalists, so these types of expressions will be common. You just have to be aware and learn to control your reactions.

Another issue that can come up is not being able to ad-lib when a guest fails to call in during a live show as planned. Yes, we have been stiffed a couple of times, which is not uncommon, even with well-known prime time talk shows. As a novice producer, I did not anticipate these kinds of issues, nor were we able to think quickly often enough, which caused panic. We would often scramble and end up cutting the show off early. This will not fare well with listeners who are expecting an hour show that is well planned and runs smoothly.

If your episode were taped, you would have time to put together a completely different show if your guest(s) did not call in or were not there when you called them. During a live show, you would definitely need to be prepared and plan for all of the possible scenarios. Through much trial and error during my years of podcasting, I learned that being organized and prepared and creating talking points for each show are essential steps for both a live and pre-recorded show. This type of planning will give you much more of a chance of having a smooth-running show, while also cutting down on the editing.

At the beginning, I did not know the difference between a recording platform and a hosting platform. I thought they were one in the same, and that each platform enabled you to record, but it doesn't work that way. In fact, there are more podcast hosting platforms than platforms for recording. Only one platform actually enables you to broadcast live and invite both guests and listeners to call in during a live broadcast: Blog Talk Radio. Unfortunately, there has not been much competition or innovation available, so a platform like this can get away with setting higher prices and not providing the best customer service. As terrific as the platform is for broadcasting with live call-ins, Blog Talk Radio comes with some challenges, such as intrusive pop-up ads, unwanted Blog Talk Radio branding, and subpar customer service. Thus, the platform is considered mediocre due to these three major issues.

Despite its issues, Blog Talk Radio is still one of the best platforms for podcasting live and pre-recording your show. It is easy to use, and you can produce a polished and professional show. As mentioned, it does not have any competition, and your subscription comes with two personal designated telephone numbers, a host line and a guest/listener line. The number never changes unless you cancel or downgrade your subscription. Blog Talk Radio also allows listeners and guests to hear the show while on hold. We have had guests call in to our show early and then comment on previous segments during their interview, which is a nice professional touch.

Guests and listeners share the same phone line, so it is important to ask your guests for their phone number ahead of time. If your show is popular, you may have quite a few listeners calling in and you will need to determine which numbers belong to your guests so that you can unmute the correct number. There have been a few occasions when I actually unmuted the wrong number and all you heard was background noise and sometimes people yelling at one another. That is not what you want your listeners to hear.

As I discussed previously, deciding whether you will be taping your show or going live is so important, because it will determine what type of platform you choose. When I decided to forego the live broadcast, I started to research different platforms that support guests and producers, and I found Zencastr, which is the platform I use with one of my celebrity clients. I initially suggested Blog Talk Radio, but his manager did not like the Blog Talk Radio branding when calling into the show. My client wanted the option to customize his own show. For example, when you dial the guest call-in number, the first thing you hear is a British woman saying, "Blog Talk Radio." She sounds nice and professional, but not when you want to brand your own show. In the beginning I did not mind it, but as my show grew I wanted guests and listeners who called in to hear "HWTP Sports Talk," not "Blog Talk Radio." Even though you did have the option to turn the Blog Talk Radio intro off before recording your show, you didn't have that option to turn it off when people called in. This was the major issue with the client's manager, and I could not blame her. We then decided to use Zencastr as the recording platform.

Zencastr is terrific for pre-taping your podcast. One negative, however, is that Zencastr is completely computer based and doesn't support access through mobile or tablet devices. This is actually an odd concept in this mobile-centric world, where half of Americans access the Internet via their mobile devices. Zencastr works strictly through your desktop computer or laptop. Another thing to note with Zencastr is that it only works with Google Chrome or Microsoft Edge browsers. If you don't have either of these two browsers, it will prompt you to download one of them. In addition, if you do not have an updated computer or laptop speaker, it will either prompt a warning signal in its studio, or it will not allow the platform to access your computer at all. If you receive an audio warning prompt and you do not fix it, you will, on occasion, sound like you are in a tunnel.

This type of selectiveness from Zencastr is probably the reason why the sound quality is superior to other platforms. It sounds as though the guest and host are in the same room. We have had some sound quality issues with this platform, however, because not everyone has an updated browser, computer or quality microphone. In addition to the issues you will have using an outdated computer or browser, you will have to remember to make sure that your microphone is unmuted. You would be surprised that something as simple as unmuting your mic could be a big problem, but it is a common one. Another issue I came across while using Zencastr is that the voices are sometimes not recorded in sync. What I mean by this is that Zencastr records each voice separately as individual tracks. It has a feature that is called "Automatic Post-production," which allows you to select all the tracks you want listeners to hear. You have the option of producing your final tracks as a WAV file or an MP3. During this automatic post-production, when you select the tracks you want finalized, Zencastr will automatically do it for you. This happened twice with my show when the host's and the guest's voices did not match up. For example, my host David Weinstein interviewed the *Washington Post*'s sports reporter Ben Golliver, and after Zencastr did the post-production I replayed the final audio and, to my surprise, I heard David start to ask a question, but before he could finish I heard Ben's voice automatically playing and literally talking over David's voice. Because the voices were not in sync, I would hear Ben answering a question followed by a long silence before David asked another question. Through trial and error, I found out what was causing this. All parties have to be connected when you stop recording. If they hang up before you stop recording, everyone will have a different record time. Each voice has its own track which is recorded separately, so if you're being interviewed for a 20-minute segment and the show is an hour, there are still 40 minutes remaining. Your recording is 20 minutes, while everyone else's recording is 40 minutes. When you do the post-production and you select all the tracks, your voice is not going to line up with the others. In order to fix this issue, you will have to either stop the recording once the 20-minute interview is over and then start up another recording for the rest of the show (which we do), or it will be an editing nightmare if you're not an experienced editor.

When I contacted Zencastr creator Josh Nielsen, he assured me that the issue has been fixed: "We have recently deployed a fix for the track syncing issue.... All tracks should line up perfectly now." He continued, "Also, we have mobile support in the plans for later this year [2020]." Hopefully, by time this book is released the mobile support will be in full effect. Another option is Ringr, a podcasting platform that is pretty similar to Zencastr. I found the platform a little complicated and not that user-friendly. Remember, all of this is subjective. What works for me may not work for you, so research the various platforms and see what best fits your needs and wants, both artistically and financially.

Another great platform that can be used to record your show is your mobile device. Be it an Android or iOS phone, each is made for this digital age. They come with high-quality sounding microphones. The phones also allow you to plug in a Lavalier microphone, which is basically a clip microphone. It is more sophisticated than the microphone that comes with your mobile device, and it is also used in broadcasting and public speaking. Before hiring me, one of my clients would record his show on his Android phone. I was totally surprised at the sound quality. It had such a professional sound that I actually thought he produced it in a recording studio. The drawback for using your phone is that it does not promote guest call-ins. The guest will have to be in the same room, or you will have to figure out a way to conference everyone into your phone.

Now that you have a feel for the different recording platforms, let's now discuss the hosting platforms. There are more hosting platforms than recording platforms, the most popular ones being Podbean, Podomatic and Libsyn. In fairness, both Podbean and Podomatic have recently added a recording feature to their platforms. Again, the platforms are for single-person recording and are not set up for more than one person. These platforms, for the most part, offer similar features, including hosting, a customized website and publishing services. Once your podcast is uploaded to their site, they will allow you to publish your podcast on the platform's website or your personal website, as well as to your social media platforms through special coding. The platforms offer customized hosting packages that include (depending on your subscription level) a customized podcast website. It will allow you to add your logo as well as choose from attractive templates that are specially made for podcasting. In addition to offering special codes for social media platforms, they also offer customized embedded codes if you want to direct listeners to your personal website. (See images below.) These hosting platforms are inexpensive and a great starting point. They range from free to about $250 per month, depending on your podcast needs. Just start small and build.

In addition, most of these hosting podcast platforms, as well as the platforms that offer automatic recording, add your podcast to streaming platforms such as Apple Podcasts, Spotify and others through RSS feed. This

Examples of embedded codes (author's collection).

allows more visibility and accessibility for your podcast, which equals success.

RSS stands for Really Simple Syndication, and most hosting platforms automatically create this for you. It is customized, up-to-date information about your podcast. It organizes your podcast in one spot and includes the headline and description of your shows. As mentioned, RSS feed is what Apple Podcasts and other streaming platforms use to add your podcast to their platforms. Your listeners could even subscribe to your RSS feed if you have access to the link. Most platforms have this feature, but you should be sure to do your research, because it's crucial to have in terms of promotion and visibility.

An extremely important note and something I found out the hard way: When you decide to discontinue your podcast hosting subscription, remember to ask customer service to help you keep your RSS feed. Otherwise, you will lose all of your shows. This happened to me as a novice, before I understood the power of RSS feed.

Another thing to note is audio quality. Audio quality is everything when it comes to podcasting. Poor audio could make or break you. See *Insights* by Jacob Bozarth and Alex Kontis for tips on audio quality.

I cannot express this enough: Determine whether you plan to stream live or record your podcast, and thoroughly research the various podcasting platforms to ensure that the platform you choose meets all your needs.

Insights: The Importance of Audio to Your Podcast

Alex Kontis

Alex Kontis is a freelance audio producer based in the UK (May 2019).

Alex Kontis.

Imagine turning up to the cinema after hearing great reviews for a film only to find out that the video quality is the same as a phone camera from 2003 would produce? You'd be pretty disappointed, to say the least. We should have the same mentality around podcasts, too.

One of the biggest turnoffs when I listen to new podcasts is the quality of the audio. Within the first few seconds, it's possible to tell that the audio has been recorded badly and, if so, then I'm out.

This isn't because I might have a higher threshold, as I produce my own show and work with others—it's because quality audio reveals that the show was created diligently and should be taken seriously.

Let's run through why high-quality audio is important and how you can achieve it with your show, too.

Why is Audio Quality Important?

Take a listen to some of the top-ranked shows on Apple Podcasts or Google Podcasts. What do they all have in common?

They all sound like they've been recorded well with a consistent standard of audio quality. Dialogue is clear and without distractions, sound effects might be tastefully used, and music is appropriately used where necessary.

High-quality audio doesn't distract you from the content of the show; it welcomes you in, and thus you're able to enjoy listening, learning, or being entertained.

How to Achieve High-Quality Audio

You might think that achieving a high-quality sounding podcast starts with recording. You'd *almost* be right. Before you even press record, it's important to make sure the environment you record in is as controlled as possible. This is the first thing you should do. It's no good having the best microphone and the most eloquent guests if you're recording with a window open next to a building site. You also don't need the "best" microphone, either. The best microphone is the right one for the job at hand. If you're recording an interview at home over Skype, a microphone that costs less than £100/$100 would work for you in a controlled environment.

After recording comes what is often the most time-consuming part of the process—editing.

You probably get frustrated hearing hedging, pauses for thought, or sentence restarts when you listen to podcasts, and your audience will likely be the same, too. Cutting them from your interview can be time-consuming and arduous, but the investment in time or hiring a podcast editor can make the difference between a well recorded conversation and a great sounding, memorable interview.

Insights: How to Improve Podcast Sound Quality (Without Spending Any Money)

Jacob Bozarth

Jacob Bozarth is the cofounder and CEO of Resonate Recordings, a comprehensive podcast editing service & production source (February 2019).

While everyone agrees that high-quality audio will benefit a podcast, not everyone can afford to purchase expensive podcasting equipment or to upgrade their current equipment. If that's you, we have good news. There's a way to improve the audio quality of your podcast without spending a dime.

By optimizing three parts of your recording process, you can immediately boost your podcast's audio quality for absolutely free!

1. Recording Environment

Where you choose to record your podcast will have huge implications for the audio quality of your podcast. Environment is everything. In our experience, your recording environment can break or make the quality of your podcast recording more than any other single element.

Jacob Bozarth.

Find a room with as little background noise as possible. When you put on headphones to record, you will be surprised at what may produce unwanted background noise that may make it into your recording. A few common culprits we are too familiar with are HVAC units, highways/traffic, trains, kids, pets, sump pumps, fluorescent lights, external hard drives, computers, fans and refrigerators, just to name a few. If possible, turn off all items with an off switch before you record.

It's also best to choose an environment with natural sound-absorbing materials such as curtains, carpets, couches, etc. Rooms with hardwood or concrete floors and blank walls may have an unpleasant echo. A good way to test your room to see if it is a good room to record in is to clap your hands and listen for a slap back echo. If you hear an echo, then you need to choose another room, or move some natural sound-dampening materials into the room.

2. Mic Technique

Regardless of whether you're recording a podcast with your iPhone or a ten-thousand-dollar mic, you can drastically improve the audio quality by optimizing a few simple things around mic technique.

First, experiment with the distance between your mouth and the mic. You generally want to be 3–5 inches from your mic, but every mic has its own slightly different sweet spot. A good rule of thumb is to make a fist with your hand and put your fist between your mouth and your mic. This will be a good starting point distance.

Next, make sure that you don't bump your microphone stand or your microphone. Even the subtlest bumps on your mic can create a thud or pop sound in your recording.

Lastly, if you don't already have a pop filter, then you can reduce the likelihood of picking up plosives or pops caused by bursts of air by putting your microphone on a 45° angle and pointing it slightly off-center towards your mouth.

3. Recording Levels & Monitoring

The third piece of the recording process that you need to optimize to improve your podcast's sound is gain and monitoring systems.

First, you want to adjust the gain of your recorder (or DAW) so that the level of your voice peaks around -12 and -10 db. This is a very heavily researched number, but we won't go into that right now. The main idea here is to leave headroom in your recording to avoid clipping (distortion) and not record at a level so quiet that you have to drastically boost the gain in post-production and end up raising the noise floor (unwanted white noise) of your audio.

Next, you must monitor your podcast in real time. This may sound a little too obvious, but a surprising number of people don't take advantage of this tool. If your current recording setup doesn't have a monitoring system, then you can get around this by recording a short snippet and talking as loud as you think you may speak during your recording. Then play back your test recording and make appropriate adjustments to your gain, mic placement and all the other factors we mentioned in this section. And while we suggest using high-quality closed-back headphones, any pair of headphones or earbuds is better than not monitoring your recording at all.

Conclusion

So there you have it! Three simple ways to immediately improve your podcast audio quality. Pouring more money into your podcast will undoubtedly improve the quality, but even the best equipment can sound bad if you don't know how to use it correctly.

We hope this section has given you advice you can implement today to make your next episode the best one yet!

Chapter Review

Many factors will go into choosing your podcasting platform, including your audience, your format, and your motivation behind starting a podcast. Deciding whether you want to stream live or pre-record is also important. Most platforms do not support a live stream. There is a difference between a hosting platform and a recording platform. It is important to know what these differences are in order to make sound decisions in choosing your podcasting platforms. Remember, knowing if you plan to stream live or record your podcast will require thoroughly researching the various podcasting platforms to ensure that the platform meets your needs.

The next chapter might make you feel a bit overwhelmed. I will discuss the daunting task of editing your podcast. This also directly relates to choosing the proper podcasting platform, because you have to understand the types of audio files the platforms supports—for example, MP3, WAV and MP2, to name a few. All this will be explained in the next chapter, but in the interim, look to the chapter discussion questions and exercises to assist you.

Exercises and Discussion Questions

a. Describe the pros and cons of pre-recording your show or going live.
b. What is your programming preference, live or pre-recorded? Explain why.
c. Research the various podcasting platforms mentioned in this chapter that support your preference of either going live or pre-recorded.

- Provide three platforms that fit your streaming needs.
- Compare and contrast the three platforms in terms of features and price points.
- Be prepared to discuss in class.

Resources

Anchor: https://anchor.fm/
Blog Talk Radio: www.blogtalkradio.com
Libsyn: https://libsyn.com/
Podbean: www.podbean.com
Podomatic: www.podomatic.com
Ringr: www.ringr.com
Spreaker: www.spreaker.com
Zencastr: www.zencastr.com
Zoom: www.zoom.com

Chapter 7

Editing Your Podcast

If your goal is to produce a polished show, the ability to edit is a very important skill to acquire. Every podcaster knows that editing is not an easy task. Rather, it is one that requires a skill set and time. For podcasters who decided to stream live, do not assume that just because you are producing a live show that you will not need editing skills. You will. Many scenarios may arise that require editing, such as inviting a guest who may not be available for the live show, but can do a pre-tape. Then there is the possibility of a guest or you or your co-host saying something that can be construed as offensive to listeners, or you may simply have to deal with an obnoxious caller.

Let me give you an example of something that happened to us live and on the air. We were discussing the NFL's "don't ask, don't tell" unofficial policy concerning LGBTQ players in the league. The caller started out well, making some interesting points, but suddenly began spewing out extremely ignorant and homophobic comments. Fortunately, I was able to drop the call. After the show, I immediately edited the caller out of the show. Even when you work very hard at producing a polished show, mishaps will happen that will cause you to want to pull your hair out. It is part of the business.

If you plan on pre-recording your show, there are usually pre- and post-discussions outside the actual interview itself, as well as some "retakes." Examples of these retakes could be adjusting sound quality, or mispronounced words, or call drops that will create dead air, or comments like "Hello, are you there?," "I can't hear you," or "Where did they go?" All of this will obviously need to be edited out.

Here's another example of the importance of having an editor (or the skill to edit) if you're not comfortable hosting a scripted show. Some people are more comfortable talking off the top of their head and are skilled at that. One of my clients had a great sense of humor that showcased well on-air, but for his new show he wanted it more polished with high production, so we tried the scripted route. The problem was that he had a hard time with his on-air delivery in a scripted environment. Because of his busy schedule, he was unable to rehearse and attend production meetings. This created a ton of tension and retakes. Eventually, we went back to a format that was a mix of scripted and creative freedom, and it was my job to fix things up in post-production. Because I had the editing skills, I was able to remove all kinds of undesirable background noises, including the occasional snorts and sniffles when he had a cold, making the show more polished.

What if you do not have editing skills or the proper editing software? This situation will affect the quality of your show, and that is not a desirable outcome, especially if your goal for a podcast is to make money. So you have got to remedy the situation by learning the skills or hiring someone who already has them.

Before we get into the types of editing platforms, let us take a deep dive into two important qualities you need to effectively edit your podcast: (1) attention to details and (2) patience.

Attention to Details. This is what I call having listener intelligence. Listener intelligence is being able to identify not only background noises, which are common in editing a podcast, but also long gaps between discussions, undesirable noises such as snorting from a cold or allergies, "ums," and other quirks that we as humans often have when talking. These types of noises can turn off listeners and, quite frankly, be viewed as unprofessional, especially if they are excessive. As an editor, it is your job to limit them. You may not be able to eliminate all of the noises, but you can limit many through editing. One of my personal pet peeves is hearing a gulping sound when a host or guest takes a drink of water, or excessive clearing of the throat (especially when it can be easily fixed by taking a simple cough drop). For you it might be something different, but you have to pay attention to the details and identify the various noises and long pauses, also known as dead air. What works for me is to listen to the entire show first and take notes as I go along. Then I go back and listen again, not only to fix the issues but also to see if I missed anything. You will find your own process and do what works for you.

Patience. Another important quality to have, believe it or not, is patience. They say it's a virtue and here is why. The editing process can be one of the most frustrating and time-consuming steps, even for those who are experienced. Once your show is over, you will want to edit it quickly and upload it for your listeners. But it is not that simple. Remember, a poorly edited show will affect the integrity and professionalism of your podcast, so take your time and carefully edit your show no matter how long it may take. Also keep in mind that if there are too many errors, it might just be easier to re-record your show, especially if you don't have a guest. Keeping these skill sets in mind, it is essential to select the right editing platform.

There are many editing platforms available, with some being easier to use than others. I personally use both Adobe Premiere and Audition to edit my podcasts. If you are a student, there are some editing software packages that offer student discounts. There are also many editing software programs that are actually free to use. Most podcasting platforms will have a section on their website that offers tips about creating a great show and will include a list of free and paid editing software packages. YouTube is also a very good source of how-to's for your particular editing software. I use it all the time.

Adobe's Audition and Premiere are two professional-level editing platforms that I highly recommend, but they are expensive. These two products are a part of the Adobe Creative Cloud, and they do offer considerably discounted student subscriptions at $19.99 per month, as well as helpful tutorials that teach you how to use their products.

Some parts of the editing process are time-consuming and tedious, thus something that should be planned for weekly. The more rehearsed that you and/or your host are, the less editing you will need to do. Conversely, the more ill-prepared you or your hosts are, the more editing you will have to do, and the more tedious the task will be.

As mentioned, there are many free editing software packages out there, and most are likely included on your mobile devices or computer package. For example, if you have a Mac or an iPhone, then you are most likely familiar with GarageBand, which comes standard on most iOS devices. This software is free and great for beginners to experienced podcasters. It is lauded for its user-friendliness and features. The software comes equipped with a complete audio library that includes instruments, presets for guitar and voice, as well as a selection of session drummers and percussions. These sounds can be used for audio transitions, breaks between your interviews, and station identification, both during live shows and in post-production of your podcasts. GarageBand is also downloadable for non-iOS computers.

Audacity is similar to Audition by Adobe. It has a similar interface. One notable difference is that it is free, whereas Audition is not. Audacity describes itself as a free, open source, cross-platform audio software. This software is also lauded for its easy to use interface as well as its quality. A reviewer at Techradar.com, a website that provides user technology reviews, wrote, "Amazingly powerful and feature-rich, Audacity is a great free alternative to costly audio editors—and it is surprisingly simple to use." Audacity allows you to record live audio through a microphone or mixer, and also allows you to import and edit your audio files. Like GarageBand, Audacity is available on both Mac and PC. An interesting point: Audacity relies on donations and advertising to keep their product free.

Power Sound Editor is another free software, one that I'm not familiar with, but like the others it is free and offers audio creation, recording and editing. One of the highlighted features of this software is that it is not very technical. In fact, the website states that it is "a welcome departure from more complicated software such as Audacity or WavePad." So for those who are not tech savvy, this software might be for you.

Editing is just as important as putting out interesting content. Poorly edited shows or a show that is not edited at all could really compromise the show's integrity and, most importantly, turn off listeners. Investing in a good editing software, be it free or paid, is essential.

Some important takeaways when editing:

- Decide whether or not you would like to learn the software yourself or outsource your editing.
- Research editing software and editing companies that meet your podcasting needs.
- Most editing software, such as Adobe, have terrific tutorials and student subscriptions, which means less money you have to spend.
- When deciding whether to outsource editing, consider your podcasting schedule and see if the company aligns with it. For example, if you air live on Wednesday evening at 7:00 p.m. and there is an obnoxious caller that you want edited out, make sure your editor is available after your show so that he or she can edit out any undesirable language or sounds. If you record your show, make sure that the editor will be able to turn around your show in a timely manner.
- If you would like to do the editing yourself, there are platforms such as Lynda.com, now a part of LinkedIn, and YouTube that offer user-friendly tutorials.
- There are many free software programs out there, so make sure you research to see which software fits not only your needs, but your technical ability or lack thereof.

Remember to carefully vet each platform and experiment to find which program fits your needs and comfort. In addition to the software I highlighted in this chapter, there are inexpensive and sometimes free classes offered by your local library, community college and places like BOCES, a local adult education program in New York that may offer editing courses. My local library as well as BOCES distributes a newsletter once a month that highlights the various events and courses they are offering. Interestingly enough, my local library actually offered a one-day course on how to start a podcast. Use a search engine and research educational centers in your area.

Look to the Resources section in this chapter for links to free editing software, even some that were not mentioned.

Chapter Review

Editing can be the most daunting and time-consuming task one has to endure when podcasting. If you want a polished sounding show, it is a task that cannot be ignored. Luckily, as outlined in this chapter, there are software and web-based platforms that can help you in this process. Remember, do not assume that just because you are producing a live show that you will not need editing skills. If you are not tech savvy or do not pay attention to details, there are companies out there that will do that task for you. You just have to remember to carefully vet these companies and be sure that they meet your needs in terms of hours, as well as have the ability to provide a reasonably quick turnaround so that your podcast can be uploaded to the masses on time. Sometimes it might be more cost and time effective to re-record the podcast if the errors are too complex to edit quickly.

The next chapter will be a lot less stressful and will examine the host and producer roles. But before you go there, look to the discussion questions and exercises from this chapter to assist you.

Exercises and Discussion Questions

Research three companies that provide podcast editing services.

a. What are the benefits of each company?
b. What about pricing? Is comparable student pricing offered?
c. Does the company match up with your schedule?
d. Is 24-hour customer service offered if something goes wrong?

- If so, is it a forum with a list of questions, or is it live customer service assistance?

Research at least three editing software programs.

a. List the pros and cons for each program.
b. If paid, is their pricing reasonable? Do they offer student pricing?
c. Research each software program you found and see if it has a tutorial on YouTube or Lynda.com.
d. Based on YouTube or Lynda.com, did you find the software user-friendly?

- Does it offer the features that you need to edit your software?

e. Finally, based on your research and analysis, which software program did you find most useful and are most likely to use in a real-world scenario?

Resources:

GarageBand: http://www.garagebandforpc.com/
Audacity: https://www.audacityteam.org/
Power Sound Editor https://power-sound-editor-free.en.softonic.com/
Music Maker: www.magix.com/us/music/music-maker/
Studio One: https://www.presonus.com/products/studio-one/
WavePad: https://www.nch.com.au

Part III

The Host(s), Listener, Producer Factor

Chapter 8

Be the Host, Get a Host or Co-host?

Left to right, caricatures of author, David S. Weinstein, and Thomas "Pepper" Johnson (author's collection).

As discussed in a previous chapter, hosting your own show, finding a host, or working with a co-host is something you should consider very carefully before creating your podcast. As you may recall from chapter 6, "Choosing Your Podcasting Platform," deciding on your hosting choices will also help determine which podcasting platform you choose, because not every podcasting platform supports more than one host or a guest.

However, the upside to hosting and producing your own podcast is that it will allow listeners to really feel your personality, the passion for your content, and the way you present it. The podcast will be a true reflection of you. However, knowing yourself, your personality, and your ability to host your show in an outgoing and intelligent way will be the key to deciding whether you should or should not be the main host.

According to a report by Westwood One, an American radio and podcast network, personalities matter to listeners. The report is titled, "The Relationship Between AM/FM Radio Personalities and Listeners Is Personal" (see *Insights*: Lauren Vetrano). In that report, some 2,617 consumers were surveyed and asked how they felt about AM/FM radio personalities. The results showed that 68 percent were able to name their favorite personality and show, while 52 percent chose to listen to their radio shows because of the personality of the host or disc jockey (DJ). These results can also be applied to podcasts, because radio and podcasts have the same basic elements.

The report further stated that listeners tune in because they resonate emotionally with the personality of the host/DJ. According to the same report, this emotional connection develops into loyal relationships based on humor and trust. Familiar hosts and DJs behind the microphone give listeners an actual person to connect with, no matter their other reasons for listening.

Further statistics from the report show the following:

- 87 percent listen because "they make me laugh."
- 64 percent say if the host and/or DJ went to another station, they would follow them.
- 61 percent say that the host and/or DJ make them think.
- 51 percent say the host and/or DJ are like friends and family.
- 46 percent say that they consider hosts and/or DJs "opinion leaders."

These statistics speak volumes about the importance of personality when working in the audio field. They also highlight the fact that listeners feel connected to the radio hosts and their shows because of the way the host is able to connect with them through humor and thought-provoking content.

If you really want to host your show but know that your personality might not be the strongest for audio—perhaps you are too laid back or shy—I would suggest that you look into having a co-host. But not just any co-host—rather, a co-host that you strategically seek out, someone who would complement your personality and perhaps even enhance it. Most importantly, the co-host should be someone who is interested in and knowledgeable about your show's content. When I started my podcast, I knew I did not have the personality to speak on air. In fact, when I become nervous I tend to stutter and stop thinking, which makes me lose credibility with the audience. In my case, it was imperative that I enlist a host or hosts. At the same time, I do have that behind-the-scenes mentality, so I knew producing would be my ideal position. In fact, one of my college professors said to me, "Jackie, you are a producer through and through … always taking the focus off yourself." And when she said that, it really struck a chord in me because it was true.

The *HWTP Sports Talk* podcast was launched in April 2014, and I decided to enlist my brother, Maurice "Mo" Parke (see below). When

I presented the idea to Maurice, he loved it and asked if he could have a co-host because he did not feel comfortable hosting the show by himself. He told me that his good friend Jason Lee would be perfect as his co-host since they had a common love of sports (including the New York Jets football team, poor guys) and talked about them all the time. Because of their connection, I felt it would work. They were by no means polished, but you could hear the chemistry and respect that existed between them, as well as the fun they had together, which resonated with our listeners—the few we had at the time. It was a good starting point for the show.

Maurice "Mo" Parke (left) and Jason "Jay" Lee (author's collection).

Another thing to consider is the types of hosts or co-hosts you may encounter. There are hosts that will be great collaborative partners, and there are those that will be high maintenance and expect you to do everything for them. Although it is part of your role as a producer, a high-maintenance host may require you to write an entire script for each show, as well as do all the research. If you are fortunate to have enough money to create a show without working a full-time job, then you might not find these tasks problematic. But if you do work a regular job or happen to be a full-time student, these scenarios can eat up your time. In these cases, it is extremely important that you recognize your wants and needs when seeking out your host. If you seek out a host or co-host without vetting them properly, this can create an undesirable situation that could compromise the integrity of your show. It will also be important to be well organized and know how to manage your time, especially when others do not.

It is also extremely important to find a host who is well versed on the topic of your show, even if it's a close friend or family member. Having a host who is unfamiliar with your show's theme will obviously compromise its integrity. You could actually lose credibility, because the host will not be able to comment outside of their planned talking points or script.

Here is a possible scenario with an inexperienced host. Suppose you have a guest who unexpectedly reveals some personal information which might be of interest to the audience that is connected to the topic being discussed. The inexperienced host might not be able to engage the guest in a meaningful and intelligent way or quickly ask important follow-up questions. Suddenly, an opportunity has been lost and your show goes flat. Thus, when vetting a host, it is also important to ask the right questions so you can acquire someone who is in tune with your schedule and passion for the topic of your podcast.

It is also important not to have too many hosts on air at the same time. I learned that the hard way while producing my show, with the result being quite chaotic. The podcast actually once had four hosts. If you have too many hosts, you will have to carefully structure the show in a way that would provide ample airtime for each. In addition, each host may have different levels of knowledge with respect to your topic, so as the producer you'll have to treat each one individually. Some hosts may be high maintenance, while others will come prepared with their own talking points and storylines. You also have to be mindful and respectful of everyone's process in preparing for a show. Even if you have just two hosts, it is necessary to have a production meeting at least once a week. That will allow you to discuss the topics you are considering for the upcoming show, as well as address breaking news that may have been released that day or in real time during the meeting. With multiple hosts, it is also important to be organized and set a formatting timeline and talking points. These tools ensure that your host(s) will not only be prepared but knowledgeable, because credibility matters.

In fact, not only does credibility matter, it is actually everything. Remember that Westwood One survey that said 46 percent of radio listeners consider their hosts "opinion leaders." This speaks to credibility. If your listeners believe your show is credible, they will remain loyal. Credibility is also important when seeking guests. Your previous podcasts will be your best selling points to agents, publicists and journalists in the respective industries.

If you do not have a notable and well-qualified friend or family member, you may also find a potential host among one of your guests, as I did with David S. Weinstein, the current host of my podcast.

News broke in the summer of 2014 that the Drug Enforcement Administration was considering an investigation on the misuse of opioid prescriptions by National Football League trainers and doctors. The trainers and doctors were allegedly obtaining and distributing prescription drugs to the players, which included addictive narcotics such as Vicodin. As I was looking for an expert to speak on this topic, I read a terrific article in the *New York Daily News* called, "Grilling NFL Trainers Could Kick Off Drug Enforcement Administration Probe." The article quoted a former Assistant U.S. Attorney who had prosecuted numerous drug cases. I thought, "We have to get this guy on the show." "This guy" was none other than David S. Weinstein. I reached out to him, and he agreed to appear. Naturally, he provided great insight on the topic. When his segment was over, he actually stayed on the line and listened to the rest of the show. There was another segment that piqued his interest, and he texted me and asked if I would mind if he participated in that discussion. He brought so much credibility to the topics we were discussing that I didn't mind at all, so I unmuted his call. After that show, I asked him if he would be interested in joining the show as a co-host. He agreed immediately.

I paired him up with the show's host, Bill Gutman. Bill's passion complemented David's lawyerly intellect, and together they created podcast gold. Their knowledge and chemistry were undeniable. Reporters and guests, including the athletes, would write me after or even state on air how different our show was and how they learned something new from their conversations with David and Bill. Bill, the consummate author, eventually left us to focus on his writing. If you have a great idea for a podcast, people will follow you and want to be a part of it. Call it human nature.

As you can see, the decision to host your own show or get a host (or multiple hosts) is not a simple task. Now that you received some food for thought, let us get into the specifics of each role, beginning with the host.

Insights: The Relationship Between AM/FM Radio Personalities and Listeners Is Personal

Lauren Vetrano

Lauren Vetrano is director of content marketing at Westwood One (December 2019).

A source of music discovery. The latest news and traffic information. Mood booster. Escape from the day. Catching their favorite program.

The reasons why listeners tune in may vary, but overall, people turn to AM/FM radio because it resonates emotionally. One of the major factors? Personalities. Familiar DJs behind the microphone give listeners an actual person to connect with regardless of why they listen.

Lauren Vetrano.

In November 2017, CUMULUS MEDIA | Westwood One conducted a study with researcher MARU/Matchbox. It asked 2,617 consumers what they felt about AM/FM radio personalities. The results show a strong affinity and trust that marketers can use to their advantage in audio creative.

Listeners Feel Connected to Their Favorite AM/FM Radio DJs, Personalities, and Shows

On-air talent is a huge draw. A massive 68 percent of listeners are able to name a favorite DJ, personality, or show. Over half of listeners (52 percent) say the main reasons they choose to listen to their favorite station are their favorite DJs, personalities, and shows.

But having a connection with AM/FM radio personalities is about more than just preference.

Listeners Develop Loyal Relationships with AM/FM Radio Personalities Based on Humor and Trust

- **Comedic relief:** 87 percent of respondents strongly or somewhat agree that their favorite DJs make them laugh.
- **Thought-provoking:** 61 percent agree that they make them think.
- **Strong loyalty:** 64 percent of listeners would follow their favorite DJs to another station if they moved.

- **Like family:** 51 percent consider them to be like friends or family. AM/FM radio continues to prove itself as an important one-on-one form of communication (CUMULUS MEDIA | Westwood One and MARU/Matchbox, 2017).

Perhaps the most important finding for advertisers: almost half of listeners believe that their favorite personality or show is an opinion leader that they trust. Personal live reads and endorsements are a staple of AM/FM radio advertising. Building upon this trust is a smart way for advertisers to get results.

Best Practice: Leverage the Appeal and Trust of Radio Personalities to Create Meaningful Audio Creative

Listeners already trust your station and your personalities. Trusted personalities can provide immediate credibility, endorsement and relevance to ads. Use reliable voices in live reads, endorsements, and recorded spots to create an affinity between your brand and listeners.

Key Takeaways

- Listeners feel connected to their favorite AM/FM radio DJs, personalities, and shows.
- Listeners develop loyal relationships with AM/FM radio personalities based on humor and trust.
- Best practice: leverage the appeal and trust of radio personalities to create meaningful audio creative.

Chapter Review

You may have noticed by now that all of these chapters correlate with one another, and chapter 8 is no different. Choosing whether you have the personality to host your show or have more than one person participating in your podcasting will determine the recording platform you will use. Do you think you have the personality? Remember this chapter taught us that personality matters to listeners more than you having a great broadcast voice. In fact, listeners want to be able to connect emotionally to their host/disc jockey. This emotional connection promotes loyalty and trust, also known as branding.

We also looked at having a co-host to help complement your personality if you do not have the ability to host the show on your own. It is important to not just grab any co-host or host—you have to strategically vet them. Everyone comes with their own agenda and could undermine what you are trying to build. And finally, make sure the host has knowledge of your podcast content. After all, you do not want to have someone on your show who has no knowledge of your topic. That will undermine the credibility of your show.

Before you get into the next chapter, work on the discussion questions and exercises below to assist you.

Exercises and Discussion Questions

a. Record the answer to this question on your cell phone or one of the podcast platforms: Do you have the personality to be a host or producer? Explain why (no longer than 3 minutes).
b. Here is a fun exercise: Take the Myers-Briggs personality test, located here https://www.myersbriggs.org/my-mbti-personality-type/mbti-basics/
c. What did your test reveal?
    - Were you surprised by the results?
    - Based on your results, are you a host or a producer?
    - Be prepared for class discussion.
d. What have you decided? Be the host, get a host or co-host with someone else? Explain your decision.
e. What podcasting platform best supports your decision?
f. List three major factors why listeners tune into their favorite radio show.

CHAPTER 9

The Host(s)

Role and Expectations

Former *HWTP Sports Talk* co-host Laina Stebbins (author's collection).

The *Houston Chronicle* describes the role of a radio personality/host as being "to entertain an audience during a given time slot." It sounds simple, but it is not. No matter what your podcasting goal, you want to be able to keep your audience captive by connecting with them. Unfortunately, there is no real cookie cutter recipe to do this, but you do not need a formal education or a big budget. I read a terrific book, *Talk Show Magic*, by Raven Blair Glover. In it, she describes successful talk show hosts as having "talk show magic." She says successful talk show hosts' "recipe for success is a combination of an attractive personality, great listening skills, authenticity, a clear vision of their audience's pain and joy, and what they are hungry to learn." (See *Insights*: Raven Blair Glover.)

According to podcaster and writer Rachel Corbett, the following attributes are most important for a podcast host. She writes, "When you are trying to connect with people you have never met, your content, delivery and authenticity will matter a million times more than your voice" (Corbett, 2016). By no means is she suggesting that voice doesn't matter, because it does. She also states, "Being in control of your voice and thinking about how you sound is an essential part of being a good presenter. That means controlling things like your volume, pitch, and intonation."

As I have mentioned, there was a point during the development of *HWTP Sports Talk* when I had a total of four co-hosts. David and Bill were joined by two young, smart but inexperienced interns who would serve as co-hosts. In the beginning, one particular intern was very eager and, during production meetings, would provide terrific storylines that we could discuss. His personality was so outgoing during the meetings that I felt he would sound great with David and Bill, who really led the show. He expressed to all of us that he wanted to participate in the on-air discussions, so we obliged. I even had him attend some NFL and NBA press teleconferences. One day I decided to dial into one of the press calls. The National Basketball Association's San Antonio Spurs held a media call for the announcement of Becky Hammon as their first female coach. I listened in and found that all of the other big media outlets, such as ESPN and Fox Sports, were on the call. To my surprise, I heard my intern state his name and say he was from *Huddlin' with the Pros*. He not only asked a terrific question, but he sounded confident and concise. It was a proud moment for me. But when airtime rolled around, he suddenly became shy and reserved. Our listeners were not really appreciative of his personality and let us know. We received feedbacks like "give that guy some coffee." He was extremely knowledgeable, yet very dry on the air. I do not know whether it was the fact that the show aired late (9:00 p.m. to 10:00 p.m.) and that he had had a long day at work, or whether he was just nervous. These types of examples are important to note, because one dry personality can turn off listeners.

Another big draw for hosting is someone with a comedic bent. Some talk shows and podcasts look to fill the hosting/co-hosting slots with someone who can be funny. A host with a sharp wit will lighten up a serious conversation by following with a joke. Listeners sometimes have short attention spans, and humor can always liven things up. No one wants to listen to someone with a dry, monotone personality who is also devoid of humor. I'm not suggesting hiring a comedian, but everyone knows someone who has a humorous personality with a quick wit, which I found with my initial host, my brother Maurice (AKA Mo). Maurice not only had a vibrant personality, but he also brought a humorous element to the show that resonated with our listeners.

As I discussed previously, if hosting is something you really want to do but you are not sure that your personality is right for the job, then seek out a co-host who will help provide your audience with just the right balance.

In addition to assisting with finding storylines, hosts can also bring productive feedback to your program behind the scenes. For example, my host, David S. Weinstein, is an attorney, and he brings a legal perspective to our show that not only adds credibility, but also gives us a unique angle. During a production meeting, we discussed the Twitter statistics that found 93 percent of our followers regularly read factual sports news. Our show discusses social issues and politics, more off-field content, but based on this stat, the host suggested we create a five-minute segment in the beginning of the show to go over the vital sports stats our listeners were craving. I thought it was a great idea. He came up with the name for the segment, "HWTP's Hit List," and even the show's new tagline, "the top stories on and off the field." This kind of productive feedback is priceless and really promotes an overall positive creative team environment.

A host or co-host can promote the sharing of ideas in a creative environment as well as share the workload, especially if you are a full-time student and/or a professional in the workforce. You can best share by each taking on tasks based on your individual strengths and skill sets. David is excellent at finding useful articles and also creating his own talking points and notes, which helps me out tremendously. Both tasks are extremely time-consuming. When I started *Huddlin'*, I had to do everything, and so will you with your podcast if you do not have access to the proper resources, such as a partner or team to assist you. By going it alone, you will sometimes run out of time because of your day-to-day obligations. I did, and it showed. Those early shows were not professionally produced. We did not have many listeners back then, so I was glad the trial and error phase began when our listener numbers were low. If we had had the listeners that we have now, one poorly produced show could have actually set us back tremendously.

On the flip side, working with a host or co-host sometimes comes with input and ideas that might not align with your vision. Sometimes, however, what you think is a great idea for a topic might not sound as good to your host. Then you should discuss it and try to have a meeting of the minds. You don't have to always agree, but since both of you want to have the best show possible, an honest exchange of ideas can be mutually beneficial.

Remember, if you decide to host and produce your own show, it will allow you to have complete control over both style and content, and thus the podcast will be a total reflection of your vision. But again, you will have to consider whether you have the personality to captivate an audience. In addition, the show's content and guests will all be your responsibility. To wear both hats of producer and host, you will have to learn good time management and organization skills. See *Insights* with David S. Weinstein to see how he handles his day-to-day responsibilities.

The next chapter will explain the producer's role and perhaps will help you determine if you are more of a producer, a host, or maybe both.

Insights: A Week in the Life of a Podcast Host, Who Also Happens to Have a Full-Time Job

David S. Weinstein

David is the host and legal analyst of HWTP: Sports Talk with David Weinstein *featuring five-time Super Bowl champion Pepper Johnson (April 2020).*

"Hellooooo, *Huddlin'* fans!" That is how every Wednesday evening starts at 9 p.m. Eastern. But what does the rest of the week look like? The show does not create itself. There is quite a bit of work that has to be done on the other days of the week. This work often fills the empty spaces on the weekend and after working hours, since hosting the *Huddlin'* podcast is not my full-time job. However, as a sports fan and sometimes fanatic, sports are always on my radar. The often difficult part is finding the time to get ready each week when my day is already full from the job I have representing my clients.

When I began hosting *Huddlin'*, we aired a live show every week. That provided both the benefit of having a scheduled time for the show and the potential conflicts that might arise if a matter took me out of town, or if I was preparing for a hearing that would be taking place the next day. Over time, we realized that we could pre-tape segments, but for the most part, Wednesdays at 9:00 p.m. were *Huddlin'* time. Even pre-taping presented scheduling issues, since most of the interviews had to take place during the day.

David S. Weinstein.

Unlike a traditional workweek, my week for *Huddlin'* starts on Friday. Unless there is a breaking story, Thursdays are usually a day off and time to put podcasting aside. Nevertheless, on Friday mornings when I get on the treadmill, I begin looking for stories that will provide a topic for discussion, or that will lead to an angle for an interview request. My producer and I have a "no fear" attitude and believe that no matter how big or small the subject of an interview request is, we will reach out and send an email. In some instances, we get no response, but in others we receive replies that result in some great interviews. We have also been able to build up a stable of regulars who we can call on to discuss a story or topic.

When I'm not preparing for an upcoming hearing, trial or filing deadline, I spend time on Saturdays and Sundays surfing the web and reading sports stories, trying to find one or two stories that represent a controversial hot-button issue from the world of sports, which has been our trademark. *Huddlin'* is not a sports podcast about X's and O's, so we look for a social issue or other topic that intersects with the world of sports.

By Sunday night, I have a general idea what the subjects will be for one or two interviews. I send an email to my producer, and we cross our fingers for a positive response. I also begin to assemble some other top stories from the week for a discussion during the podcast. By Monday morning, it is back to my regular job and, aside from some time at lunch or during a break, my pre-show research is done.

On Monday night, we get together for a production meeting to try to nail down the interview subjects and topics. We also begin to outline and determine the format for that week's podcast. We have found that having a video chat with the entire podcast team gets us all on the same page and we can start preparing some of the social media that will generate hits for us and interest in the show. Tuesday night brings a near final draft for the show. On Wednesday, after five, it is time for a tweet and a final draft of the outline for the week. Then it is 9 p.m. and *Huddlin'* time.

Chapter Review

A podcast host should keep the audience captive by connecting with them. This is an important role and a skill that not everyone has. Here are some important takeaways from this chapter:

a. Content, delivery and authenticity matters more than your voice.
b. Record yourself and try to control your volume, pitch and intonation.
c. Find a co-host with a comedic bent.
d. If you go with a co-host, seek out one who will complement your personality and help provide listeners with just the right balance of humor and gravitas.
e. If you go with a single host, make sure he or she will be knowledgeable about the content of your show and will fit its format and culture.
f. Remember, if you decide to host and produce your own show, it will allow you to have complete control over both style and content, and thus your podcast will be a complete reflection of your vision.

Before you move on to the next chapter, look to the discussion questions and exercises in this chapter to assist you.

Exercises and Discussion Questions

a. Record this answer on your cell phone or a podcast platform (no longer than 3 minutes):
    - Do you think two highly bubbly personalities will come across to listeners as exhausting or exhilarating? Explain.
b. Analyze, compare and contrast the host(s) of three popular podcasts. Try to find a podcast with a solo host and one with a co-host.

- Write down the title of each podcast and determine what, if anything, they have in common.
- Which host(s) did you prefer and why?
- Did you find the host(s) credible? Explain your answer.

c. What have you decided? Will you be the only host, or will you have a co-host? Explain your answer in detail.

Chapter 10

The Producer

Role and Expectations

The author (author's collection).

A producer oversees the entire production of your show, including content fact checking, and research, while also creating the vision of the show. In addition, the producer is also in charge of booking guests, including getting their bio and photo, creating scripts, doing the pre- and post-production formatting and editing. If you have a workable budget, you could have more than one producer and split up the workload.

Even if you have the oratorical skills and content to captivate your audience, hosting and producing your own show will not be easy. All of the hard work that goes into producing a proper podcast, especially one that sounds professional enough to invite guests and pitch to advertisers, falls solely on your shoulders. Producing a polished show entails being organized and planning ahead. You will have to make sure that you are well researched, rehearsed, and prepared. After all, as the host and producer you are not only the face of your podcast, but also the voice.

The following is a perfect example of a poorly produced show. As the producer, I should have prepared my original hosts, Mo and J. Lee, better. We had done about four shows when I booked the founder and executive of the NBA Orlando Magic and basketball Hall of Famer Pat Williams as a guest. We were so green then, and it showed. Mr. Williams came on the show to promote his recently released book. When talent comes on a show to promote something, their publicist usually sends you a press kit. In Pat Williams's case, his press kit consisted of his bio, a copy of his book, an overview of his book that highlighted key takeaways, and a one pager filled with questions that an interviewer could ask if there was insufficient time to read his book.

As novices, we thought we were in the clear because we believed that we did not have to worry about coming up with our own questions or reading the book. This wasn't the way to go. Once Mo asked him the first question off the sheet, Mr. Williams's answers started to flow into the other questions, not allowing Mo or J. Lee to ask another question. The two of them started to panic, as did I. We also did not get any unique perspective from the book, because the interview was controlled through these set public relations questions. The Williams interview took place during the NBA playoffs, so the guys were able to get some interesting perspectives about the games. But if they had had a journalistic background, been better prepared, and had an experienced producer, the interview would have been longer and more polished. Incidentally, Pat Williams came back on the show two more times, so he could not have been too upset by our unpreparedness. He got to say what *he* wanted to say about his book, which obviously made him happy.

According to *The Radio Producer's Handbook*, written by Rick Kaempfer (see *Insights*: Rick Kaempfer), a producer's job is multi-faceted, and he cleverly uses the title as an acronym. He states, "Each letter in the word will give a glimpse into some of the producer's daily duties."

P is for Psychologist
R is for Researcher
O is for Organizer
D is for Director
U is for Understudy
C is for Creative Writer
E is for Engineer
R is for Right-Hand Man

Let's take a look at each letter and how it applies to podcasting.

Psychologist. Kaempfer interviews Dr. Ed Dunkelblau, psychologist and director at the Institute for Emotionally Intelligent Learning. When describing the producer-host relationship, Dr. Dunkelblau interestingly states, "From what I have seen the producer needs to be a therapist, child psychologist, marital counselor, and specialist in treating post-traumatic stress and addictive disorders." He goes on to say with a little humor, "The biggest difference between producers and psychologists is that a psychologist's effectiveness is hard to measure and at times hard to even see. The producer's effectiveness is revealed immediately, every day. The other difference is that we get paid better."

Researcher. This is something that is mentioned frequently throughout the book. You may even think it has been overstated, but it is one of the most important skills you will use in everyday life and as a podcast producer. Research aids you in making informed decisions and providing invaluable insights on a variety of topics and your potential guests.

Organizer. Being organized is another theme that is discussed throughout the book. Kaempfer goes one step further by saying, "Creative personalities are not organized. Ever." I'm not sure if I agree totally with his characterization of creative people. It sounds so definitive, and there is always that one creative person, like myself, who prides herself on being organized. But he is trying to make the point that more creative types, who may feel more comfortable as a host or DJ, will typically rely on (or at least very much appreciate) the organizational skills of their producer. If your guests are creative types, you again will thank yourself if you go the extra mile with organization ahead of time.

Director. A true partnership arises here. As the producer, you will be making sure each segment of the show runs smoothly. During show time, a producer plays the role of the director with things like on-the-spot fact checking, or contacting a relevant guest to patch him into the show, or fielding listener calls. This leaves the host free to focus on what he/she does best: entertaining and engaging both guest(s) and listeners.

Understudy. According *to The Radio Producer's Handbook*, the producer needs to understand everyone's job, including the host's, in order to do his or her job effectively. For example, what happens if the host is sick or goes on vacation? Will you cancel the show until the host gets back? Kaempfer suggests that the producer could fill in, and there are many producers who have gotten their "big break" as an understudy before moving on to host their own show. We at *HWTP Sports Talk* always canceled our show when David or I were unavailable to do the show that week, or even for more than a week. As I have explained earlier, I do not have the personality to host a show, but another alternative would have been to invite one of our previous guests to host, perhaps a reporter. Make sure it is a guest that you have a good rapport with and one who has an outgoing personality.

Creative Writer. As a producer, you are responsible for all of the creative writing and preparation for your host. The creative writing could include a script for the entire show, as well as content for the website or social media channels, and even pitch letters to guests or advertisers.

Engineer. Unless you have a big budget and record your podcast in a recording studio, it is highly unlikely that you will need an engineer. An engineer, in this case an audio expert, is responsible for maintaining, repairing, and operating the recording equipment. On the smaller scales, a producer takes on this role.

Right-Hand Man. A producer and host work in concert to produce a quality and entertaining podcast. As Kaempfer puts it, "The producer is the host's Man Friday, and also his Man Monday, Tuesday, Wednesday and Thursday." (Throughout the book he refers to a producer as a man, but we know there are some really extraordinary women producers—present company included.) This last point serves as a catchall, because when there are just two people on a podcast team, the producer needs to be willing to take on whatever task is needed to consistently produce a quality show.

Managing Your Time

When you are hosting and producing your own podcast, you will need to manage your time properly, and the best way to accomplish this is by being organized. In podcasting, an easy and simple way to organize your time is by creating pre- and post-production schedules. You can use an editable calendar template or create a table (which most word processing software offers) to help you organize a smooth-running show. Below is a simple example of a pre- and post-production bulleted schedule, which is also effective.

Friday, July 3, 2020

- All subscriptions and equipment should be purchased.
- All artwork relating to the show including logo should be completed.
- All marketing materials including tag line and show description should be completed.
- All website and podcast website materials should be up and visible to the public.
- Production meeting at 7:00 p.m.

Monday, July 6, 2020

- 12:00 p.m. Production meeting to discuss topics and guests.
- 6:00 p.m. Recording of podcast.
- 7:00 p.m. Work with editing team.

Tuesday, July 7, 2020

- 10:00 a.m. Production meeting to go over episode, or listen for any additional issues for post-production.
- 7:00 p.m. Upload completely edited and approved podcast.

In addition to production schedules, you should also plan for when the final form of the podcast will be posted, or, if you're streaming live, when you will stream each week. The best practice for organizing yourself before recording or streaming your show is to create scripts and talking points. You can use talking points and a script even if you do not have a guest. These tools will keep you on task and organized.

Talking points and scripts are two different things. Talking points are used for interacting with your guests, or for you as host without a guest. Usually laid out in bullet points, talking points form a list that highlights the information you want to put forth, either by yourself or with a guest, and they will keep the topic and conversation seamless. A script is more specific and usually contains the standard language you use for each show. It involves the introduction of your show, the breaks, and the "outros," also known as the ending of your show. Scripts will be fully examined in chapter 12. For the purpose of this chapter, creating a script is an important tool and should also be kept in mind if you are the producer.

When both producing and hosting, all the work will fall on your shoulders. You will be required to develop show topics, find guests that align with your topics, write scripts and talking points, and handle branding and messaging. The upside to this is that even though everything will fall on your shoulders, you will have full control and listeners will feel the passion you have for your own show.

I touched on pre- and post-production in this chapter, but the next chapter will go into more details about this all-important process.

Insights: The Importance of the Podcast Producer

Rick Kaempfer

Rick Kaempfer is author of The Radio Producer's Handbook *(Allworth Press, October 2004) (December 2019).*

Rick Kaempfer.

Not every podcast is fortunate enough to have someone exclusively tasked with producing it. I'm one of the lucky ones. I co-host two podcasts, *Minutia Men* and *Free Kicks*, on the Radio Misfits Podcast Network. Having a producer allows me to concentrate on what I do best, and that is creating the actual content of the podcast.

In our case, the producer's job is to make the content sound as good as possible. That is almost as important as the content itself. Studies have shown that bad sound quality is the number one reason people stop listening to podcasts.

Our producer has had a big hand in virtually every element of the sound quality of our podcasts. The first thing he did was set up the recording equipment in my house to make the process as convenient and easy to use as possible. This had been the biggest hurdle to my entering the podcasting world. I'm not exactly a technical marvel. He stays on top of this by adjusting the audio of every individual podcast before posting it. Our producer also helped us realize the vision of our audio ideas. We have professionally produced audio clips that transition us from topic to topic. These clips make the show sound professional and streamlined. Finally, our producer is responsible for editing and posting the final file. We send him raw files containing the various different elements of the show, and he edits the few mistakes we make (ahem), puts the segments together, inserts the commercials and/or promos, and posts the final podcast on the Internet. Obviously, it is not an exaggeration to say we would not have a podcast without our producer, Tony Lossano.

There are other types of podcast producers who help with content, guest booking, and directing the talent. That is what I did as a radio producer for over twenty years. We obviously do not need to have that kind of help with our podcasts because of my previous experience, but podcasters without a similar background would find this type of producer invaluable. Still other podcast producers are responsible for promoting the podcast. They can make the podcast a multi-media experience by recording it on video or taking pictures and sharing them via social media. Adding this element can make a podcast larger than life.

Even podcasters who can handle the technical side, the content, and the promotion of a slick and professional sounding podcast would benefit from a producer to help. I always recommend that podcasters take stock of what they do best and concentrate on that. Delegating the rest of the podcast to a producer will allow the show to be the best it can be.

Chapter Review

A producer wears many hats and oversees the entire production of the show. This includes content, scripts and research. The producer also books guests and edits the show. Juggling all of these tasks, a producer must know how to manage his or her time properly. There are many tools out there to help you organize and manage your time effectively. These tools could include a schedule, talking points and scripts. Depending on your budget, you could break up these tasks by hiring a scriptwriter or a guest booker, to name just two.

Before going to the next chapter, look to the chapter discussion questions and exercises below to assist you.

Exercises and Discussion Questions

a. What big takeaways did you get from this chapter?
b. Do you think you are organized enough to produce your own

show, or will you get someone to produce your show? Explain your reasoning.

c. Throughout this chapter, there were various teachable moments. Pick one and explain how you would have handled the situation differently.
d. Explain how you would prepare for your show:
   - With a guest.
   - With a guest who fails to show up.
e. Create a simple production schedule. Be prepared to discuss this is in class.

Part IV

Let's Create Your Podcast!

Chapter 11

The Production Process

In the previous chapter, I gave you an example of a very basic pre- and post-production schedule. But what I did not mention is that a production schedule, especially a pre-production schedule, can be simple or detailed and complex, depending on how you plan your show. Keeping this in mind, let's take a deeper look at the creation of your podcast—in other words, the production process. Production comes in three stages: pre-production, production, and post-production. All are very important stages for planning and implementing. Remember, every podcast production will vary from the simple to the complicated depending on your needs and wants, and also your budget and time, so use this as a guide.

***Phase 1.* Pre-Production:** The first step to tackle is pre-production, which is the planning and development of your show from every angle. This includes programming format, scripting, format outline, recording platform, as well as including a timeline of deadlines and/or completions. For example, I knew I wanted a show that discusses social issues and politics with a sports focus. I also knew that I wanted to stop using a particular podcasting platform, so I did some research and came across a platform that was computer based and sounded great. In addition, I was trying out a new format—a more one-on-one discussion with just the host and a guest or two. No more panel discussions.

I also needed to re-brand the show because, as I mentioned earlier, at one point, I restructured the show with only one host and then finally settling on having two hosts. Therefore, I had to get new artwork and marketing materials, as well as a new website. I also wanted to add a production meeting so that we could discuss the upcoming shows each week. I needed to consider a script and which day I would record and upload the finished podcast. I also needed to plan the topics I wanted to discuss and the guests I would invite on the show. All of this had to be detailed in my pre-production schedule, along with a realistic timeline for completion.

Now, if you are creating a pre-production schedule for a newly developed show, as I did with *The Luke Show*, your production schedule might be a little different. In this case, I was not the decision maker—Luke and his manager were. So, my pre-production schedule had options, including detailed explanations of podcasting platforms and links for him to listen to, sample voice over artists that he would use for his show, and a deadline for him to decide on his selections and a roll out timeline. The package that I put together for *The Luke Show* looked like an actual business plan.

Programming Format: A programming format is your show's content and how it will be structured and eventually presented to your potential listeners and advertisers. For example, will it be live or taped? Will you be the sole host, or will you have a co-host? Will you produce the show yourself or hire a producer? Will you invite guests? What will be your show's theme? Will it be fiction, nonfiction, documentary style, or something different? How long will your show be—thirty minutes, forty-five minutes, one hour? Let's not forget your timeline to roll all of this out.

These are the types of questions a properly thought out programming format answers. Look at it as sort of a marketing plan where you clearly define the objectives and strategies of your podcast. Having a well thought out programming format will ensure an organized and well-executed show. It will also manage listener expectations and promote consistency for your show, which will enable you to successfully build an audience as well as build your brand.

According to Jeff D'Anza, a design consultant and author at Learning Solutions, an educational website for business professionals, "The decision of how you want to tell your story can have an impact on your timeline, as different types of podcasts can dictate different time commitments" (D'Anza, 2018). In other words, if you are producing a documentary style podcast, it might require more out of studio (or home) recording that could take you away from job commitments and other day-to-day life responsibilities, not to mention incurring additional travel expenses. If you produce an interview-driven podcast like *The Luke Show*, one that involves a host, a guest, a mic, a computer and simple scheduling either by telephone or email, it will not take up as much of your time as a documentary type format.

D'Anza also describes the various common nonfiction and fiction formats, including examples of podcasts, which I found beneficial enough to share.

This is exactly how D'Anza explains it:

Fiction

Fireside storytelling: Straight-forward, linear narrative storytelling. The kind of story you could imagine someone telling around a campfire (example: *Lore*).

Self-aware storytelling: Use of the medium as a part of the story. The podcast itself acts as a character in the story. These podcasts are very up-front about being a podcast and speak directly to the audience (examples: *Welcome to Night Vale, Limetown, The Message*).

Non-linear storyline: Use of timeline editing that makes the listener piece together the overall narrative. Not as straightforward in their storytelling style. Like a Quentin Tarantino style storytelling format (examples: *Homecoming, Alice Isn't Dead*).

Nonfiction

Documentary style: This one follows a linear timeline like a feature film documentary. Often have high production values (example: *Crimetown*).

Non-linear/documentary hybrid: The most popular type of podcast. Similar to documentary style, these, however, use timeline reorganization to push the story progression. Often use hosts/producers as characters (examples: *Serial, S-Town, In the Dark*).

Tent-pole thematic: Rather than having a single story throughout an entire podcast, this type uses multiple, stand-alone stories within a single episode. These stories reinforce or investigate a central theme (examples: *Radiolab, This American Life*).

Storytelling is an integral part of journalism, and these types of show formats can garner a huge listening audience. This also points out the many programming formats you can consider other than the straightforward interviewer and interviewee scenario (fiction podcasts are explored more in chapter 13).

One more note: if you are going to invite guests, make a list from the realistic to the unrealistic and create a show around them. This is great for planning ahead and keeping a wish list to be included in your pre-production schedule.

Let us take a closer look at a podcast programming format and address the theme of your show and what you need to think about before you select your show's length. A key question is whether you have enough content to fill the desired length of the podcast. I'll use *The Luke Show* as an example. *The Luke Show* with Luther "Uncle Luke" Campbell is an opinionated podcast that discusses pop culture as well as breaking and current news from the worlds of politics, sports and entertainment. We decided that the show length would be one hour. As producer of the show, I decided to research current news from pop culture to politics beforehand and saw that there was a ton of information out there to fill an hour-long show—probably even a two-hour show. Now, if your particular show talks about something more arcane like, say, hieroglyphics, I'm not sure you will be able—or even want—to fill an entire hour. That is a topic I personally might not want to touch because it's so specialized, but if your mind is set on discussing a very niche area, you might consider a half-hour show or even a fifteen-minute show per week.

Luther Campbell is smart and has a larger-than-life, entertaining, and opinionated personality, and because of this I'm pretty sure he could easily have fun talking about hieroglyphics, if he had to. With that being said, this is the type of mindset you must have when deciding the length of your show, because you don't want to fill an hour-long show with a topic that might bore listeners after a half hour or, for that matter, within fifteen minutes. You also do not want to force discussions to fill the show. If, for example, your show is an hour and the first half hour starts out strong because you have interesting content, you have to make sure you have enough of that interesting content to also fill the second half. If you don't, your natural instinct might be to wing it and fill that segment with nonsensical and redundant chatter. It is important to be well versed in your subject matter and carefully consider how much of the show it can realistically fill. Remember that podcasts are an intimate forum with a fully engaged, intelligent audience, and any type of forced discussion to kill time will be noticed and could essentially turn them off.

The Outline: After you have decided on the length of your show, now consider creating an outline. An outline is a schedule of what will happen on-air for each broadcast. Creating an outline of your format promotes consistency and organization, and will keep you on track for each broadcast. As discussed previously, you will need to figure out how long you would like your show to run and whether you are planning on having guests. Let us use a very simple example of a sixty-minute show that will air at 9:00 p.m. once a week with an invited guest. Here is a basic draft of what the outline for that show might look like:

9:00 p.m.: Intro jingle
9:01 p.m.: Host introduction
9:02 p.m.: Hot topics
9:15 p.m.: Break jingle
9:16 p.m.: Host introduces guest
9:17 p.m.: Host and guest discuss today's news
9:30 p.m.: Break jingle
9:45 p.m.: Host thanks guest and takes caller questions
9:55 p.m.: Host wraps the show and thanks the guests and callers, as well as giving the credits (i.e., thanks producer, editor and staff), and calls to action (i.e., listener engagement—how they can post questions about the show, follow the show on social media, and contact you)
9:58 p.m.: Outro music plays out the show

Building an audience requires consistency. Listeners want to know what to expect week after week, and creating a show outline will help you to achieve this goal and meet the all-important listener expectations.

Production Schedule: Now that you have developed a complete plan to implement and create your podcast, you have to give yourself a timeline and create a production schedule. If your pre-production planning is complicated and includes equipment, software, podcasting platforms or even artists, you need to have a realistic deadline for the completion of each task. You will divide your production schedule into three phases of production: pre-production, production, and post-production. Your production schedule tells you what happens before, during and after your show. This process requires good time management and organization, so be as realistic as possible and give yourself enough time to complete each phase.

Production: The next step is production. Using your production schedule, this is where you or a hired producer will implement the items you outlined in pre-production. At this point, you will have purchased all the necessary software, equipment, artwork, and voice-overs. The intro and outro theme music will have also been chosen, and all marketing and social media interns will be in place. The show's format will have already been decided, scripts will have been written, and the length of the show and the day it will be streamed have been set. All that remains is to record it and present it to the masses. Make sure to check off anything else that was outlined in your pre-production schedule before you hit record. What's left is the actual produced recording of your show. This is where all of your good hard work will show.

Post-production: This is the final step in podcasting, and it usually includes the all-important and quite daunting editing phase. Whether you are streaming live or pre-recording your podcast, you will want to edit any unwanted noise and tighten up any dead air space, which is a natural occurrence during a live or pre-recorded show. When you record your podcast, you can do retakes and then go back in post-production and edit them out. You cannot edit during a live show, but you certainly can edit quickly after the show and then upload a polished version of your podcast.

Post-production also involves promoting your episode. This may involve sharing a 30-second teaser on social media, sending the link out to subscribers, choosing the right hashtags to find new listeners, and supplying your guest(s) with ways to promote the episode. We'll get into more details on marketing and promotion in Part V.

During the production process, always keep this in mind with each phase of planning: you are only as good as your last episode.

Chapter Review

The production process comes in three stages: pre-production, production, and post-production. These stages are the business plan of your podcast. Like a business plan, some production plans are elaborate and some are basic. Your budget will determine how elaborate your plan will be.

Pre-production is all the planning that will you do to get to the production stage. Pre-production includes what staff, equipment and content you will need to produce your podcast. It will also include a budget that will help you bring all of this to fruition, as well as a realistic timeline. Production is the actual recording of your episode, whether it is pre-taped or live. By this stage, you will have the equipment and personnel you need to get this done. If you stream live, your audience will be able to listen to what you produced immediately. If you decide to record your show, then you are preparing your show for upload for listeners to hear. The final step is post-production, which involves the editing and promotion of your podcast.

The next chapter will examine scripts and the tools that can help you become creative. Writing scripts is another part of the production process and is done during the pre-production stage. As always, before moving on to the next chapter, look at the discussion questions and exercises carefully, as they will assist you.

Exercises and Discussion Questions

a. Pre- and post-production package:
    - Record a 3-minute segment describing your show's content.
    - Based on your show's content, and using what you learned in this chapter, create a programming format.
    - Create a pre-production schedule.

b. What sorts of fiction and/or nonfiction storytelling formats are you most drawn to, and why?

Chapter 12

Writing Scripts, Intros, Outros and Journaling

Podcasting does require some writing. You do not need to be a professional writer, but you do need to be able to put clear thoughts onto paper. In this chapter, we'll discuss why you will need the ability to write clearly for your scripts, intros and outros, and journaling.

Writing Scripts

I have mentioned scripts throughout the book but haven't yet highlighted what they really are and how helpful they can be. Whether you are a novice or an expert, you will benefit from a script. Scripts in the podcast world include the set language of your show, standard or "boilerplate" language that stays consistent. They are useful tools to ensure that your show runs in an organized and consistent way. They also promote listener expectations, which is very important to your show's brand.

A weekly script usually includes an introduction (intro), a break, and a closing (outro). Each segment's language stays the same each week; the only thing that changes is the guest information. For example, let us say that your show starts at 9:00 p.m. and ends at 9:30 p.m. Here is a sample of a simple script that will give you a better idea of what is needed.

9:00 p.m.: Introduction

"Good evening and thank you for tuning into *Jordan and Will Gallagher's Podcast*. My name is Jordan Gallagher and ... I'm Will Gallagher, as some of you may know, each week we highlight one veteran. We do this because we think that veterans are often overlooked and do not get enough credit for their service and sacrifice. This week's guest is firefighter pilot, Zayn Logan."

Give an overview of Zayn's illustrious career as a firefighter pilot.

- Nearly 25 years in the Navy.
- Talk about his awards.

- "Zayn is not only going to share his experience with us, but he will also give us a little insight to being a firefighter pilot in the Navy."
- "First, on behalf of myself and our listeners, Zayn, I'd like to thank you for your service."

Every 10 Minutes: Break

"You are listening to *Jordan and Will Gallagher's Podcast*. We air live Wednesdays at 9:00 p.m. Tonight we're speaking with Zayn Logan. If you have a question or comment, please post it on our social media pages at hashtag GallagherForVets."

9:25 p.m.: Closing

"Thank you for listening to another edition of *Jordan and Will Gallagher's Podcast,* where we highlight all things U.S. Veterans. I'd like to thank Zayn Logan for joining us this evening. You can follow Zayn on social media @ FirefighterZaynLogan."

"Be sure to follow us on social media *@Jordan&WillForVets*. Remember, we'd love to hear from you, so please post your questions and comments at hashtag GallagherForVets. Good night everyone, and we'll see you next week."

We can again benefit from looking at the similarities between podcasts and radio broadcasts. Besides the obvious fact that they're both audio-only media, there are many other features that they both share, including how they are formatted. I mention this because I used radio as my guide when I set up my first podcast. They both have a DJ/host and include an introduction (intro), breaks, and a closing (outro). Most radio shows and, for that matter, television shows have producers who write the scripts or hire a script writer. The reason for this is they know the talent, i.e., host(s), will benefit from guidance.

Think of a script as a screenplay of sorts, a roadmap of what you plan to say to your listeners. Whether or not you are comfortable talking off the cuff, a script will enable you to sound professional. Here is another example, from a recent script at *HWTP Sports Talk*:

Intro

Female voiceover plays. "Welcome to *HWTP Sports Talk with David Weinstein*. We air live every Wednesday at 9:00 p.m. Eastern. Recognized by our guests and listeners for our hashtag No Holds Barred conversations. Now, here is David Weinstein."

David starts talking immediately after Carrie's introduction. "Hello, Huddlin' Fans. Thanks for tuning in. We have an exciting lineup of guests for you tonight. We are going to speak with civil rights activist, Baptist minister and politician, the Reverend Jesse Jackson."

"As some of you may know, by day I practice criminal defense law with Jones Walker LLP in Miami, Florida. BUT once a week I'm HWTP's legal analyst and your podcast host."

"We'd love to hear from you, so post your questions using hashtag AskHWTP.

In addition to our guest, I'll be going through HWTP's Hit List, the top stories on and off the field for this week."

Transitions, Every 10 Minutes

"You are listening to *HWTP Sports Talk with David Weinstein* and I am in the middle of my conversation with the Reverend Jesse Jackson."

Transitions, Every 20 Minutes

Play the break with female voiceover. "You are listening to *HWTP Sports Talk with David Weinstein*. Don't be shy—post your questions and comments at hashtag AskHWTP. Now back to you, David."

Outro

"As a reminder, the *Huddlin' with the Pros Sports Talk* podcast is posted every week on our website at hwtpradio.com."

"We're the podcast that tackles all the controversial, hot-button issues from the world of sports, recognized by our guests and listeners for our hashtag No Holds Barred, good questions and informed conversation.

The show is produced by Jacqueline Parke and is a Sweet G Communications production."

"Special thanks to our guest, the Reverend Jesse Jackson."

"Thanks also to our great *Huddlin' with the Pros* team."

"Be sure to like us on Facebook and follow us on Twitter @ hwtpsportstalk. Missed a show? Visit our website at hwtpradio.com and download our podcast on your smart device."

"Well, goodbye everyone, and we'll see you next week."

Music plays.

Each week we discuss different topics and have guests that are appropriate to those topics, so those details (as underlined above) are changed in your script for each show. The rest of it stays the same. Again, consistency helps with branding and builds listener loyalty.

For a show I produced for one celebrity client, I used to provide a script for his interviews. He would often go off script and also use just some of what I wrote, which was perfectly fine because you do not want to sound stiff, like you are simply reading. You should sound as natural as possible. For my client, the script was his security blanket, yet he was not comfortable in a fully scripted environment, since he was at his best when he was speaking informally and conversationally. But because he wanted a more professional show and more structure, he wanted a scripted show combined with free talking. This is another example of using a script for a better show. It is not a cookie cutter situation. You have to know yourself and know what will get the best interview from your guest, as well as the most polished show as the host. So use scripts and even talking points as a guide, but don't be too rigid, especially if you as a host may not feel comfortable using them. Another important note: be sure to read your script beforehand and get familiar with it by recording yourself and playing it back. You can even send it to friends and family for honest critique. Practice makes perfect.

Journals: Creativity and Decision Making

Another helpful tool for the beginning podcaster is to create a journal. A character in one of nineteenth-century playwright Oscar Wilde's plays said, "I never travel without my diary. One should always have something sensational to read in the train."

A great quote—funny and true. When you find yourself in a podcasting rut, keeping a journal is a great way to get out of it. Many people use journals. Writers and artists keep one handy to jot down ideas and thoughts. Those with emotional or mental health issues are often told to keep track of their moods and triggers by writing them in a journal. In fact, journals can work for most everyone and be helpful in many walks of life.

For a beginning podcaster, a journal is a great way to get your creative juices flowing and is helpful when you have decisions to make. It promotes relaxation and lessens stress by allowing you to just write down your thoughts and ideas, your concrete plans as well as your dreams. And once you write something down, there is no chance you will forget it.

According to a recent article on the mental health website Psych Central (Maud Purcel, 2018), there are many health benefits to keeping a journal. They include the following: to "clarify your thoughts and feelings," "know yourself better," "reduce stress," "solve problems more effectively" and "resolve disagreements with others."

I'm also a professor at a local college in Hudson Valley, New York, where I teach an online class that I designed called "Podcasting: Creation and Strategy." I asked the students to introduce themselves and to explain their reasons for taking the class. All of them gave terrific responses and outlined the type of podcasts they would like to create. A couple of weeks later, I discussed the importance of journaling and asked them to jot down their wish list of guests, as well as their passion/interests. They had a week to do this. When I compared what some of the students wrote in the introduction to what they wrote in the discussion post, there were differences. The journaling actually made them see what their true passion was. It was really astounding for me and for them to see.

All these benefits will enable you to think more clearly, which, in turn, promotes creativity and thoughtful decisions when performing pre- and post-podcasting tasks.

Here are some useful tips for keeping a journal from *BuzzFeed* (Lee, n.d.):

Always carry your journal with you.

- Keep your entries short.
- If you are skeptical about committing to a journal, purchase an inexpensive notebook.
- Do not write on the first page.
- Do not stress about writing every single day.
- Create a relaxing routine around keeping your journal.
- Or incorporate it into your existing routine.
- Keep it simple.
- Make lists.
- Do not beat yourself up over mistakes.
- Create your own layout.
- Practice your handwriting.
- Try bullet journaling.
- Try many different methods to see what works for you.
- Do not try to be perfect.

BuzzFeed is known for its great lists, but I'm only including this one here for guidance, not for you to feel obligated to follow its points exactly. Keeping a journal is supposed to be stress-free and fun. If you truly feel that writing in a journal is too difficult a task for you—a burden instead of a help—then simply don't do it.

Jingles: Intros, Breaks and Closings

Often associated with advertising, jingles are described as "a short verse or song marked by catchy repetition," per the Merriam-Webster dictionary. When watching commercials or even television sitcoms, a catchy tune is often played. As consumers, people equate these catchy tunes with a product or a television show. Answer these questions and then discuss in class:

- What catchy tune do you think of for Folgers Coffee?
- What catchy tune do you think of for the TV sitcom *Friends*?
- What catchy tune do you think of for ESPN's *SportsCenter*?

For number one, you probably thought of "the best part of waking up is Folgers in your cup." For number two, you probably thought about The Rembrandts' song "I'll Be There for You." And for number three, well, it is hard to write in words the theme song for *SportsCenter*, but those who watch it will have no problem humming the tune. These shows and products are a perfect example of successful branding and show how important jingles can be to your podcast and your brand. (See *Insights*: Izabela Russell.)

One of my favorite podcasts is ESPN's *30 for 30*. It really captures the essence of storytelling with interesting and thought-provoking content. Give it a listen. One thing you will notice with each episode is that the podcast host and producer, Jody Avirgan, starts each show by reading an advertisement with music in the background. This is followed by their theme music before Jody thanks his audience for listening. Finally, he introduces himself and then begins the episode by giving the listener some background on the subject or theme of the show. In the background, there is usually a smorgasbord of soundbites from news coverage that relates to the episode's storyline. Every episode is set up this way. *30 for 30* is creating continuity and listener expectations with each of their episodes. Intro jingles, breaks, and closings go hand in hand with scripts, and that is why they are so important to your brand and listener expectations.

There are many jingles and voiceover production companies available with fees ranging from $100 on up. The company I went with and refer my clients to is Music Radio Creative. It is a British-run firm that offers reasonable pricing for a jingle or voiceover. Depending on what you want, the fees range from $50 on up. You have the option to pick the voice of your preference, be it a male or female, high or low energy, or even just go with instrumental music. Most production companies provide links to samples of their work that you can listen to on their website. Do your research and select a company that is reliable, professional and cost effective for you.

Insights: Podcasts: Audio Branding with Jingles

Izabela Russell

Izabela Russell is the CEO of Music Radio Creative. (November 2019)

Podcasting is one of the fastest growing content platforms, and one that is currently still heavily underappreciated. In early 2019, Google announced that it would now surface podcast episodes in search results based on deep AI analysis of the covered content. This means that you have the potential for even more free Google real estate up for grabs, but only if you are willing to create content good enough to appear there. Starting a podcast can also bring the additional benefit of community building. Podcasting can give you and your company a public, open voice, showing that there are real human beings behind the brand and allowing people to connect with the brand on a personal level. As it directly speaks of you (and potentially your brand), you want to make sure that your podcast sounds great. In the same way as you would want to make sure your business logo looks good, you want to ensure your podcast "logo," or signature audio, sounds good. That is what good podcast branding is for.

What Is Podcast Branding?

Podcast audio branding is a relatively recent development that has increased with the number of podcasters seeking development of their own brand and exploring this relatively new niche. Podcasters who decide to have their podcast branded with audio jingles do so because they want to sound professional and make great first impressions. Podcast branding includes the following potential elements:

- Podcast intro: professionally recorded introduction that summarizes the podcast and its purpose to the listener in usually no more than 30 seconds.
- Podcast outro: the last recording you play on the podcast—it should provide clear next steps for the listener (call to action).
- Podcast jingles: short audio transitions that can be used to switch between the segments, introduce guests or change the topic without awkward pauses.
- Podcast ads: commercials that can advertise your own products and services or those of your sponsors.

How Much Audio Branding Is Enough?

Audio branding should complement your content and not take over the entire podcast. Its purpose is to subtly and gently bring together every episode you make and subconsciously introduce the listener to your brand. Having produced over 9,000 podcast elements via Music Radio Creative over the past decade, I would recommend under 30 seconds for the intro, up to 60 seconds for the outro, and between 5 to 10 seconds for each jingle. Any more than that just distracts from the content and often leads to the "skip 15/30 sec" button being used.

The Most Important Element of Audio Branding

In my opinion, even more important than the music is the voice that delivers the message. Make sure to use a professional voice actor who is experienced in delivering short messages. Think about it—radio stations do not ask friends to record their radio jingles. Why? Because they know that a good voice is a brand investment that will bring new listeners. Consider the following:

Izabela Russell.

- Age of the voice artist
- The energy in the artist's voice
- Locality of the accent
- Suitability of the voice to the script itself (they should go hand in hand!)

Do not assume that one size fits all. The fact that one voice works great on your favorite podcast does not mean it will be equally effective on yours. One thing I never, and I mean never, recommend is pre-recording your own intro. It doesn't sound right. You can have the best voice in the world, but the harsh reality is that the concept itself truly sucks.

Good places to look for a variety of voices:

Music Radio Creative: https://www.musicradiocreative.com/

Voiceover Facebook groups: there are many of them out there—good place to tap the talent directly. Simply search voiceover in the Facebook search bar.

Have Fun in the Process

Do not forget to enjoy the process. Mistakes happen to the best of us, and it can take some time to figure out your very own audio brand. Approach this with a smile on your face. Enjoy the learning curve.

Chapter Review

Scripts are beneficial because they manage listener expectations. They also promote organized and professionally sounding podcasts. A weekly script usually includes an introduction and an outro, which are the first and last things that listeners hear when they tune into the show, as well as breaks that play between discussions. During a break, you will normally remind listeners how to post questions and comments, or dial-in if it is a live show, as well as who you are talking with and the topic. Sometimes listeners tune in late in the middle of a discussion, and a break will get them up to speed. The final step is the outro, which is what you say when you are ending the show. The outro should always include a call to action—that is, encouraging your listeners to share the episode and stay connected via social media or by subscribing to the show.

Another important tool, especially if you get in a rut, is to create a journal. Journals are a great way to awaken your creativity and release stress. Jingles are also an effective way to help make your podcast sound highly professional. There are a few companies out there that create jingles and voiceovers for a great price. As I mention throughout the book, research is always one of the best tools to use.

We've been discussing mainly nonfiction journalistic podcasts up to now, and it's time to take look at another type of storytelling podcast—fiction podcasts. Before moving on to the next chapter, look to the discussion questions and exercises below to assist you.

Exercises and Discussion Questions

Journaling Exercise

Using your class notebook, write down a few words about the following without editing your writing:

a. List three words that best describe your mood right now.

b. List three professional goals you would like to accomplish over the next five years.

c. Shoot for the moon. List three guests whom you would love to have on your podcast.

Recording Exercise

a. Create a script that will introduce your podcast to the world.

b. Following your script, record a two-minute (or shorter) introduction to your podcast.
c. Post the recording on your various social media platforms, including relevant hashtags (be sure to turn on Twitter analytics and any other available analytics).
d. Monitor and analyze the response, if any.
e. Note the number of people who saw the post.
f. Write a three-paragraph essay on the results of your podcast introduction.

Resource

Music Radio Creative: https://www.musicradiocreative.com/

Chapter 13

Fiction Podcasts

When podcasting first became popular as a genre, the nonfiction form was the most prevalent by far. But as the medium expanded, a rich variety of fiction podcasts, also called narrative or storytelling podcasts, began to appear. These podcasts are designed to provide pure entertainment, and can exist on their own or serve as another means for a company to increase brand recognition and loyalty.

What Makes a Popular Fiction Podcast?

The first step to creating a successful fiction podcast is—you guessed it—research.

Listen to every narrative podcast that you might find interesting. You can focus on the specific genre you're interested in creating, like comedy or science fiction, but keep in mind that you can learn a lot from shows that are very different from yours as well.

A good place to start is the most popular fiction podcasts, such as *Welcome to Night Vale* and *Homecoming*.

Welcome to Night Vale is the story of a small town in a desert "where all conspiracy theories are real." Created by Joseph Fink and Jeffrey Cranor, the bi-monthly episodes are structured like a local radio show, with "news" updates that frequently feature paranormal activities. Its popularity marked a turning point in podcasting, as it was the first fiction podcast to gain popular appeal. The first episode aired in 2012, and the podcast is still running ten years later, along with a touring show and several spin-off novels and other podcasts.

Homecoming, the story of a caseworker and a veteran in a mysterious facility, is a suspenseful drama created by Gimlet Media. Gimlet is a leading digital media company and podcast network founded in 2014; *Homecoming* was the company's first narrative podcast, debuting in December 2016. The podcast, which starred luminary actors, including Catherine Keener, Oscar

Isaac, David Schwimmer and Amy Sedaris, was so popular it became an Amazon Prime Original series starring Julia Roberts.

Both of these podcasts are worth listening to because of their popularity alone. They also each provide interesting formats for this type of narrative. *Welcome to Night Vale* uses direct address to the audience, harking back to the radio shows of the Golden Age. It uses music, but is sparse when it comes to other sound effects. *Homecoming* is structured so that audience members feel like they're peeking into a different world. Scenes include telephone calls, therapy sessions and snatches of conversation, which work together to pique listeners' curiosity as they try to piece together what's happening in this strange facility.

Don't just listen to the most popular podcasts, though. Shows that didn't do very well can be highly educational, too. Get yourself a playlist that includes low-budget, short-lived shows alongside the most successful ones.

As you listen to these various podcasts, take notes about what works and what doesn't. Are the actors believable? Are the storylines engaging? How's the soundscape (more on that below)? Are there missed opportunities for music or sound effects?

Be sure to listen to several episodes in a series, because a key component of fiction podcasts is their serial nature. "Serial" simply means each episode is part of a series—that is, the narrative flows from one to the next. The other option is an "episodic" structure, which means that each episode is complete and can be listened to in any order. As a creator, these terms become important when you're publishing your podcast, because most platforms give you the option of organizing your shows either by the most recent one displayed first (for episodic) or the first one displayed initially (serial).

The Function of Fiction

It's important to consider the purpose behind creating your fiction podcast, as that will determine your approach. If you are a writer with a story inside you that needs to be told, creating an episodic narrative podcast can fill that need and may boost or even launch your writing career. If you are a content professional at a company, a storytelling podcast can be a powerful way to get your message out and build your customer or client base.

For individuals, the podcast medium can be a relatively budget-friendly way to tell your story—certainly simpler than producing a film, for example. There is a higher production value needed than with a nonfiction podcast, between voice actors and sound design, and arguably more work up front than, say, a news-based podcast that is developing scripts and securing guests on the fly. With fiction, you'll be smart to spend a lot of time and effort in the planning stage. When you're ready to launch, the product is already complete and you can focus on marketing.

Some storytellers have been encouraged by the trend of fiction podcasts being picked up and turned into television series or films. In addition to *Homecoming*, more prominent examples of this trend include *Lore*, a podcast that uses traditional folklore and historical events that was turned into a series on Amazon Video; and *Limetown*, a fictionalized crime podcast that was adapted into a series for Facebook Watch, starring Jessica Biel and Stanley Tucci.

Having your podcast become a major television show or film is an exciting possibility. However, a few words of caution about this trend: the best fiction podcasts fully embrace the medium. If you have a story that you always imagined as a feature film, it may be tempting to release it as a podcast in the hopes that it will be picked up by a major film studio that has the budget to bring the story to life in the way you always wanted.

The issue with this is that you may end up giving short shrift to the podcast production, thinking that this is just a teaser for the "real deal." That's a mistake, because you will miss out on unique storytelling aspects of the podcast medium.

However, the podcast-to-screen transition can be tricky. *Homecoming* in particular was critiqued by some for not being properly adapted to the on-screen format. The original podcast was clearly designed to be told with only audio and no visuals, with the action taking place largely via phone calls and "found" recordings of therapy sessions. This pared-down approach works brilliantly for audio, but on-screen there is suddenly a lot less happening.

So while the possibilities of future versions of your story may be appealing, it's best to stay in the now and enjoy the reach that the podcast itself will create. You can gain critical acclaim as a storyteller by embracing the audio medium.

On the business side of things, a smartly positioned fiction podcast can build brand recognition and ultimately drive profits. *The Message* is a good example of a company using a fiction podcast to increase brand recognition and loyalty. *The Message* is a science fiction podcast written by playwright Mac Rogers and produced by General Electric. The story surrounds a recovered alien transmission that needs to be translated.

Unlike a nonfiction branded podcast, there's no direct appeal for listeners in *The Message*. However, it is a well-made and compelling drama that explores the uses and limits of technology in our modern world and its future possibilities, which is perfectly in line with GE's brand. *The Message* was so popular with audiences that the company produced a follow-up, *LifeAfter*, which won a Cannes Gold Lion.

Linda Boff, the chief marketing executive at General Electric, told the *New York Times* that the motivation behind creating these podcasts was to make sure GE's brand remained "relevant ... contemporary... [and] interesting." She also offers this nugget: "We get on the radar of future employees, young people who are making a choice as to where they want to work." Recruiting efforts are a crucial focus for many large companies and may offer a compelling reason for executives to agree to your podcast idea.

It's also notable that the writer, Rogers, started his career as a playwright. His plays have appeared on stages throughout New York City and other major venues, and have won awards and critical acclaim. It goes to show that if you are seeking a writer for your fiction podcast, you don't necessarily need someone with experience in the medium. What's most important is that your writer is a true storyteller, because the story itself is what will draw in listeners.

The McDonald's podcast *The Sauce* (also discussed in chapter 3, "Industry Trends and Statistics") is another good example of a company using a fiction podcast to communicate with consumers and employees, both current and future. *The Sauce* was designed to mimic a true crime investigative series, but was really an elaborate—and memorable—apology to consumers over a sauce shortage. And people really listened to it: it cracked into iTunes' Top 100 chart within a day of its release in 2018.

Telling a Story with Audio Only

Audio fiction is a unique storytelling medium, with both limitations and opportunities to consider.

As discussed above, a successful branded fiction podcast can be a powerful platform for a company, as it promotes brand awareness, increases customer or client loyalty, and/or serves as a recruiting tool. However, just like fiction podcasts that are not tied to a brand, the success of these podcasts hinges on compelling storytelling.

What doesn't work is if it sounds like one long advertisement for the product or company. Consumers are regularly bombarded with advertisements, and many people make efforts to minimize or avoid ads as much as possible. There's no faster way to get someone to turn off your podcast than to make it sound like an ad.

So, how do you create an engaging story in the podcast realm?

The key elements are soundscape design, cliffhangers, and the use of professional actors.

Your soundscape has two main components: music and sound effects. As a creator, you may favor one over the other, but most fiction podcasts have a mix of both. As with nonfiction podcasts, you can use music for your intro and outro. You may also add it as background music to play beneath the dialogue, which can set the tone and help draw out the emotions of the scene.

For sound effects, the sky is really the limit. That doesn't mean you overdo it and have a sound effect alongside every piece of dialogue. The best approach is to go through the script and make note of any opportunities for sound to be added. If you're writing the script yourself, always keep sound effects in mind. How can they enhance your storytelling? Build them right into the script. If it can be done with sound, do it with sound.

A smart area of research here is to read old radio play scripts, many of which are available in full online. Simply Scripts is a good resource for this.

Here's a sample of the *Flash Gordon* radio play script from 1935, as posted on Simply Scripts:

> **SFX:** Plane goes down, then siren.
>
> **ANNCR:** The plane lurches into a spinning nose dive. Flash Gordon's trained muscles carry him across the aisle to the frightened girl, to gather her in his arms and then leap free of the falling plane. And pulling the ripcord of his parachute, glides to Earth.
>
> **SFX:** Siren out.
>
> **FLASH:** Don't be frightened, Dale. The plane has crashed, we're safe.
>
> **DALE:** Yes, thanks to you.
>
> **FLASH:** Hold fast, we're landing now … careful … easy …
>
> **BOTH:** GRUNT AS THEY LAND
>
> **FLASH:** Are you all right, Dale?
>
> **DALE:** Yes.
>
> **FLASH:** Good.
>
> **DALE:** Oh, look, Flash! There's a large steel door. It's closing!
>
> **FLASH:** Why, that's the laboratory of the great scientist, Dr. Hans Zarkov. He's coming this way!

"SFX" is an abbreviation that is still used today, meaning "special effects." As you can see, the sound effects directly called for here are the plane going down and a siren. Do you see other chances for a sound effect? They talk about a large steel door closing. Is that something that could be done with sound rather than being described in dialogue? How about the parachute being deployed? Could you create that sound in a way that's recognizable to an audience so that the narrator doesn't have to describe it?

Radio plays are a good education in this way because they were a nascent form of the medium. It can be a fun place to start because as modern audience members, the retro style is underscored by the technological limits. Audio storytelling has come a long way.

In addition to moving the plot along with sounds like a ringing telephone or crashing cars, sound effects can also create ambiance, sometimes more effectively than background music. If you have a peaceful or cozy scene that takes place in a cabin in the woods, maybe you have a soundscape that includes birds singing, wind rustling trees and crickets chirping. If it is an urgent scene in a hospital emergency room, you could have medical devices beeping, wheels rushing over tile and patients moaning in pain. The two effects create vastly different moods.

In the *Flash Gordon* script, there is also an instruction for the actors to "grunt as they land." This brings us to the important element of professional actors in a fiction podcast.

You may not have the budget to hire Stanley Tucci to act in your podcast, but don't let that deter you. Use a website such as Backstage to create a casting notice, which should include your production dates, rate of pay, information on the characters and storyline, as well as whether the actor will be recording in-studio or at home. You can also "double cast" with podcasts, which means that one actor can play multiple characters if they have the vocal range. This can be a helpful way to save some money. Much of your casting decisions will be determined by your budget.

Keep in mind that you may be able to get very good actors for low pay, especially if you are casting in a large film or television market such as Los Angeles, New York or Atlanta. Many actors these days have full recording equipment in home studios, especially those who specialize in voice work. Some will work for very little money if they think it will be a valuable addition to their resume or reel, or if they are drawn artistically to the character or story. For this reason, your casting notice should be as compelling as your future marketing material.

Again, based on your budget, you may have your actors record from home. However, you may find it's worth it to rent a studio and have the actors come in and work with a director. The actors can then do dialogue in real time, which makes it easier to sound believable. A director can create a consistent tone that is in line with the story goals and help each actor deliver a compelling performance. The director can also be helpful in auditioning actors, as they will know what qualities to seek.

Once you have your actors in the studio and, for example, you want them to "grunt as they land" like in the *Flash Gordon* script, of course it's not practical to ask your actors to jump out of a moving plane just for the sound effect. But you could ask them to jump in place in the studio, grunting as they hit the ground. The bottom line with sound effects is to be intentional, get creative, and have fun.

The other crucial element of sound design is the quality. As covered in other chapters, top-quality recording equipment and good software are crucial for a podcast to reach audiences in any meaningful way.

Then there are cliffhangers. Among the many important elements to good storytelling in general, cliffhangers are particularly useful in the podcast realm. A cliffhanger in storytelling is when an episode ends in suspense, without resolution of the conflict. Often, the cliffhanger involves a new conflict or roadblock for the characters, introduced during the final moments of an episode. The idea is that, when an episode ends, the listener immediately plays the next one—or waits eagerly for it to be released—because they just *must* know what happens next. It's a highly effective way to retain listenership.

Cliffhangers are most effective once an audience has grown invested in a character's story and drawn in by the emotional journey. Once you are rooting for Flash Gordon to save the world, you will be left in suspense when an episode ends with him, say, literally hanging from his fingertips on the edge of a cliff. You want to tune into the next episode to see how, or if, he pulls out of it.

Chapter Review

Fiction podcasts, whether as a stand-alone offering or tied to a brand, are all about compelling storytelling. The audio medium presents unique challenges and opportunities for getting a message across. With no visual element, the soundscape becomes crucial, as does the participation of professional actors.

The most successful branded or company podcasts have little to do with the product or service being sold, at least not overtly. Instead, the goal is to connect with consumers, clients and/or employees, both current and future, in a way that's aligned with the company's identity. Podcasts can be a unique and memorable way to communicate with the people who might ultimately be interested in your product or service.

Creating a fiction podcast can be an effective and relatively cost-friendly way to build a career as a writer. The medium is exploding in popularity, and writers, designers and actors from all different professional backgrounds are becoming drawn to it. The most successful fiction podcasts embrace the audio-only format in creative ways.

Telling a story without visuals means the audio element is crucial. High-quality sound equipment, professional actors and a thoughtful sound design are essential to telling your story in an effective and compelling way.

The next chapter will take a look at show topics. Depending on your show's subject matter, this process can either be a breeze or quite daunting. Before you go there, work on the discussion questions and exercises here, which will help you.

Exercises and Discussion Questions

a. *Welcome to Night Vale* uses similar narrative techniques to Orson Welles's 1938 radio drama, *War of the Worlds*, which caused mass panic in the U.S. as discussed in chapter one. Why do you think our modern audiences didn't experience similar hysteria?
b. What's the difference between an episodic and a serial podcast? Which one do you think works better for fiction, and why?
c. What makes a successful branded fiction podcast? Explain both in terms of format and the goals it can achieve for a company.
d. Choose a scene from an old radio play and rewrite it for production as a podcast. How many actors do you need? What sound effects can be added? Do any scenes call for ambient sound? If so, what kinds of sounds would you use?

Resource

Simply Scripts: www.simplyscripts.com

Chapter 14

Show Topics

Plan Ahead of Time

You will find that research is a common theme throughout this book. It is one of the most important things that you will need to do if you want to have a successful podcast. This section will put an emphasis on developing content and procuring guests for your show.

A few fellow podcasters who have listened to my sports podcast have asked me, "How do you get such great guests and topics?" My answer is always the same: research. It may sound simple, but it's not. Proper research will enable you to develop the knowledge to create content that is well-thought-out and informed, and that will allow you to effectively plan ahead.

Planning ahead is important to your show because it is another tool that will keep you organized and allow you to hopefully have insightful guests and quality discussions. There were times where, as the producer, I missed opportunities because of poor planning. Instead of becoming dismayed because I did not have the right person to discuss a timely topic, I made it a teachable moment. With thorough research, I began to plan ahead effectively by looking at the time of the year, and then going month to month so that I could determine what was important and newsworthy. A good example is February, which is an important month since it features the Super Bowl, one of the biggest events in professional sports, and it is also Black History Month. For each show in February, we researched African American athletes who were game-changers in their sport. In addition, while researching the Super Bowl, we also realized that it is more than just a game. The Super Bowl is really a week-long celebration. The National Football League has really done a great job in sponsoring events that help the hungry and also plan for some special promotions that allow fans to meet notable players.

Thus, we do not only report on the game, but we also discuss events like the "Taste of the NFL," a star-studded attraction during Super Bowl week that offers dishes by chefs from each of the 32 NFL cities. The proceeds from this event benefit selected hunger relief organizations. The NFL Experience is another special event during Super Bowl week, one where fans are invited to participate in games and activities, as well as having the opportunity to meet football players from the past and present. Keeping all this in mind, we had a February segment highlighting one African American athlete per show and featured the Super Bowl by discussing all the activities surrounding it while reporting on any post–Super Bowl positives or incidents. Planning ahead gave us ample opportunity to link our coverage to key events and themes throughout the month, giving listeners the deep dive into the stories behind the sports that they've come to expect from the podcast. This is just one example, but it should give you an idea of how to plan ahead.

While researching, I also found that most major newspapers have a public relations department that disseminates emails reporting their top stories to producers and other media professionals. The *Washington Post*, for example, sends out emails once or twice each day listing the leading headlines along with a summary of each story. The summary allows you to review each storyline and decide whether or not it fits into your show's format. Some storylines will be time-sensitive and will need to be discussed right away to keep your show current, such as is if the New York Yankees win the World Series. If you have a sports-based podcast, you would probably flag that news item as something to mention during the intro to your next episode. Two weeks later, that story simply wouldn't be news anymore. Other storylines will be "evergreen"—that is, not tied to a particular event but of general interest to your listener, and they hold up over time. An example is the history of women in politics. Someone interested in that topic would click on the episode whether or not anyone else was talking about it, even if there wasn't a news hook. It's good to collect those evergreen stories and always have a few on hand. They can always be pushed to a future show to make room for breaking news, or used when a guest backs out on you or a story goes bad for some reason.

Newspapers disseminate these headline emails to producers for several reasons. First, it is great publicity for the reporters and the news outlets, positioning themselves as experts and, second, most reporters want to have a medium where they can discuss the stories they write. Obviously, broadcast media is a great place for this. It is a win-win situation and the reason why a reporter will likely agree to be one of your first guests.

Breaking News

Depending on your show's programming content, it is sometimes difficult to plan ahead because of breaking news, which primarily affects news-driven show formats, such as sports, politics and entertainment. On the other side of the coin, it could also affect something as offbeat as hieroglyphics via an announcement of an important cutting-edge software or utensil that was released.

Super Bowl LIII, which was held in Atlanta, had some controversy surrounding it because many critics view the National Football League as having hypocritical policies with respect to how they treat their players. Let us use Colin Kaepernick as a prime example. Kaepernick, a well-known quarterback who had taken the San Francisco 49ers to the Super Bowl, gained notoriety, but not because he was involved in any criminal activities. His only blemish was that he got down on one knee during the national anthem in protest of the treatment of minorities in the country, a right that should be protected by the First Amendment to the Constitution. Kaepernick's kneeling gave rise to a number of hate messages and conspiracy theories, resulting in him being blacklisted by the league's owners. Here is where the hypocrisy lies. The league appears to be more forgiving of players who have conducted felonious crimes against women, including battery and sexual assault.

The podcast I produce is more interested in the social and political issues of off-field/off-court activities, and the controversy surrounding Kaepernick and Super Bowl LIII was a perfect storyline for us to tackle.

Here's what happened: Soul singer Gladys Knight was invited by the National Football League to sing the national anthem before Super Bowl LIII. As aforementioned, the game was held in Atlanta. Ms. Knight was born in Atlanta, a city that is well known as the cradle of the civil rights movement. With the National Football League holding the Super Bowl in such a historic city, Ms. Knight made some cringe-worthy and surprising comments. She said, "I'm here to give the anthem back its voice," which many thought was a direct dig at Colin Kaepernick. For a singer not only known for her soulful voice, but also for her civil rights involvement, her comments seemed out of touch and, quite honestly, contrary to her stated beliefs. Needless to say, a backlash quickly formed in the press.

The show we had planned for that night was a series of hot topics that included a sports reporter from *USA Today* who was covering the Super Bowl. I quickly scrapped the plan after hearing Ms. Knight's comments and seeing the resulting reaction from the media and the public. I knew we would need to address the incident if we wanted to stay relevant to our listeners. But it was a risk, because I would have to ask the *USA Today* reporter to come on later in the show—basically "bump" him, which doesn't always go over well—in order to make room for a new guest.

I began thinking about who we could invite to talk about Ms. Knight's comments in light of Kaepernick's actions, beyond the excellent reporters who were our usual guests. I wanted someone solid who could speak to the civil rights movement, someone like the Rev. Calvin Butts, a well-known civil rights activist and minister, or another civil rights activist and minister, the Rev. Jesse Jackson. Admittedly, both reverends were a long shot, so I wasn't hopeful but reached out to them anyway. If neither could participate, I could always go back to the original plan with the *USA Today* reporter.

But then the Reverend Jackson accepted. It was perfect. He was an integral part of the civil rights movement, walking side by side with Dr. Martin Luther King, Jr. He obviously had a high public profile, was a strong advocate for Colin Kaepernick, and very vocal about how the National Football League was treating him. The Reverend Jackson was one of the critics who said publicly that the National Football League owners had colluded to keep Kaepernick out of the league, essentially blackballing him. Given all of these facts, we were naturally excited that he agreed to join the show. It was a stroke of luck, and we were able to address breaking news on the show. But it would not have happened if I had not decided to pursue him.

Generally speaking, getting guests is not easy, much less at the last minute, but that is what's required if you want someone special to discuss breaking news. It is one of the biggest issues you will face as a new podcaster, and may often leave you disheartened. You will receive more nays than yeas from high profiled guests (and not so high profiled ones), but our motto has always been "go big or go home." Sure, you may be forced to go home more often than not, but that's all part of the game, and you need to stick with it if you want to build a solid show. You cannot stop trying because, as with the Reverend Jackson, you will sometimes be rewarded.

Just a small note to remember: when you are recording your podcast, as opposed to streaming it live, covering breaking news is not always ideal. You will have to re-record portions of your show or, in some cases, the entire show to accommodate that breaking news story. You will need to be sure that you have not only the time to re-record before you upload your podcast, but also a solid editor on hand to assist in this process. Sometimes it is better to just leave your show as is and record a 30-second to a one-minute segment addressing the breaking story so it can stream before your show or as an add-on. That can also be very effective.

Now that you have a grasp of breaking news, the next section discusses evergreen stories, another helpful tool that will fill your show when you run short of story ideas.

Evergreen Stories

The Balance Careers, a website that focuses on job search and career planning, describes evergreen stories as "content that is always relevant, much like the way evergreen trees retain their leaves all year round." In other words, evergreen stories have a long shelf life with no expiration date. They are the types of stories that will be relevant today or a year from now. A good example of an evergreen story is "Women in Sports: Is There Still a Pay Gap?" This is a story that you could examine and find experts to discuss today or six months from now. Why? Because it is an ongoing issue that unfortunately may never fully go away. It may improve league by league, but there will still be some remnants of pay inequality among women in sports for a long time.

Let us do a 360-degree turn and go back to our offbeat subject of hieroglyphics as another example. You could plan several shows ahead with this topic, because most of the information related to this subject is not breaking news, but would help create evergreen stories. For example, the *Sun*, a UK newspaper, ran the headline, "Dead Strange: Mysterious Egyptian coffin covered with 'nonsense hieroglyphics' baffles archaeologists" (Pettit, 2019). The headline pretty much speaks for itself, but from that article I could create an upcoming show topic by asking the question, "How common is it for nonsense hieroglyphics to appear on precious artifacts?" This story could be done tomorrow or a year from now and it would still be relevant. Like the gender pay gap example, this storyline is not time sensitive and could be discussed at any time—making both the perfect types of stories around which to plan episodes.

Create Talking Points

Talking points are a good reference tool to use when hosting or co-hosting your podcast. They promote an organized, flowing conversation. You will know exactly what you will discuss and in what order. As I mentioned previously, talking points are not scripts and shouldn't be confused with them. By contrast, they are supposed to be concise bullet points that include relevant information about your topic so that they will guide your conversation. The best practice when creating talking points is to keep each one concise and simple to best assist with organizing your information, and to make them readable at a glance.

Here are some best practices for creating talking points:

- Simplicity wins. The purpose of your talking points is to guide you or your hosts.
- Discussion in a concise manner. Bullet points will help you organize your thoughts in a brief, to-the-point way. Your points do not even have to be full sentences—they just have to contain enough information so that you as the interviewer will be able to

understand and convey questions effectively. You may find that short words and then a link to the relevant article might be useful. Everyone will have their own process when they create talking points. Find yours and do not get hung up on formalities. For you, it could only be one word per bullet point that may spark your conversation. Experiment and rehearse with your producer or a friend.

- What are the main points you are trying to convey? Ask yourself what is it that you want your listeners to learn from this interview and start jotting those things down. For example, if your show is about veterans living on the streets in your community and you have invited a local politician on the show, your talking points may look like this:

    a. Discuss the homeless problem in the community.
    b. What are you doing about it?
    c. Are there programs out there to help veterans on the street? Food/housing?
    d. What can we do collectively as a community to help veterans?

The key is to lay out what you want your listeners to learn or know about the issue or interviewee. Do not get caught up with formalities because everyone has their own way of remembering, so feel free to play around and figure out what will spark your (or their) memory.

Chapter Review

The most important takeaway from this chapter is to plan ahead. Planning content for six months to a year ensures fluidity and continuity. Keep in mind holidays and health days when planning shows during certain months. Evergreen stories will assist you in planning ahead, because these types of stories have a long shelf life. They will be relevant for months, sometimes years. Reach out to media outlets or influencers that relate to the topic of your show. There are unexpected events, such as breaking news, that will alter the programming of your show, so be ready to change things around. Do not forget to create talking points that can help guide your discussions, especially when you have a guest.

Now that you understand how to gather information about the topics for your show, the next chapter will guide you through the process of interacting with your guests on and off the air. Before you read the next chapter, look to the discussion questions and exercises below to assist you.

Exercises and Discussion Questions

a. Whether or not you have come up with a real-life theme/name for your podcast or one for the purposes of this book, do research using your content theme and find articles that are examples of an evergreen story and breaking news.

- Based on these articles, create story ideas and plan for four shows.
- Identify potential guests from these articles—people who you would like to invite on your show. Explain why. How do they relate to your subject matter?
- Be sure to list their affiliation and contact information.
- Create talking points for each show. Remember that the points should be bulleted and concise.

Resources for Story Ideas

Yahoo News: www.yahoo.com
Google News: https://news.google.com
New York Times: https://www.nytimes.com
Washington Post: https://www.washingtonpost.com

Chapter 15

Interacting with Guests (On- and Off-Air)

Another important factor in putting together a good show is the way you interact with your guests, both on and off the air. Whether you have a host, host the show yourself, or have someone else join you, it is important to have thoroughly researched your guest(s) and the topic(s) you will be discussing. While interviewing your guests, you want to be able to properly engage them with professional questions that will yield informative responses and promote follow-up questions, as well as listener participation both on and off the air.

There are certain scenarios that may have you interacting with your guests off-air. The process of inviting a guest to your show generally begins with a pitch letter. You are often pitching your show to a publicist, agent or representative of your potential guest. You want to appear respectful and business minded, showing them that this is a collaboration that makes sense for their client. Draw parallels between your show's themes and the potential guest's interests. Do your research and see what connections you can find. Most celebrities have causes they care about and interests beyond what they're known for, which can serve as great entry points for getting them on your show.

Sometimes their representatives will respond with a quick yes or no. Others will completely ignore your email, which happens more often than not. Be sure to follow up, but don't become a pest. Use your judgment, but generally two follow-ups are a safe maximum. After all, if you don't get a certain guest, his or her agent or publicist may have lots of other clients who could be a good fit, so you want to remain professional and start building relationships with them. Some guests may not have a publicity team, so you can write them directly.

If you receive an affirmative answer, your guest or their representative may ask you for the talking points or questions in advance of the on-air interview. A direct inquiry could result in the guest asking you these same questions. In both cases, the purpose is to allow the future guest to be fully prepared before they come on the show. But it's not a requirement, and some producers will decline this request because they don't want the guest to rehearse their answers or come in over-prepared. With some shows, they may even deliberately want to put the guest "on the spot" in the hopes that they'll get interesting new material that will promote listenership. Personally, I prefer the guests to have an overall picture of what will be discussed, but without seeing the exact preset questions and talking points that the host has. That way, the guest has a level of comfort, but you can still get those more interesting, off-the-cuff answers. I have found that sharing a more general overview of the topics and themes with the guests promotes spontaneity and gives rise to an organic discussion.

Depending on your show's format and content, as the host or producer you may want to do pre-interviews with your guests to learn some interesting facts about them that will be different and entertaining, and maybe even surprising. If you watch any of the big talk or radio shows, most of their famous guests are pre-interviewed by a producer. The next time you watch or listen to an interview, see if you can identify a leading question from the host. By "leading question," I mean whether a host already knows the answer to a question he is about to ask. He may start the question with, "I understand that you..." Then the guest might say, "Oh yes, this happened when I was younger," and begin talking about something more personal that might be interesting, humorous, or even off-the-wall. These types of stories are designed to create headlines or go viral, which is something you want for your show and something that will get your podcast placed front and center in the news for what the industry calls "earned" media, as opposed to "paid" media, which is paid advertising. Pre-interviews can be very important and may be a great marketing and promotional tool.

There are some on-air gaffs that can also happen when conducting interviews. For example, hosts may not be prepared, or could ask inappropriate questions or conduct themselves in a self-serving manner. Having discretion and being prepared is tantamount to a professional and credible show, as well as fostering excellent guest relations. After all, you want those guests to come back.

Interacting with your guests should also not be approached as an opportunity for self-promotion or self-interest. It should be for the betterment of your show and its credibility. Each podcast that you produce is essentially a promotional tool for getting other guests on your show. Remember: you are only as good as your last show.

When you "hire" a host, it is often difficult to determine if the person will be working for the betterment of your show or have a hidden agenda to self-promote and gather contacts for his or her own self-interest. These types of people will learn fast that guests and their representatives will not have any use for them outside of your proven show. I have seen it firsthand. I even had a guest tell me what the wayward host was trying to do. Everyone has their own self-interests, which is fine, but you need to find a team that knows the meaning of teamwork and loyalty, and is willing to use your organization as a place to truly learn as well as assist you with your goals.

The right team for you is out there. You just have to vet your applicants carefully. You do this by asking pointed questions, such as their goals for the future and what they are trying to achieve from hosting or any other position you need them to fill. Having a host who does not put a premium on the best interest of your show will create issues. I had a co-host who had ulterior motives beyond the podcast. He went on to create his own podcast, which did not do well. He learned, however, that hosting and producing your own podcast is not as easy as it seems.

If you are hired to produce a show for others, preparing the client/host for an important interview is essential. You will have to not only do research on the invited guest, but you will also have to prepare your client by presenting the research on the guest and discussing it during the production meeting. Sometimes as a producer you may have to work with clients who are extremely busy or difficult to work with, and this will make preparing for the show a bit harder. A great example of an ill-prepared host from a producer's point of view occurred when a fellow producer of mine produced a show for her client on the 2020 election. The producer not only had to prepare the host, but also had to prepare the guest, because she knew the host and guest had polar opposite political views. To combat ill-preparedness on the host's part, the producer called a production meeting, at which time she revealed that there would be a lively discussion about the qualifications of (at the time) presidential candidate Kamala Harris, now the first woman vice president of the United States. It was important for the producer to challenge the host, whose opinions, as I mentioned, were opposing, but also somewhat misogynistic, and the producer quickly found that the host wasn't open to hearing other points of view. Under these conditions, the producer thought this political expert will eat her client/host alive with facts.

Needless to say, the client refused to do another production meeting. The producer's greatest fear for her client came true. Not only did the political expert make the host look foolish, but also got him to falsely change his views right on air. When I say falsely change his views, I mean that he did not have meaningful opposing questions or answers for the political expert and ended up changing his opinion for argument's sake. This happened simply because he wasn't informed enough to challenge the expert.

Hosts do not have to be scholars, but one of their most important off-air tasks is to be informed and well-prepared. Know your guests by conducting research and creating talking points before your interview. The key is research, research, research. It is one of the most important things a producer and host must do. Without proper research, you simply cannot create an informative and entertaining show.

Teamwork Makes the Dream Work

If you plan on creating a polished podcast, a show that will promote listener growth which could lead to paid advertisements, I suggest that you assemble a team with like mindsets and a similar work ethic. You do not want to just randomly put people together and create your podcast; you want to strategically assemble the right team, people who will work hard and believe in your show. The right team will come with great ideas and constructive criticism that will help grow your podcast. As the great basketball player Michael Jordan has said, "Talent wins games, but teamwork and intelligence win championships."

According to a *Forbes* magazine article (Rodriguez-Zaba, 2019), you should define the team culture for your organization. The article emphasizes that "by fostering a strong team synergy, you create a work environment that minimizes conflict and maximizes success. Differing ideas become problem-solving collaborations, and shared visions bring the future into better focus." The article also states, "Your Company's team culture is a reflection of your strengths." Another advantage of having a strong team is their willingness to share the workload. That allows you as the producer to assign tasks by the strength of your members. It will also enable you, as the creator of your content, to focus on the tasks that you know best, which will ease stress levels and any feelings of being overwhelmed.

Getting staff for your podcast will not be easy, especially if you do not have the budget to pay them. There are resources out there that could help, and one of the avenues that I found useful was contacting my local colleges and universities. I applied to be part of their internship programs. Students need internship credits, and most schools are happy to work with you if they find you credible. Universities and colleges use a terrific student recruiting platform called Handshake. When I started recruiting, Handshake wasn't widely used, so I worked directly with the recruiting director at the universities. Handshake allows you to list a job posting at participating universities across the United States. The caveat to this is that the participating colleges and universities have to accept you and will naturally vet your organization. This vetting process will be worth it, so carefully fill out the form provided. Seek out schools that fit your needs. Don't randomly contact schools that have nothing to do with the jobs you are posting. Remember that schools and students want positions that will help them learn and create solid work experience that they can add to their resume. My suggestion is to create a job description as well as a brief description of your company before participating in Handshake. This will allow you to effectively fill out the form as well as answer questions that the prospective schools may ask. Do not be afraid to recycle job descriptions from other websites, especially if they fit. When I was looking for a social media coordinator, I conducted a search using the key words "Job Description of a Social Media Coordinator." Many websites showed up in my search result. I was able to copy and paste relevant descriptions that applied to what I was seeking. The Internet is an incredibly useful tool.

In my years of experience of being in business, you will come across people that will try to undermine your authority and do things their way. So it is very important to thoroughly do your research and know who you are hiring for your co-host, host, producer, or any staff member, for that matter. You must clearly and thoroughly explain your vision for the show and how you plan to execute it. Be sure to define your expectations, hours, and roles to your interns or employees, because an organized and well-prepared show and staff is a successful one.

Chapter Review

Interacting with guests on- and off-air is essential to putting together a good show, and it is also the best way to cultivate and maintain a solid lineup of guests. You want them to be willing to return as well as refer their friends and colleagues. At *HWTP Sports Talk*, there are a few go-to reporters and athletes whom we can call on regularly, and this was made possible by our professionalism, excellent content and host. Since my podcast host is a lawyer, it is a nice trade off because reporters look to cite him in their articles outside of the show.

The other side is interacting with guests and/or their representatives through pitch letters and phone calls. It is also important to make sure that when a guest comes on your show, you and/or your host(s) are intelligently engaging them and not indulging in self-promoting behavior. These types of things can turn off guests and make you look unprofessional. When hiring personnel for your show, be sure to thoroughly vet them by asking the right questions. Assembling the right team will enable your podcast to soar.

The next chapter works in conjunction with this one in that it will examine the tools needed to find guests for your show and highlight the best practices to keep them open to returning for future shows. Before moving on to the next chapter, work on the discussion questions and exercises below to assist you.

Exercises and Discussion Questions

a. What scenarios may have you interacting with your guests off-air?
b. The next time you watch or listen to an interview, see if you can identify a leading question that the host asks the guest.
c. Imagine you have a podcast with a specific theme, and you have secured a dream guest. The person would like to see the questions ahead of time. How would you handle this scenario? If you decide to send the questions to the guest, include those with your answer.
d. Why is it important to be prepared for an interview?
e. Assemble your podcasting team:

- Make a list of the titles you would like to assign.
- Seriously think about your dream team. Who would it consist of and why?
- Explain the roles of team members and why each person would be perfect in a particular role
- Using the Internet, try your hand at writing one job description.

Resource

Handshake: https://www.joinhandshake.com/

Chapter 16

The Guests

Creators, Experts and Influencers

Having great guests on your show can make all the difference. Because of my entertainment and journalism background, and my roles with two critically acclaimed magazines (*The Four One-One* and *Huddlin' with the Pros*), I had access to notable experts and high-profiled people in the publishing, sports and entertainment fields. One was former National Football League player and coach Pepper Johnson, who won two Super Bowls with the New York Giants as a player in the 1980s and three Super Bowls as a coach with the New England Patriots. Another was Bill Gutman, a notable biographer and sportswriter. Knowing them gave me an advantage—something that most beginning podcasters may not have.

What I mean by "an advantage" is that I had people I could call immediately to come on my show. Having them on early gave my show credibility. "Perception is reality" is a marketing phrase I swear by, meaning what people see is what they perceive to be true. Having well-known guests as soon as the show launched created the perception that my podcast was a lot bigger than it was. Other potential guests might think that if Pepper Johnson was on the show, then there is no reason why they shouldn't be on the show, too. I was also able to use these shows in my pitch material to agents, publicists, and journalists. My podcasts were my best selling points.

If you do not have a well-known friend, the first people who are most likely to come on your show will be journalists. Journalists write captivating stories that are often very personal to them, so they will usually be open to discussing them on an even broader scale. Some journalists can be selective as well, especially the well-known ones, but if you produce a solid show with interesting content that fits in with what they report on, they will support it. If you are not comfortable reaching out to national media, start with your local ones. You would be surprised by the support you will receive, especially if you have solid content.

In addition to editing and promoting the show, I was in charge of securing the guests wanted by my podcast host for the topics he was going to discuss. One of our guests joked on Twitter, "David, do not forget to give Jackie credit for convincing guests to spend time with you."

Find the Right Fit: Research, Research, Research and More Research

How do you find the right guests for your show? A one-word answer: research. It is important to invite guests appropriate for your content. For example, if your show is about technology and you are putting together an upcoming episode about the impact that intellectual property law has on technology (i.e., patents and copyright infringement), you may not want to invite a guest attorney who practices family law. Just because the guest is a lawyer doesn't mean his or her area of expertise is the right fit for the type of law you will be discussing. As a producer, I certainly would not invite a family law attorney on to discuss patents and copyright issues in the tech world. Do your research to try and find an expert or an attorney who specializes in intellectual property.

Using the *Sun* newspaper headline that I referenced previously—"Dead Strange: Mysterious Egyptian Coffin Covered with 'Nonsense Hieroglyphics' Baffles Archaeologists"—if I were to create an upcoming episode with a guest speaking about how common it is for nonsense hieroglyphics to appear on precious artifacts, I would start with that article. I would read the article for context, see who was quoted, and then try to get that person on the podcast. I would also try and find similar articles in other publications. In addition to the *Sun*, another UK newspaper called *Express* and an Iranian newspaper called *Iran Daily* also reported on this story. Because of the wide variety of media coverage, you can usually find several experts and journalists to contact. In this case, since Dr. Kamil Kuraszkiewicz was the original source of the story, it makes sense that he's the only one quoted in the article.

I did a quick search on Dr. Kuraszkiewicz and found that he is an Egyptian expert from the University of Warsaw, which is six hours ahead of New York time. Unfortunately, Dr. Kuraszkiewicz's contact information was not on the University of Warsaw website because the staff directory link was not working. What do you do in this case? Contact the university directly. If you run into another obstacle, like a time difference or language barriers, go back to the drawing board by researching universities/colleges with solid archaeology or Egyptian studies departments. Seek out professors with PhDs. Most professors have their curriculum vitae (CV) listed with their profiles. Review them and see if they are knowledgeable enough to discuss the topic—in this case, nonsense hieroglyphics.

On the other hand, if you were able to reach Dr. Kuraszkiewicz and he was not available to do your show, sometimes you might get lucky because he may refer you to a colleague who is just as reputable and knowledgeable. If the person does not offer a recommendation, don't be afraid to ask. Having an expert as a guest is a terrific way to bring credibility to your show.

As a side note, time zones are very important to consider when scheduling interviews. I invited the Istanbul, Turkey, bureau chief for the *New York Times*, Carlotta Gall, on my show to discuss the Turkish government issuing an arrest warrant for National Basketball Association star Enes Kanter. She agreed to participate, but there was one problem: Istanbul was eight hours ahead of the Eastern Time zone. I had to pick a time that was suitable and convenient for everyone. She was only available at 3:00 p.m. Istanbul time, which was 7:00 a.m. in New York. I knew she was a good guest to have, so we made that time work.

The Cold Pitch: How to Reach Out to Someone You've Never Met

Writing the infamous "cold pitch" emails may sound daunting, but don't let it be. It is about knowing your target audience and reaching them. If you are considering creating a podcast that highlights new music from artists—let's call it "Open Mic"—you will need to have the actual artists' music to play in order to get this podcast rolling. So, how do you get access to this music? Research.

Research the small independent labels right up to the major labels. All you need is just one label to buy into it. Every major recording label has a public relations department, and most of their websites have contact information for their respective publicists. If you do not see an email address on the website, call them and ask if they will give you an email address.

It is the same for any kind of content. I have found during my years in the sports and entertainment industries that people will support projects that they feel are not only great ideas, but also beneficial to them. So it is important to write a strong pitch email that emphasizes the opportunity you will present and how your platform will present it. The pitch letters that I send out always state why I'm writing in the first paragraph, and then go into the details. Over the years of fielding press and other requests, I tend to ignore the emails that start out with what I call rambling. They go on and on, and you don't know why they are writing until you get to the end of the email—a huge turn off for me. People are busy and they don't want to read a five-page pitch letter. Get to the point quickly. A typical pitch email may look like this:

> Dear Sir/Madam:
>
> I'm the producer of an upcoming podcast called *Open Mic*. The podcast will provide opportunities for upcoming artists to showcase their music in an otherwise competitive and selective process by program/music directors. **I am writing to invite you to send us your new artists' music.**
>
> As you know, program directors can be extremely selective about what music gets added to the rotation, and the music that is added tends to be from the same popular artists, which leaves many talented new artists unheard. *Open Mic* wants to change this by giving new artists a solid platform for their work.
>
> *Open Mic* will stream Sunday through Saturdays each week from 2:00 p.m. to 6:00 p.m. EST. Once a month, we plan to highlight a new artist(s) and invite them on the show for an interview.
>
> Thank you for your time and consideration. We look forward to working with you in the future.

You will note that the "ask" is in the first paragraph. I start off introducing myself as the producer of *Open Mic*, and then I describe what the show is about in one sentence, followed by the ask. The other paragraphs I used to go into further details about how the show could benefit the musician and the label, and how it fills a void. This layout can be followed with any subject matter.

Communicating with Your Guests

Now that your guest(s) have accepted the invitation to be on your podcast, the next step is to decide how you will communicate with them. As I mentioned, I wanted to produce a live show, so the podcast platform I started out with was Blog Talk Radio, which provided a dedicated guest telephone number. I would always send a scheduled guest an email, first thanking them for accepting our invitation and also to inform them of the logistics. For *HWTP*, the first thing we asked the guest was, "Would you like me to call you and conference you into the studio, or would you like to dial in directly?" In my experience, most guests prefer that we call them and conference into the line. After that, I inform them that we prefer that they speak from a landline, but if they have good cell reception, then that is okay, too. In this mobile-centric world, 98 percent of our guests did not own a landline, and since we aired live on Wednesday evening, many of the guests call from their homes.

Even if you pre-record your show, cell phones are problematic because of poor service, and there were times when we were really frustrated by having great shows compromised because of poor cell service. David and I would tease one investigative reporter from a well-known national newspaper for his poor cell reception. It was horrible. He even changed his service, and it was no better. Because guests and callers call into the same number, we ask that guests send us the telephone number they'll be calling from. This way we can distinguish their number from the listener calls. Lastly, we ask for an after-hours contact number, if it's different from the primary number they gave us. This is necessary in case we have an issue contacting the guest, or if he or she forgets to call in. These are all great tips for a live show and a pre-recorded show.

When the Rev. Jesse Jackson was scheduled for the show, he was supposed to dial in at 9:15 p.m., but he ended up calling in a half-hour later. He simply forgot. This is another good reason why you should have an after-hours contact number, because he was not answering my calls to his primary number. I actually had to call his publicist to reach him. The Reverend Jackson calling in late pushed everything back, including the other guest we had scheduled for that evening, *USA Today* investigative reporter A.J. Perez, who is a friend of the show and was extremely understanding about the delay. Blog Talk allows you to listen to the show while you are on hold, so A.J. was able to listen to the show and told us that it was "really cool" that we had the Reverend Jackson on.

While Blog Talk has some great features, it also has some issues that I personally did not like, particularly when it comes to interviewing guests, so we eventually switched to a pre-recorded format and used Zencastr, a computer-based recording platform. This platform was not mobile friendly, however, so guests would have to use their computer to conduct the interview. The email that I sent to guests after we switched to Zencastr told them how to link to the show, gave them computer compatibility specs, and suggested a test run.

Another thing you may be asked by guests is to provide talking points (which we discussed previously) and pre-questions. Talking points are not only for you as the host, but also for the guests. Many guests, whether they are experts or celebrities, may be nervous, and talking points are great for them. They not only know what will be discussed, but knowing the talking points in advance will enable them to prepare and relax. The show will run more smoothly, and the guests will be more likely to sound more confident and authoritative in their conversation. That way, everyone wins.

Pre-questions are completely different than talking points. These are the actual questions you plan to ask the guests. You should have them ready, since some guests will want to know exactly what you are going to ask. Personally, I'm not a fan of guests receiving pre-questions because I believe in an organic, honest exchange, and providing your questions gives them a chance to prepare stock answers, which often eliminates the possibility of off-the-cuff sound bites or new discussions.

As you can see, there is more to be done than just simply inviting guests on your show. There are important steps like follow-up questions and logistics that need to be set before you go live or record in order to have a successful and stress-free-show.

Hopefully, your guest was terrific and the show turned out well. The next step for me is to always send out a quick thank you note. I don't wait. I email guests immediately after the show and thank them for coming on. Some guests beat me to the punch and tell me what a great time they had and express a desire to return. That is always a good feeling. But for the most part, I reach out to them first. It is polite and promotes good producer-guest relations. The note doesn't have to be long-winded, rather just simple and concise. If guests shared something particularly interesting with you on air, tell them. Thank you notes should always be part of the protocol. It is a great practice to have, and it is good business as well.

Insights: The Triple Threat Interview Formula

Raven Blair Glover

Raven Blair Glover is the author of Talk Show Magic *and founder of the Amazing Women of Power Radio Network. (March 2016)*

"My theory is that I'm not doing anything special. The thing I have learned, from listening to a mentor of mine, Jerry Clark, if you do not A-S-K, ask you won't G-E-T, get."

One of the biggest mistakes people make when they start their own podcast is interviewing random people with no thought as to how their guests will help them build their audience. As an interview-preneur, one of my secrets to success is my Triple Threat Interview Formula:

- Interview top influencers in your industry.
- Get yourself interviewed on other shows.
- Interview clients and potential clients.

My formula works because it ensures every interview is beneficial to the guest, the audience, and your own bottom line.

Step 1: Interview Top Influencers in Your Industry

Most people have a hard time believing they can even approach big time influencers to be on their show. I have been blessed to interview Alex Mandossian, Lisa Sasevich, Russell Simmons, Chili from TLC, Ali Brown, Jack Canfield, and Oscar winner Lou Gossett Jr., to name just a few.

Raven Blair Glover.

You want to start by doing what I call "Interviewing Up." When you interview influencers, you are connecting your name to respected people in your field, which builds credibility with your listeners.

Make a list of as many top guests as you can imagine: national and international celebrities, as well as people who are well-known and respected locally or within their field. For example, let's say your show is about meal planning. One top influencer for your list may be Food Network personality and cooking icon Rachael Ray. However, securing her as a guest can take some time. In the meantime, invite guests who are more approachable, such as a well-known nutritionist, a local owner of a kitchen store or cooking class, or even a private chef. Start small and dream big.

If you are feeling nervous about a big interview, remember the rules of I.C.O.N.:

I = Investigate. Do your research and find out as much about your celebrity guest as you can.
C = Connect. Build rapport with your guest by talking to them at least 10 minutes before you begin to record your show.
O = Own it. This is your time to shine. Take charge of the interview and be natural.
N = (Get Down to the…) Nitty Gritty. Do not waste time with fluff. Get right to the point and do a great interview.

Once you get the first guest, ask them for a referral. Just ask, "Who do you know that would be open to being a guest on my show?"

Step 2: Get Yourself Interviewed on Other Shows

Being a guest on an influencer's show will bring more people to your platform. You may think, "Why would anyone want to interview ME?" Remember, you are there to share your expertise. As long as you deliver on what the show is about, you do not have anything to worry about.

Make a list of shows that would benefit from your expertise. Again, small shows are a great place to start, but keep the big names in mind, too.

Next, pitch yourself as a guest. Let them know who you are and why your expertise is a great fit for their show. Contact them via email, their website, or even their social media accounts. Help the host by offering a couple of suggestions for the topic of the episode. Make sure your suggestions are a great fit for the host's audience—and will also draw them in to be part of your own audience, too.

Step 3: Interview Clients and Potential Clients

There is no better marketing for your business than interviewing your own clients. If you are a health coach with a podcast on healthy living, have your clients come on to talk about their own journey and expertise, and the positive changes they've seen in their lives since working with you.

On the other end, think of every guest you have on the show as a potential new client. Build rapport and let them see your expertise.

The Triple Threat Interview Formula practically guarantees that you will grow your audience and make money. Do not leave it to chance. Take charge of your interviews and start implementing this formula now.

Chapter Review

Some podcasters will have the luxury of knowing notable people to invite on their show, and some will not. If you are in the latter camp, don't let that discourage you. Do your research and take the initiative to reach out to journalists and influencers who relate to your specific content. Look to local journalists and experts in your area. If you produce solid content, people will support you. Research includes reading related materials and Internet searches. When inviting guests, keep time zones in mind and schedule accordingly. Keep your pitch letters short and sweet, because people are busy and they do not want to read a five-page pitch letter. Get to the point quickly. Once your guest accepts, remember to provide all of the logistics of the appearance on your show, including how to call in and/or login to your show. Finally, recording or streaming live with cell phones is not ideal. A landline is preferred, but in this mobile-centric world, landlines have become virtually extinct, except in the office.

The next chapter will help you to overcome some common issues that everyone goes through, from the expert to the novice. Problems are inevitable, but we have some tips to limit those issues. Before you begin the next chapter, look to the discussion questions and exercises below to assist you.

Exercises and Discussion Questions

a. Based on your research in the last chapter on creating story ideas and identifying potential guests, including contact information for the potential guests, and using what you learned in this chapter, invite a guest on your show.
   - Create a pitch letter. Be sure to include that it is a student exercise. You will be surprised how many potential guests will want to support you.
   - After classroom discussions and feedback, send the pitch letter out to the potential guest.

b. What were the results of the pitch letter? Explain what kind of response you received, positive and negative. Were you referred to another expert or potential guest?

c. If your potential guest decides to participate in this assignment, record a ten-minute interview.

d. If you were unable to get a guest, then record your own five-minute segment discussing the topic.

e. Have fun with this assignment.

CHAPTER 17

Overcoming Common Issues

Podcasting does come with issues and, like radio, one of the most common problems is guests and hosts talking over each other and cutting each other off. It's something that has always been an issue in this medium, and while it happens less frequently in video formats, it does happen there as well. Have you seen ABC's popular talk show *The View*? It is the poster child for hosts talking over each other and cutting each other off. When this happens, you are unable to hear the message, which can be extremely frustrating as a listener or a viewer.

When video is involved, you are able to see each other and act accordingly and effectively to each other's social cues. This enables you to tell when someone is finished talking or about to interject. In the audio realm, if the guest is not in the same room and is calling into your show, you are unable to see those same social cues, making it difficult to sense when someone has finished a thought or is about to interject. This creates the dreaded effect of hosts and guests talking over each other or cutting each other off.

Below are some other common issues for podcasters while streaming live or pre-recording your show.

- Host cuts off guest right before station identification or an ad spot.
- During a discussion, host, listeners and/or guests engage in a conversation that might require on-the-spot fact checking. As a host or producer, you want to get that information as quickly as possible.
- Sometimes host(s) and/or guest(s) are engaged in a great conversation and time is running out. As a host or a producer, you want to be able to send a fast-enough cue to let the guest(s) know the amount of time left so they can wrap it up.
- Background noise or poor cell phone coverage from the guests (which happens often) can leave you unable to communicate. Tell them their coverage is poor or ask if they can move to a quieter spot, either by email or text message—something unobtrusive to

the show. Stop short of cutting them off or asking them to find better cell coverage for all to hear. Ideally, you will have done a dry run ahead of time to troubleshoot issues like cell coverage, as discussed previously.

- A guest or host has volume issues.
- Not being able to identify more than one speaker in a panel discussion situation. This can be a problem for the host, producer and even the audience.
- Recording platform issues are very common.

These are some of the problems that will occur as a podcaster. They will drive you bonkers when they arise, because these issues may compromise the integrity of your show.

Let's take a closer look at some of these issues and the ways to overcome them.

Podcasting Remotely

For the most part, podcasters record or stream live from different parts of the United States and the world, whether it is in a professional recording studio or their bedroom. At the same time, guests will call into these shows from various parts of the United States and the world as well. For example, my podcast host dials into the show from Miami, Florida, and I produce the show as well as dial in from New York. Our recently added host, Pepper Johnson, also dials in from his home in Florida. Guests also call in remotely from across the United States and sometimes on assignment from Europe or Asia. There are certainly some challenges with this setup, especially when you're streaming live. Because no one can see each other, as the producer I will send my host cues via cell phone text that a guest is on the line, while I also handle listener feedback and provide on-the-spot fact checking. None of this is easy and can create a chaotic atmosphere. Recording your show would be a little less hectic, because you could do retakes and edit everything in post-production.

Cutting Off Your Guests

Cutting off guests is something that has occurred often when we're trying to insert our station identification, during question and answer sessions with listeners, or when we're navigating through guests when there is more than one on the line. We rely on texting, which is not always reliable. Texting can also be distracting if you stream live. Sometimes I cannot text fast enough for the host to react to or address my text messages, which often relate to fact checking updates or listener questions. When you record your show, you would obviously not have to deal with listener questions or calls. You could read social media comments from your listeners during your recording. The more guests you have, the more chaotic this can become, whether you stream live or record your show.

As previously mentioned, we streamed our podcast live, but the following example could apply to pre-recording your show as well. We had seven Boxing Hall of Fame inductees, including the legendary Michael Spinks, on the air at the same time. None of us, of course, were in the same room. We started the podcast with a basic introduction and then went into the Hit List segment (a roundup of the week's sports news). During the Hit List segment, I texted my host to tell him that I had some but not all of the guests on the line, so he should prolong the segment. I also told him that I would text him once everyone was on. He acknowledged. I waited for everyone to come on the line and had to personally call Michael Spinks last and conference him into the studio. Everyone was finally on the call and muted. While broadcasting live, my host cannot hear the guests, and the only person I could hear was Michael Spinks because he was on my line. Now, during pre-recording, you have the ability to freely communicate with everyone before pressing record. But since this was a live stream, we could not. I texted my host to let him know that everyone was now on the call and that I would unmute all of them to set up the boxing segment. I started to unmute everyone one by one.

The problem I noticed was that my host was not responding to my text telling him that everyone was on the line. He kept talking on his own for a solid three minutes. Remember, he's in Miami and I'm in New York, so we have no way to communicate visually, nor can I rush in and tap him on the shoulder. I unmuted each line with the exception of Michael Spinks, assuming my host would see my texts soon enough. Because the host was still riffing off the Hit List, the guests thought they were still on hold. One of the features of this podcasting platform is that when you are placed on hold, instead of hearing music you are able to listen to the live broadcast of our podcast. This is normally a great feature, but caused confusion in this instance. I heard one of the guests, thinking that he was still on hold, talking to someone else, and you could hear the conversation in the background while we were live streaming. So, I had to quickly mute each line again. Now I'm scrambling, getting more nervous by the minute when I hear Michael Spinks on my end saying, "Oh man, he's talking football now. Damn." I did not know whether to laugh or cry. I desperately continued to try and reach the host by text and by email, and he finally answered after five emails. It turned out that he wasn't receiving any of my text messages.

Another problem that arose from this very same show was that we had seven people on at one time and the host was able to effectively manage the questions to the guests, but identifying them was a huge challenge for him. In addition, there was still a lot of talking over each other, which caused some confusion and, to be honest, at some points in the segment, chaos.

Our listeners did not know who was talking, and I had a feeling my host lost track, too. Before the show, I did set the ground rules and asked each guest to please identify himself before speaking, but some of them simply forgot to say their names. Sometimes, in the middle of a good conversation, rules go out the window.

Overcoming the Challenges

We were able to overcome these challenges by using video platforms such as Adobe Connect and Zoom. Video platforms are great for the host-producer scenario, and even the host-guest scenario. Video will allow you to see each other and effectively communicate in a private offline setting. It will minimize your host cutting off the guest and vice versa, because you'll be aware of each other's visual cues, even if you record your show.

Adobe Connect was the video classroom platform that was used at the Newhouse School at Syracuse University. For a while, I would use that platform for free because I was a student, but Syracuse changed over to Zoom. In my opinion, both platforms are comparable. Personally, there are some features that I really loved with Adobe, and there are some features that I like better in Zoom. I won't go into detail, because all of this is subjective and they are really picayune points—plus, what works for me might not work for you. But, one point I will make is that the Zoom audio quality is better than Adobe Connect. With the right equipment, you could actually record a podcast on Zoom. The price points for each platform are vastly different. Adobe Connect runs from $50 to $370 per month, whereas Zoom's price points are from free to $19.99 per month. Adobe's platform is definitely a little more professional, but as a podcaster you might not need that platform. A simple platform like Zoom will work perfectly fine.

As a sports podcast, we are inspired by the hand signals often used in games when football and baseball players communicate nonverbally during a game. I created a system of signals for my host and me to relay information to each other during a show. I created a chart with hand signals and their corresponding meanings, then sent a copy to my host and kept a copy myself. Using the chart during interviews, I was able to communicate with my host effectively. Sometimes when the host is conducting an interview he won't notice certain things, such as jumping in before a guest is finished with his or her thought. The symbols worked well with us because my host knew to look up to see what I was doing. He would also see through his peripheral vision and know that I was sending some sort of hand signal. For example, a thumbs-up may mean continue speaking, and hands out may mean stop or wait. You can use whatever you feel works best. These symbols, along with your programming format, will help you produce a free-flowing show. You should create your own chart of symbols that will help you communicate effectively with your podcast team. The symbols do not have to be obvious. They can be shapes or numbers—whatever will help you communicate with your team and even guests.

Another alternative is using an instant messaging platform such as Google Hangouts, Facebook and AIM, to name a few. Do your research and see which platforms work best for you. You may not have the most current computer, which will affect the performances of platforms like Zoom and Adobe by causing delays and other issues, so in that instance one of the instant messaging platforms may work best. Remember: research, research, research.

If you are both the producer and the host, do not be afraid to set up interview rules for your show and send them to your guest ahead of time. You could even send your programming outline for that show. This way your guest will be able to see what time you will break for station identification or anything else. Often times your guests will be accommodating, especially when they know what to expect. Planning is key. Another thing to note when recording is that you can do the interview first, and then once it's done you can add the station identification, intro and outros. This way you and your guest can have an uninterrupted conversation.

The Podcast Industry Needs to Evolve

As a podcaster, I would like to see the industry evolve into a more interactive medium for both listener and podcaster. As previously discussed, there are many podcast services out there, but with the exception of Blog Talk Radio, none of them provide sufficient and reliable ways to broadcast live. You have to purchase additional software and equipment to do so, and this can be costly. Also, none of the platforms I have mentioned so far has a built-in private visual studio for podcasters to use in order to effectively communicate with their producer/staff and guests during a live stream or recorded show, creating a real virtual behind-the-scenes, in-studio feel. There's no ability for podcasters to upload VR/360 video either, which would allow for innovative creative ads, listener engagement, and news packages. Perhaps one day we'll see podcasting evolve into a true virtual in-studio medium.

Chapter Review

Producing a podcast comes with issues that are commonly seen or heard in television and radio. The most common problem is the dreaded talking over each other. It is a common issue that is frustrating for listeners and, for that matter, for all involved. When hosts and guests talk over each other, it creates chaos and your message can become lost. Unlike television, podcasts are audio only, which makes some social cues difficult to detect, especially if you are recording remotely and not everyone is in the same room. Another common issue is when hosts cut off guests right before station identification or an ad spot, which affects branding and your bottom line. Sometimes during a discussion, the host, listeners, and/or guests engage in a conversation that might require on-the-spot fact checking, or hosts and/or guests are engaged in an interesting conversation yet time is running out. Background noise or poor cell phone coverage from the guests can also be a problem. And unexpected issues can always happen, too.

These common issues are created or compounded because of the logistical fact that podcasts are mostly recorded or streamed live from different parts of the United States and even the world. With that in mind, by incorporating video platforms such as Zoom and Adobe Connect can help hosts, guests and producers communicate effectively, which naturally promotes a smooth-running show.

The next chapter will discuss marketing your podcast as well as examine a phrase I live and breathe by: perception is reality. What people see is what they believe.

Before you move on to the next chapter, work with the exercises and discussion questions to assist you.

Exercises and Discussion Questions

a. What are some of the recording and/or live streaming challenges you may face while podcasting?
b. How would you handle the infamous problem of talking over each other?
c. Create a symbol board that you might use for the host/producer scenario to communicate with each other.
d. Using the teachable moment in this chapter with the seven boxing legends, explain how would you handle identifying each of the guests in a similar panel discussion.

e. Research video platforms and pick one that you might use in a real world scenario. Be sure to discuss what you like about the platform, including pricing and whether you find it user-friendly.

Resources

Adobe Connect: https://www.adobe.com/products/adobeconnect.html
Skype: https://www.skype.com/en/
Zoom: https://zoom.us/
Google Hangouts: https://gsuite.google.com/hangouts

Part V

Marketing Your Podcast

Chapter 18

Perception Is Reality

What Does This Concept Mean?

"Perception is reality" is a widely used marketing term, but what does it really mean? According to a 2018 article written by Radhika Duggal, an experienced financial services and healthcare marketing leader, "The perceptions consumers have of a brand, its values and its products and services can have a dramatic impact on consumer purchase behavior. If a business can foster positive perceptions focused on these aspects, it is likely to build a sustainable, loyal and growing customer base."

The article goes on to say that consumer behavioral evaluations in perception are the result of physical stimuli from the outside environment and from people's expectations and motives based on past experiences. It notes that consumer expectations and motivations are formed by past experiences and are difficult to determine, but we can focus on the physical stimuli.

So what is the meaning of physical stimuli? According to MedlinePlus, a government website associated with the National Library of Medicine and the National Institutes of Health, physical stimuli "is anything that can trigger a physical or behavioral change." In marketing, these physical or behavioral changes include sights, smells and sounds. The stimulus can be a visual one, such as from a website, film or television, or an audio stimulus, such as from podcasts or radio.

Personally, this is a concept I have lived by and, as a result, I have always conducted my business in this manner. I always felt that, in addition to quality, consumers and potential guests would buy into my product if they perceived it as professional and actually larger than it was. It worked.

Believe it or not, I first heard the concept only a few years ago from my nephew, William, who is a manager at a well-known luxury car dealership. We were discussing a new project he had in mind and, because of some apprehension I had, he finally said, "Auntie Jackie, do you not know that perception is reality?" It stopped me in my tracks. I actually asked him to repeat it. At first, I thought it was a term he made up, but when doing research, I discovered that it was a commonly used saying in sales and marketing. It was a philosophy that I practiced, but I did not realize it had an official marketing name.

When I first started my sports entertainment webzine (web-based magazine), I actually began downstairs in my family room. I had a little desk and phone set up in a small corner of the room. From that little corner, I would discuss upcoming issues with my staff and the various sports leagues communications representatives over the phone. I would update the website daily and send out pitch emails, letters and faxes.

It was an effective set-up, but I didn't want people to think it was an amateur operation just because I didn't have a formal office space. I invested in an artist to create my logo and was able to design inexpensive letterhead and business cards that I printed myself from my computer, investing a little bit in "card stock" paper for better quality. I had a British co-worker, Veronica Johnson, who had an incredibly professional sounding London accent, so I asked her to record the outgoing message for the answering machine. All of this screamed professionalism. Of course, to do all this successfully you have to have a solid product. In my case, because my webzine was one of the few media outlets that focused on off-field/off-court activities of the sports industry through storytelling, the sports and entertainment industries embraced us. The facade of my webzine looked professional, and then when you took a deeper dive into the content, you saw that it was unique because it filled a void in sports reporting.

The perception and content of my webzine is what opened the door to getting great writers. Both athletes and sports industry executives supported us by allowing us to interview some great players in the industry. We also had the pleasure of interviewing many other great athletes, such as golf great Tiger Woods and NASCAR legend Jeff Gordon. None of the people we spoke with knew that I was operating from my home. Sports publicists and the leagues thought we were a lot bigger than we were. They loved the concept and thought the website and staff were professional, so they bought into it. Our editorial format at the time was unique; as I mentioned before, we were storytelling before it was the norm.

The same desire to present my podcast in a professional and unique way guided my approach when I reinvented it in 2014. The reason was simple—by then, I knew the importance of having a good public perception. While creating content for my podcast, I realized that I was no longer filling a void; I was actually one of the many media outlets using storytelling to create editorial content.

American author and former business executive Seth Godin said so eloquently, "Marketing is no longer about the stuff that you make, but about the stories you tell." Storytelling has become an integral part of journalism, both in advertising and marketing. Psychologist, professional storyteller and executive coach Vanessa Boris said, "Telling stories is one of the most powerful means that leaders have to influence, teach and inspire....storytelling forges connections among people, and between people and ideas. Stories convey the culture, history, and values that unite people. When it comes to our countries, our communities and our families, we understand intuitively that the stories we hold in common are an important part of the ties that bind" (Harvard Business, 2017).

Here are some of the best practices for creating good perception.

Website and Email

A website is your storefront. It is the first impression consumers have of you. The old saying "first impression is a lasting impression" is very true. When you create your website, it is important to make sure it is user-friendly with a clear message about you and your podcast. You will want to include your most current podcast episode along with archived episodes so that listeners have the option of listening whenever and wherever they choose. You will also want to include information about how listeners can contact you as a way to promote listener engagement.

Contact information is another opportunity to appear as the consummate professional. I cannot tell you how many small business owners have a website address but do not set up an email address that corresponds with their website. They still use Gmail, AOL or Yahoo email services for their email. In my professional opinion, your email and website should have continuity. For example, if your website is www.hwtpradio.com, your email should correlate to your web address. If people want to reach you by email, your email address should look something like this: YOURNAME@hwtpradio.com. How does it look if your website is www.hwtpradio.com and your email address is @gmail.com? It doesn't invite a positive perception. There are many platforms and products out there for creating a professional email account, including the same company you used to secure your URL/web address. You could also try Google Business Solutions, HostGator, and Network Solutions. Google Business Solutions is the product that I use for my website address and emails. This product includes G Suite, web hosting, cloud storage, and data analytics. My websites are created on Squarespace, a website creation platform. This platform has a partnership with Google and allows you to not only secure your website URL (address), but also allows you to create an email address. Google Business Solutions also comes with Google Docs, a popular cloud-based word processor that is also used in many classrooms. Docs is a great alternative to those pricey office products. The documents you create in Google Docs can be downloaded as a PDF or Word document and allow multi-person editing. Google products may not be for you, so do your due diligence. Vet and research solutions that will both meet your budget and your business needs.

Another option you have when creating a website for your podcast is using the podcasting platform's personal page that comes with your subscription. As I mentioned in chapter 6, most podcasting platforms offer a customized, user-friendly page for your website. Depending on your price point, these platforms offer well-done, professional templates from which you can choose. It is often less expensive to use the podcast platform's template than to create your own website. If you use a podcasting platform and want to have your own website apart from the platform, you will have to direct your podcasts to your new site, which you can do through coding. Some platforms do not offer these codes unless you subscribe at a higher level. In other words, the usual free level will only include basic features, such as recording and a page that will automatically generate an archive that listeners can return to whenever and wherever they want. The free option comes with a price. Visitors to your page will have to deal with intrusive pop-up ads as well as additional ads before your show plays. One of the biggest culprits for these intrusive ads and added audio ads in the beginning of your show is Blog Talk Radio. Our listener numbers significantly increased when I upgraded my subscription, which allowed me to move my podcasts to my own personal website.

The drawback to this is that you are paying for two sites. One site, Blog Talk Radio, housed my podcast archives, and the other was the customized website that I created through a website company. For me, the cost was worth it because my listeners did not have to hear annoying, intrusive ads. We were a young podcast and did not want to deal with added problems while we were trying to get listeners to buy into our content. Therefore, we took the whatever-is-necessary approach to appear and sound as professional as possible.

Sound Quality

Another part of positive perception is to record a solid, professional podcast. Whether your topic is sports, politics or any other subject, it is critical that your podcast streams in high-quality sound. Having a podcast that sounds like the host is in a tunnel, with choppy background noise, for example, will turn off listeners. It is said that listeners will be able to

Caricature of Pepper Johnson (author's collection).

judge your podcast within seconds of your introduction. The use of jingles for your introduction, breaks and outro can make your podcast sound extremely professional.

Imagery

Investing in a professional logo can really bring your website and podcast to the next level. There are many companies as well as freelancers that

High Times **Editor-in-Chief Dan Skye joined** ***HWTP Sports Talk*** **to discuss National Football League commissioner Roger Goodell. We decided to highlight a funny quote that Skye made and successfully promoted this by creating a caricature that included Skye and Goodell as well as the quote (author's collection).**

can create an inexpensive logo. Also, do not be afraid to tap into friends and family. Someone always knows an artist or graphic designer. I used Mallette Blum, a young artist who created all of my logos as well as my client's logo. I loved Mallette's work, and she met my budget. So do your homework. What works for someone else may not work for you, but if you want to be taken seriously, invest in a logo.

Promotion

There are many ways to get exposure for your podcast. On social media, hashtags are extremely important. To do this correctly, you will need to create your own hashtag. You can also make use of hashtags that are popular with your listeners (and potential listeners), which will keep you relevant and help your podcast to be discovered by people with similar interests. Google has many tools that can help grow your podcast by using Search Engine Optimization (SEO). Facebook and Instagram offer inexpensive ads that reach thousands and thousands of people for under $100. Twitter is another platform that offers reasonable ads. Be sure to turn on the analytics on all social media platforms so that you can see how well your ads are doing and monitor the reach of your posts. Turning on these analytics is also a great way of seeing how well your posts are doing in general. Make sure you understand your audience so that when you're advertising on these social media platforms, you're able to effectively use audience targeting to get the most out of your advertising dollars.

Search Engine Optimization

Blogger Rachel Leist describes Search Engine Optimization in simple terms. SEOs are "techniques that help your website rank higher in Search Engine Results Pages (SERPs). This makes your website more visible to people who are looking for solutions that your brand, product or service can provide via search engines like Google, Yahoo and Bing" (Leist, 2020). If you are not tech savvy, you will find that most website and podcasting platforms automatically build this feature into their website templates so that you can easily fill in keywords that relate to your website and demographics.

The most important and effective way of benefiting from SEO is to know your listener demographics and determine what they are looking for when using search engines. For example, if you are targeting people from Portugal, you will want to know their media consumption and whether or not they are on the Internet. According to Statista.com (Johnson, 2020), there are seven million Facebook users in Portugal, with 22.9 percent of the users being between the ages of 25 and 34. In addition, 48.8 percent of the users are male and 51.6 percent are female. Statistics like these are important when targeting, but you also have to do a deep dive and find out the psychographics, which is defined by the online dictionary Lexico as, "the study and classification of people according to their attitudes, aspirations, and other psychological criteria, especially in market research." In other words, learn their buying and spending habits, hobbies, and their values. Knowing this will determine what your target market could be using search engines for, which helps create effective SEO through the appropriate keywords, which help connect your target market to your website.

Meta tags also promote good SEO. Meta tags describe your website content by using short phrases. You add them in the header of the HTML page of your website. We're getting too technical, but here's just a short overview. HTML is the foundation of your website, and most website hosting platforms have it built right in. So you really do not need to know HTML coding, but it is important to know that these features exist and how you can make them work for you. If done properly, your target market, those searching for services like the ones you are providing, can potentially find you. Meta tags work hand in hand with SEO, because solid keywords result in increased search engine optimization.

As blogger Werner Geyser puts it, "quality should be the first priority of your podcast." Great content and audio matters because "audio and content quality will be the key factors to your podcast's success. Promotion and SEO will only work if you have a solid starting point for your podcast" (Geyser, 2021). (See *Insights*: Tereza Litsa and Todd Rengel.)

The digital age has had a direct impact on not only how we receive our news, but also how we receive our advertising with the popularity of social media. The next chapter will examine this phenomenon and what you can do to successfully promote your podcast.

Insights: Podcast SEO 101: How to Optimize Your Podcast for Search Engines

Tereza Litsa

Tereza Litsa is a marketing strategist and producer of the Reclaim Social *podcast. (June 3, 2019)*

Podcasts have turned into a very popular option for content consumption.

They are not new as a form of content type, but there are an increasing number of people rediscovering them. They can actually be an interesting medium to explore when trying to grow your audience.

"Podcast SEO" is expected to be a growing term among SEO professionals, marketers, and podcast hosts over the next few years.

What do we mean by "podcast SEO," and how can you really optimize your podcast for search engines? Here is everything you need to know.

Tereza Litsa.

Podcasts Show Up in Google Searches

Google announced earlier this year that podcasts will start showing up in search results. You will be able to search for a podcast and find some of the episodes through the search results. The indexing of the podcast will return the audio content that you can consume directly.

There is also the potential for Google and its services to analyze the audio and automatically transcribe it to highlight a podcast in relevant search results.

What's interesting is that Google Podcasts has recently started automatically transcribing the podcasts to use the content as metadata. Thus, people are able to find specific information as part of an episode without even knowing about the podcast beforehand.

This is a big moment for anyone interested in SEO to understand that podcasts are becoming more important. With Google's support, there is a clear indication that podcasts cannot be ignored as a source of content.

"Podcast SEO" is now a growing term, and there is a great opportunity for successful podcasts to build their audience through search traffic.

Thinking of SEO When Structuring an Episode

How do these changes from Google affect your podcast? A good starting point is to think of your content structure.

A podcast can sometimes feel like a casual conversation, but it still has a structure and a theme. Whether you are producing formal or casual content, you want to be able to have a clear theme. Think of what you want to talk about and how the questions can maintain a good flow. It will be easier for Google to understand the content of your podcast and how to index it if you start thinking of your audience and what they expect from you. Moreover, a clear theme also helps your listeners understand your main focus without getting lost in the conversation.

Creating a Site for Your Podcast

You do not necessarily need a site to start your own podcast. All you need is a hosting provider. However, if you want to start thinking of SEO more seriously, you want to be certain that you own the data and the relationship with your subscribers. You can also build an email list to grow your most loyal listeners.

A site can also help you improve your podcast's SEO. It is easier for search engines to discover your episodes when you provide additional context to them.

Many podcasts publish a new blog post for every new episode to describe their new topic. It is a great way to build up the content for your podcast and make it easier for search engines to pick up the main theme and the focus keywords.

You can also treat your blog content as any other regular blog post to link from one episode to the other, add related posts, and keep your audience engaged.

Adding Keywords to Your Podcast Episodes

Your podcast's title is your number one keyword. However, you won't just rank for it once you create more episodes, so you want to make sure that you increase your chances of building your audience.

When creating content for your podcast, you want to pick one main keyword that will describe it. Think of your theme, the episode's structure, and find the best keyword to describe it.

Make sure that you do not pick the same keyword on every episode, as you risk cannibalizing your own success. Even if there is a similarity from one keyword to another, it is still important to aim for one keyword per episode.

Your keyword should have a high search volume and ideally a low competition level. You can aim for long tail keywords and find inspiration by searching in Google or through the use of tools like Ubersuggest.

Decide on the Episode Titles

Your podcast titles will determine whether your potential audience will spend the time to listen to your episodes. Even when someone discovers your podcast, they won't necessarily listen to every single episode if the titles aren't appealing enough. Your titles should be clear and descriptive, while taking into consideration the limitation of characters.

A keyword can also be helpful in the episode's title, but you still want to make sure that you add it in context with the rest of the content.

Should You Include the Episode's Transcript?

Google may have just started automatically transcribing the podcasts, but the transcriptions are not yet perfect.

A transcription of your episode can help search engines understand your podcast in more detail. It can improve the discoverability of the episode through the right focus on keywords, content structure, and key topics.

A transcription also makes your podcast more accessible to people, and you can even split the topics that you are talking about in time brackets to help everyone find them easily in your podcast.

Podcast transcriptions can be time-consuming, though, and not every podcast host might be ready for this step. If you are serious about building your audience and improving your SEO, even in the longer term, it might be worth the effort.

Metadata

As with every other practice of SEO, metadata can provide additional details about your content.

A podcast's description can explain what the episode is about. It should provide further information right after the title. The description is also helpful for search optimization to allow search engines to understand the topic of your episode. You can also add your main keyword to ensure that you are consistent with it.

Tags are also useful for your podcast. They allow people to discover podcasts by looking at specific categories or genres. You can add several tags, but you want to make sure that they are still somehow relevant to your podcast.

Think of your potential audience and what they should search to discover your podcast.

Link to Your Podcast on Social Media

Sharing is caring. A good indication of a podcast's success is the number of shares and comments it gets on social media. You do not need to have an extremely popular show to see a few positive comments or shares on social media.

As with every form of content, content marketing is an important factor in improving your success. Pick your social media channels and other forms of promotion based on your topic and target audience. This can be a consistent effort with the promotion.

Encourage people to share the link if they've enjoyed your show, and create tracking links to find your best-performing channels. This can be a great way to improve your SEO through "online word of mouth," as it can improve your levels of popularity and eventually your ranking.

Ask for Reviews for Social Proof

Podcast reviews can also help your podcast's success. Reviews are not just an indication of the quality of your podcast—they can also help improve the social proof.

Ask your listeners to leave a review if they enjoyed your podcast. Start with your most loyal fans, and make the process as effortless as possible.

Social proof can be very useful for SEO as it "notifies" search engines of the most successful pieces of content.

Add Your Podcast to Google Podcasts

As Google becomes serious about podcasts, Google Podcasts is now more important than ever. If you are not uploading your episodes to Google Podcasts yet, you can quickly do it by adding your podcast's RSS feed.

It is the easiest way to start improving your SEO presence while monitoring your rankings, and you will show up as an audio snippet in search results.

Quality First, SEO Next

I assume that we'll start spending more time with "podcast SEO" as podcasts keep growing as a content type. The fact that Google is paying more attention to them and the way that they can show up in SERPs is a good indication that the podcast market will only grow stronger. What you need to remember, though, is that quality should still be a priority for your podcast.

Audio and content quality will be the key factors to your podcast's success. Promotion and SEO will only work if you have a solid starting point for your podcast.

Find a creative title and a unique topic, and pay attention to your sound's quality. These things will help your future audience connect with you and your podcast, making success easier through marketing and SEO.

Insights: The Importance of SEO

Todd Rengel

Todd Rengel is president of Animus Rex (www.animusrex.com), *a digital agency in New York City (December 2019).*

Todd Rengel.

Two websites walked into a bar. "What'll you have?" the bartender asked one website. She took his order and walked off, then returned with the drink. The other website waited for his turn. And waited. And waited. He waved at her, held up a wad of cash—nothing worked. Finally, fed up, he left the bar, thirsty and frustrated. The first website asked why his buddy hadn't been served. "Did not see him," the bartender answered honestly. "Are you sure he was even here?"

The simple fact is this: if your website, podcast, or app does not appear on the first page of Google, it is invisible. Google has 92.95% global market share in 2019. So, when we talk about Search Engine Optimization (SEO), we are really talking about ranking well on Google searches, even though other search engines do exist, like Bing and Yahoo!

But just how important is search engine page rank?

The #1 organic result of any search has an average Click Through Rate (CTR) of between 30–35%. Then the CTR drops rapidly: the #2 result is down to about 18%, #3 drops to 11%, and #10 falls even further, to 2.4%. Less than 10% of all searches ever go past page one.

Ideally, all websites want to be ranked #1. But only one website can do that for any given search phrase, and only a handful of the 1.5 billion websites in existence today make it to page one. This is where SEO can have a significant impact.

In May 2018, Dr. Judith Meer started The Pelvic PT, a specialized physical therapy practice primarily serving pregnant and postpartum women in Hoboken and Jersey City, New Jersey—towns just across the Hudson River from lower Manhattan.

We helped The Pelvic PT with a new website, a search engine optimization strategy, and the SEO implementation.

Dr. Meer knew a good website was critical for explaining what she did and who she served, but our primary business strategy was to help her rank well on Google in order to get the phone ringing. Market research showed that most of her potential patients were under 40 and had the latest iPhone in their pocket. We knew that 68% of consumers started health-related searches online, which is a trend echoed across most industries.

Our strategy focused on several key areas:

- Focusing on a niche market (being #1 in a specialized field in a specific geographic area)
- Relevant and quality content (useful, friendly, and informative)
- Good website usability and clear naming of pages (call it what it is)
- Google Analytics and Google Search Console (using Google tools to rank well on Google)
- Google My Business (being very specific about geography and offering)
- Studying what people were actually searching for and optimizing for those terms
- And, more recently, mobile page speed

The results speak for themselves:

Searches for "Pelvic PT Hoboken" ranks her website #1 and shows the Pelvic PT's Knowledge Card to the right. Similar searches for Jersey City and Hudson County and variations, like postpartum care Hoboken, 4th trimester Hoboken, etc., all rank within the first three organic results.

Business is booming. The Pelvic PT gets a large percentage of its business from Google searches, and patients regularly comment about how helpful and easy the website is to use. They provide an incredibly valuable service, have many repeat patients and patient referrals—and sport a 5-star rating on both Yelp and Google.

Does SEO matter to The Pelvic PT? Dr. Meer notes that "ranking well on Google has put my clinic above physical therapy practices that have been in town much longer. As far as my patients are concerned, I suspect there is

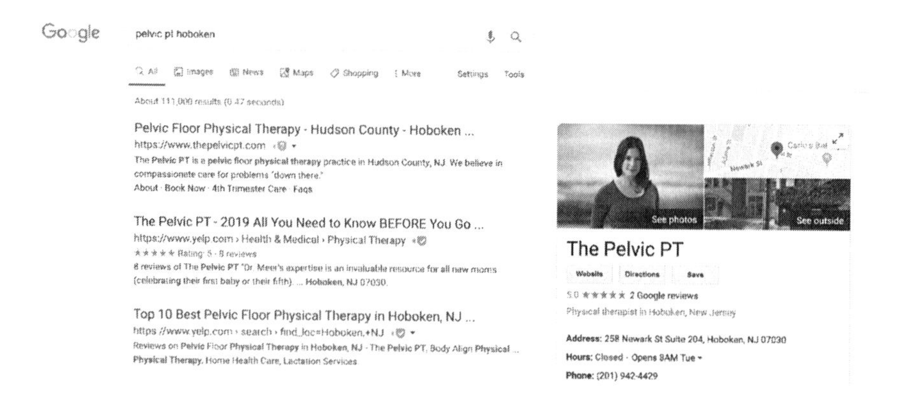

Google search results for Pelvic PT Hoboken (author's collection).

a perception of higher quality because of our ranking. While their expectations are often exceeded when they come in for appointments, having stellar SEO was instrumental in the rapid growth of my business and in its continued success."

Chapter Review

"Perception is reality" in a nutshell means that people believe what they see. If people believe in your values and content, they will support you, so it is important to make a good first impression, which starts with your website and email. Stay away from creating emails @gmail.com or @aol.com, to name a few. Try to have your email address match your website address. There are many inexpensive website and email platforms out there that will meet your needs and budget. The most important part of creating good perception is your podcast. That will be your ultimate marketing tool, so it is important to produce a professionally sounding quality show. Investing in a professional logo can really bring your website and podcast to life. Use social media hashtags to get your podcast noticed, and remember to keep the hashtags short and not too complicated. Facebook and Instagram offer inexpensive advertising that will reach thousands of people for under $100. Using the proper keywords will ensure effective SEO.

The next chapter will examine advertising and social media in this digital age. But, before you go there, look to the chapter discussion questions and exercises below to assist you.

Exercises and Discussion Questions

a. Describe ways in which you could create good perception using your podcast vision.
b. What does SEO stand for? Describe what it means.
c. Create a SEO plan for your podcast including keywords you would use.
d. Research both website hosting and podcast hosting platforms and describe in 200 words what type of SEO and metadata options they offer.
e. Describe the platform you would most likely use in a real world scenario and explain why.

Resources

Google My Business: https://accounts.google.com
Google Podcasts: https://podcasts.google.com/
Ubersuggest: https://neilpatel.com/ubersuggest/
Keywords Everywhere: https://keywordseverywhere.com

Chapter 19

Advertising and Social Media

As a podcaster who is seeking advertising dollars, you will need to produce a show that not only has solid content, but also has high-quality audio. I cannot stress this enough. These are two necessities for a professional digital presence. Here are some best practices for increasing your presence and creating a positive perception.

Social Media: Social media is a great place to promote your podcast. It is also a great place to engage with your listeners. Hashtags are one of the most important tools of social media. They are the most effective on Twitter (not as effective on Facebook, but they do work there as well). The Twitter culture is all about the hashtags. Instagram is the same. Instagram allows you to follow your favorite hashtag. Hashtags allow you to get your content in front of people you may not normally reach, well beyond your followers.

According to Twitter, "A hashtag—written with a # symbol—is used to index keywords or topics on Twitter. This function was created on Twitter and allows people to easily follow topics they are interested in."

The useful tips and information about hashtags listed below was taken directly from the Twitter website. The link is listed in the Resources section of this chapter.

Using Hashtags to Categorize Tweets by Keyword

- People use the hashtag symbol (#) before a relevant keyword or phrase in their Tweet to categorize them and help them show more easily in a Twitter search.
- Clicking or tapping on a hashtagged word in any message shows you other Tweets that include that hashtag.
- Hashtags can be included anywhere in a Tweet.
- Hashtagged words that become very popular are often trending topics.

Tips for Using Hashtags

- You cannot add spaces or punctuation in a hashtag or it will not work properly.
- If you Tweet with a hashtag on a public account, anyone who does a search for that hashtag may find your Tweet.

- We recommend using no more than two hashtags per Tweet as the best practice, but you may use as many hashtags as you like.
- Type a hashtagged keyword in the search bar to discover content and accounts based on your interests.

Here is a good example of the power of a hashtag. I connected one of my celebrity clients, Uncle Luke, with former 2020 presidential candidate (and current Vice President) Kamala Harris. She wanted my client to appear at a few media appearances and events. I tweeted out a video and photos from a South Carolina homecoming campaign event at which she appeared with him. Though I have just under 300 followers on Twitter, thanks to the hashtags, more than 6,000 people saw my post. Had I not used the hashtags shown in the image below, my post would have been restricted to my followers. The hashtags took it over the edge.

Another thing to note is to use the appropriate hashtags for your posts. If your post is on sports, you are not going to use #2020KamalaHarris. Your hashtags have to be appropriate to your content. Even though Twitter recommends using only two hashtags per post, it is okay to use more. Since my podcast is on sports, if my social media intern posts on the Twitter page relating to, say, the NBA, besides a #NBA hashtag I also have them include one for Major League Baseball, the National Football League, and perhaps other sports-related institutions. Hashtags do not always result in new followers, but they do put you in front of people who may not otherwise know you exist.

× **Tweet Analytics**

Jacqueline Parke @SweetGcomms
#Kamala2020 Uncle Luke (**@unclelukereal1**) representing!
#SCStateHomeComing pic.twitter.com/58jiFjwtb0

Impressions 6,183
times people saw this Tweet on Twitter

Total engagements 523
times people interacted with this Tweet

Twitter analytics results showing use of hashtags (author's collection).

Another important thing that I haven't discussed is social media listening tools, which are a great way to monitor your digital footprint. These tools are especially helpful for communications professionals. If your company tells you that it is interested in your podcasting idea but would like you to do a test run and ask you to produce three shows, you will want to monitor the results of your hard work by having access to tangible reports that show who is listening along with trends.

There are many social media listening tools out there, such as Hootsuite, HubSpot, and SproutSocial, to name a few. All of these platforms provide reports and an interface that allows you to publish and schedule your posts. Hootsuite is a very popular and user-friendly platform. Subscription levels run from free to $129 per month. HubSpot offers social media listening and much more. Its subscription levels run from $50 to $3,200. SproutSocial is an elaborate platform whose subscription levels run from $99 per month to $249 per month.

As you can see, prices and services vary, so you will need to do your research and determine which platform will make good business sense by meeting your needs and budget.

Offline Promotion: Engaging with listeners offline is just as important as social media engagement. Despite its name, social media can be impersonal even though it casts a wider net, but offline promotion leads to more personal engagement and promotes one-on-one relationships. If you have a sports podcast, your offline promotion could include going to local football games, setting up a tailgating tent and creating contests and promotions surrounding these events. Taking advantage of local events like this will allow listeners and potential listeners to fully engage with you.

There are many grassroots initiatives you can use for promoting your podcast offline. Let us say you are creating a podcast to support United States veterans and your content is geared towards highlighting veterans who overcame adversity. Through these stories, you are hoping to help other veterans who are having a variety of problems. A good grassroots promotion for this could be creating flyers that clearly display the purpose of your podcast. Do your research and try to locate veterans' support groups in your area, which are places where you could hand out flyers promoting your podcast. You could even place the flyers on their cars. This is a really basic grassroots promotion that could yield very positive results. You might also seek out members or founders of the support groups to invite them to share their stories of hope on your show. This is another way of raising awareness for your podcast. I find that if people like your content, they will support you and spread the word about what you are doing. Word-of-mouth is a powerful form of grassroots promotion. Be creative and do not be afraid to reach out to people and influencers well versed in the subject area of your content.

Keeping Consistent Hours: Another important way to raise the perception of your show is setting your hours and sticking to them. Being consistent will allow listeners to follow you and not have to guess when you are going to live stream or upload a new podcast. If you are accepting callers, let listeners know how to contact you and the best times to do so. If you do not have a telephone set up for your podcast, ask listeners to post their questions and comments on social media using a custom hashtag that is affiliated with your podcast—nothing too long. We used to have a long hashtag: *#AskHWTPSportsTalk*. We began receiving feedback asking us to shorten it because it was too long. Many users simply could not remember it. We then settled on *#AskHWTP*.

Advertising and Promotion

In this digital age, you might expect that online marketing would be enough to reach your audience. Unfortunately, it's not. A hybrid marketing strategy is the most successful one. Depending on your budget, you can combine an inexpensive grassroots plan with an online marketing strategy. Social media platforms, such as Facebook/Instagram and Twitter, provide cost effective plans that meet any budget. I combined Facebook and Instagram because (1) Facebook owns Instagram and, (2) when you purchase a Facebook ad and your accounts are linked, the ad will also appear on Instagram.

Google, although proprietary, offers a lot of great tools to help your business grow. They have leveraged the strength of their search engine and created some powerful tools to get your company noticed. Google Ads is a product that may assist in promoting your podcasts.

Google Ads are very powerful because they bring your company front and center in Google searches. I conducted a Google search on podcasts, and the first results I saw were Spotify, Pandora and NYC Studios. Trust and believe that these companies paid handsomely to receive that prime positioning. Google says, "you are in charge of your online advertising costs. Never pay more than your monthly budget cap, and you can stop any time." Although you may not have the budget for prime positioning, do your homework and figure out the best return on your investment based on your budget.

Another advertising option is what's known as native advertising. These types of ads are designed to have the same look and feel of the webpage or social media feed on which you are purchasing your ad. Native ads are widely used because they have more reach than traditional advertising. I prefer these types of ads because they are not intrusive and read more like an article than an ad. Some native ads use compelling storytelling, while others are written as if experts are reviewing and recommending products.

Let us return to my sports podcast as an example of using native ads. Say I decide to purchase a native ad in *Sports Illustrated*, which is known for their great feature articles that are often highlighted by compelling storytelling. I'm also aware that it is Black History Month in the United States, and I decide to put the two together. Thus, my native ad will highlight an exceptional African American female athlete named Florence "Flo Jo" Griffith Joyner, who passed away in 1998. She is considered the fastest woman of all time, setting track and field records in the late 1980s that still have not been broken. The native ad, which will have the same look and feel of *Sports Illustrated*'s website, would be about a 500-word article highlighting Flo Jo's accomplishments with quotes from the 2017 interview with her family. The ad would look as though *Sports Illustrated* wrote it, but the quotes in the article would be attributed to my sports podcast as, "Al Joyner told *HWTP Sports Talk...*" or "Flo Jo's daughter, Mary Ruth, stated on *HWTP Sports Talk....*"

Although the article has the same feel as an actual *Sports Illustrated* article, it is highlighting not only the Joyners, but also citing *HWTP Sports Talk*. This is a good example of a native ad that is giving us credibility, partially because it looks like a *Sports Illustrated* article. At the end, it would inform the reader that the full interview is available at hwtpradio.com. That is the power of native ads. The same concept is in play when you look at native ads in newsfeed form. The ad will have the same look and feel of, say, Twitter, if that is where you purchased the ad.

Like any new technology, native ads have come under fire. Department stores, such as Lord & Taylor, were using notable fashion bloggers to promote the release of new products and fashion. It is no surprise that consumers were having trouble determining whether the product reviews were ads or actual blogs. Having consumers read what are perceived to be actual articles on Lord & Taylor's website when, in fact, they are advertisements disguised as editorial/journalistic works is considered deceptive advertising by the Federal Trade Commission (FTC). Consumers were unaware that these fashion bloggers, who had millions of followers, were actually paid to blog and recommend Lord & Taylor clothing on their website. The FTC had to step in and file lawsuits against Lord & Taylor because there were no disclosures listed on the blogs to let consumers know that they were ads. (See *Insights*: Lesley Fair.)

Insights: FTC's Lord & Taylor Case: In Native Advertising, Clear Disclosure Is Always in Style

Lesley Fair

Lesley Fair is a senior attorney with the Federal Trade Commission's Bureau of Consumer Protection. Reprinted with permission from the Federal Trade Commission (Fair, 2016).

It is a fetching frock with spaghetti straps, an engineered paisley print, and an asymmetrical hemline. And it is at the center of a law enforcement action against department store chain Lord & Taylor for its allegedly deceptive use of native advertising—the first case of its kind since the FTC released its "Enforcement Policy Statement" in December. The lawsuit also challenges Lord & Taylor's "product bomb" campaign on Instagram as misleading.

Lord & Taylor used an extensive social media push to launch Design Lab, its own apparel line aimed at women between 18 and 35. The strategy was interesting: Focus on just one item—that paisley asymmetrical dress.

For the native advertising part of the campaign, Lord & Taylor signed a

FTC website (*www.FTC.gov*).

contract to have Nylon, an online fashion magazine, run an article about the Design Lab collection featuring a photo of the paisley dress. Lord & Taylor reviewed and approved the paid-for Nylon article, but did not require a disclosure about their commercial arrangement.

In addition, Lord & Taylor contracted to have Nylon post a photo of the paisley dress on Nylon's Instagram page. Again, Lord & Taylor reviewed and approved the paid-for post, but did not require a disclosure.

That was only part of the campaign. Lord & Taylor also recruited a team of fashion influencers, all of whom had two things in common: a sense of style and a massive number of followers on social media platforms.

Lord & Taylor gave the dress to 50 influencers and paid them between $1,000 and $4,000 to post photos of themselves in the dress on Instagram on one specified "product bomb" weekend in March 2015—the same weekend when Nylon posted its Lord & Taylor-approved photo. Style the dress any way you like, Lord & Taylor told the influencers, but in other aspects, the contract was all business. The influencers had to: (1) use the @lordandtaylor Instagram user designation and the campaign hashtag #DesignLab in the photo caption; and (2) tag the photo @lordandtaylor.

Lord & Taylor's reps preapproved each of the influencers' Instagram posts to make sure they included the required hashtag and Instagram designation. The company also edited some of what the influencers planned to say.

But despite the company's punctilious approach to hashtags, handles, and the like, Lord & Taylor was curiously silent about other key aspects of the campaign. For example, according to the FTC, Lord & Taylor's contract did not require the influencers to disclose that Lord & Taylor had paid them. Furthermore, none of the Instagram posts Lord & Taylor approved included a disclosure that the influencer had received the dress for free, that she had been compensated for the post, or that the post was a part of a Lord & Taylor ad campaign. And as the complaint alleges, Lord & Taylor did not add a disclosure to that effect to any of the influencers' posts it reviewed.

The Instagram campaign reached 11.4 million individual users, resulting in 328,000 brand engagements—likes, comments, reposts, etc.—with Lord & Taylor's Instagram handle. And the paisley dress sold out.

The FTC complaint charges Lord & Taylor with three separate violations: (1) that Lord & Taylor falsely represented that the 50 Instagram images and captions reflected the independent statements of impartial fashion influencers when they really were part of a Lord & Taylor ad campaign to promote sales of its new line; (2) that Lord & Taylor failed to disclose that the influencers were the company's paid endorsers—a connection that would have been material to consumers; and (3) that Lord & Taylor falsely represented that the Nylon article and Instagram post reflected Nylon's independent opinion about the Design Lab line, when they were really paid ads.

Under the terms of the proposed settlement, Lord & Taylor cannot falsely claim—expressly or by implication—that an endorser is an independent user or ordinary consumer. If there is a material connection between the company and an endorser, Lord & Taylor must clearly disclose it "in close proximity" to the claim. And Lord & Taylor cannot suggest or imply that a paid ad is a statement or opinion from an independent or objective publisher or source.

What does the Lord & Taylor case suggest for your company's social media campaigns?

If you use native advertising, consider the context. As the FTC explained in "Native Advertising: A Guide for Businesses," "The watchword is transparency. An advertisement or promotional message shouldn't suggest or imply to consumers that it is anything other than an ad." Review your native ads from the perspective of consumers who do not have your industry expertise about new forms of promotion.

If there is a material connection between your company and an endorser, disclose it. What's a material connection? According to the FTC's Endorsement Guides, it is a connection between the endorser and the seller that might materially affect the weight or credibility a consumer gives the endorsement. Read "FTC's Endorsement Guides: What People Are Asking" for nuts-and-bolts compliance advice and apply those principles if you enlist influencers, bloggers, or others in your marketing efforts.

Disclosures of material connection must be clear and conspicuous. What about explaining a material connection in a footnote, behind an obscure hyperlink, or in a general ABOUT ME or INFORMATION page? No, no, and no. As with any disclosure of material information, businesses should put the disclosure in a location where consumers will see it and read it. The terms of the Lord & Taylor settlement apply just to that company, of course, but for prudent marketers, a good rule of thumb is the standard in that order: "in close proximity" to the claim.

Train your affiliates and monitor what they're doing on your behalf. If your company uses social media campaigns like this, make your expectations clear at the outset with influencers and follow through with an effective compliance program. There is no one-size-fits-all approach, but "The FTC's Endorsement Guides: What People Are Asking" lists elements every program should include:

- Because advertisers are responsible for substantiating objective product claims, explain to your network the claims you can support;
- Instruct them about their responsibilities for disclosing their connection to you;
- Periodically search to make sure they're following your instructions; and
- Follow up if you spot questionable practices.

The FTC eventually released "Native Advertising: A Guide for Businesses." The guide begins, "Marketers and publishers are using innovative methods to create, format, and deliver digital advertising. One form is 'native advertising,' content that bears a similarity to the news, feature articles, product reviews, entertainment, and other material that surrounds it online. But as native advertising evolves, are consumers able to differentiate advertising from other content?" This very question is the reason for regulation. The guide continues, "Because ads can communicate information through a variety of means—text, images, sounds, etc.—the FTC will look to the overall context of the interaction, not just to elements of the ad in isolation. Put another way, both what the ad says and the format it uses to convey that information will be relevant. **Any clarifying information necessary to prevent deception must be disclosed clearly and prominently to overcome any misleading impression**" (emphasis added).

Native ads are widely used on social media and have a high click through rate, but because of the FTC regulation you, as a consumer, will now be able to determine what posts are paid advertising and what posts are created from the owner of the social media page. As a consumer, look for words such as "Advertising," "Promotion," "Sponsored," and "Suggested Post," just to name a few.

As a content creator wanting to purchase native ads, know the laws and adhere to them. Make sure you clearly disclose that the content you are placing on another site is not misleading or deceptive.

Content Advertising: Content advertising is a marketing strategy that produces value-added content with its primary function of distributing the content through a paid channel. A perfect example is having an important guest on your podcast and wanting as large an audience as possible. In one of the podcasts I produced for Luther "Uncle Luke" Campbell, we had an episode that included an interview with former University of Michigan men's basketball standout, former NBA player, and ESPN analyst Jalen Rose. He came on the show to discuss a young NBA player, Zion Williamson, as well as other sports news. The conversation was informative and funny, which created several great sound bites that I could promote. Before the interview started, Jalen did an impromptu rap of one of Uncle Luke's hit songs. It was an incredible moment, and while it was not part of the interview, I thought it could be a great 30-second teaser to encourage listeners and potential listeners to tune into the show. Unfortunately, I dropped the ball as producer and did not hit the record button before the interview started, so the rapping was not recorded. A missed moment for sure, but a mistake I'd never make again. Fortunately, I was able to use another funny clip that turned out just as good.

But let's look at what I could have done with that missed moment. Keeping content advertising in mind, the clip could have been set up this way: *The Uncle Luke Show* introduction jingle, Jalen rapping, then an outro with a call to action: "Full interview this Wednesday at 9:00 p.m. EST at LukeRecord.com." Once this had been completed and cut down to exactly 30 seconds, I would then purchase ad space on the various social media platforms such as Twitter, Facebook, and Instagram. If we had the budget, we would have probably bought ad space on ESPN or another sporting website, or even a music site to promote the interview. This example is what content advertising is all about.

Banner Ads: Banner ads were the first ads on the Internet. They began in 1994 with AT&T, which bought a rectangle ad on a website called HotWired.com. According to the *Atlantic*, "About 44 percent of the people who saw it actually clicked on it" (LaFrance, 2017). Nowadays, banner ads receive a dismal 1.91 percent click rate.

The *New York Times* published an article called, "Fall of the Banner Ad: The Monster That Swallowed the Web" (Manjoo, 2014). The article examines the rise and fall of the banner ad and states, "These days, finally, the banner ad is in decline. Why? … because the web, the medium in which it has thrived, is also in decline. Today we live in a mobile, social world, spending most of our time online using apps that load faster and are much prettier and more useful than websites." An important factor in the decline of the banner ad was explained, in part, thusly: "Instead of banners, many of these apps, including Facebook, Twitter and Instagram, make money through ads that appear in users' social feeds, rather than off to the side of the page."

Banner ads are budget friendly, but not cost effective. This is the very reason why you need to do your homework to find what meets your needs and gives you the best return on your investment.

Pop-Up Ads: Pop-up ads, in my opinion, are the most intrusive and annoying ads in digital advertising. Whether they consume a quarter of your screen or the entire screen, I find them extremely annoying and will purposely avoid brands that run them. I'm not alone. This consumer reaction is typical and accounts for the fact that pop-up ads only represent two percent of all online advertising. It is probably why Google hates them. Google, along with other web based platforms, has come together with the Interactive Advertising Bureau ("IAB") to tackle the pop-up ad issue. In 2018, Google installed an ad blocking extension to their web browser Chrome. This didn't come without controversy. According to Marketing Land, "Critics of the move say it gives Google the power to favor its own ad formats on its own browser and dictate what makes a good ad experience" (Marvin, 2017).

According to the IAB (IAB, 2016), users block ads because:

> Consumers want uninterrupted, quick browsing and a streamlined user experience.
>
> - Among those that already use an ad blocker on their PC, the top reason for using it on a computer is the perception that sites are easier to navigate without ads.
> - Among those that already use an ad blocker on their smartphone, the

top reason for using it on a phone is the perception that ads slow down browsing.
- Consumers that use ad blockers tend to blame ads for slow loading pages, while those not currently using ad blockers tend to blame the content for slow loading pages.
- Most annoying ad elements are: Ads that block content, long video ads before short videos, ads that follow down the page as the user scrolls.
- Consumers that use ad blockers are even more annoyed by these ad elements, especially auto-start ads (audio, in-page video, in-stream video).
- Users of ad blockers are less tolerant of ads.

Despite all this, pop-ups are the advertising method that some podcasting platforms still use, as well as online newspaper websites. These types of ads can actually turn off potential new customers. I know this firsthand because my podcasts have lost listeners because of our early use of pop-ups. A lot of browsers, like Google, are incorporating ad blocker software to their browsers to address the intrusiveness of pop-up ads.

Research the various options that fit your needs and wants. The key to successful advertising and promotion on and offline is to plan, research, know your goals, and know the demographics and psychographics of your targeted market.

Chapter Review

Producing a well-thought-out podcast with quality audio is essential to getting listeners and advertising dollars. Here are the best practices to increase your presence:

- Social media is a great place to engage with listeners and share content. Hashtags are very important when posting content.
- Interestingly enough, in this digital age, promoting and engaging with listeners offline is just as important. A hybrid marketing strategy is the most successful approach.
- Grassroots initiatives are inexpensive and extremely effective.
- Keeping consistent hours is crucial, because listeners will know when you are going to stream live or upload your podcasts. Consistency helps in branding and cultivates and maintains listener expectations.
- Advertising options: **Native advertising** is the most effective online advertising method, but be sure to prevent deception by clearly disclosing and prominently displaying the proper language in order to prevent misleading consumers. **Content advertising** is a marketing strategy to distribute your content through paid

advertising. **Banner ads** are still being purchased and appear on the top, side, middle and bottom of a webpage. They are the least effective, having a 1.91 percent click through rate. **Pop-up ads** are one of the most intrusive ads on the web and have a two percent click through rate.
- Research all of these advertising options to see what fits both your needs and budget. The key to advertising is planning, using targeted demographics, and knowing your goals.

The next chapter will examine podcasting in the business world. Before you move on, look to the discussion questions and exercises below to assist you.

Exercises and Discussion Questions

a. What are some best practices for increasing your presence and creating a positive perception?
  - Using your own podcasting idea, write a one-page essay applying these best practices.

b. Twitter exercise: Find an article that relates to your podcast content. Summarize it and use appropriate hashtags. Be sure to turn on Twitter Analytics before you post.
c. Describe some grassroots initiative that you would create for your podcast.
d. How would you use native advertising in promoting your podcast?
e. How would you guard against deception with your native ad?
f. Create a 30-second teaser for your podcast.

Resources

How to use hashtags: https://help.twitter.com/en/using-twitter/how-to-use-hashtags
Lord & Taylor, LLC, In the Matter of (Complaint): https://www.ftc.gov/enforcement/cases-proceedings/152–3181/lord-taylor-llc-matter
The FTC's Endorsement Guides: What People are Asking: https://www.ftc.gov/tips-advice/business-center/guidance/ftcs-endorsement-guides-what-people-are-asking
Native Advertising: A Guide for Businesses: https://www.ftc.gov/tips-advice/business-center/guidance/native-advertising-guide-businesses
Google Ads: https://ads.google.com
Google Business Solutions: https://www.google.com/services
LaFrance, A. (2017, April 21). "The First Ever Banner Ad on the Web," *Atlantic*: https://www.theatlantic.com/technology/archive/2017/04/the-first-ever-banner-ad-on-the-web/523728/
Manjoo, F. (2014, November 6). "Fall of the Banner Ad: The Monster that Swallowed the Web," *New York Times*: https://www.nytimes.com/2014/11/06/technology/personaltech/banner-ads-the-monsters-that-swallowed-the-web.html

CHAPTER 20

Podcasting for Business

Podcasts are a viable marketing tool for businesses and, slowly but surely, companies are catching on. The fact that companies are lagging behind, however, could provide opportunities for communications specialists and marketers to pave the way and stand out, enabling them to become authoritative voices in their respective industries. Another advantage is the fact that podcasts can build strong relationships with an audience, create brand awareness, and give listeners an opportunity to enjoy spending quality time with excellent content while learning something new in an intimate setting. They can also increase traffic to your company's website, bring in new business and create brand awareness. Podcasts allow listener flexibility because they have the option to listen whenever and wherever they like. Podcasts are cost effective to create, have a global reach, and can be a great tool for media training for executives because they build strong communication skills.

Companies also use podcasts for internal communications with their employees. American Airlines created the podcast *Tell Me Why* specifically to communicate with their 120,000 plus employees across the United States. The company eventually made the podcast public to address policy changes, strategic direction and bad public relations. I have listened to a few of the podcasts from American Airlines, and they contain straightforward interviews with no music transition, which may seem a bit dry for the average listener. However, internal podcasts are a great way to engage and share company goals and strategies with employees, and even to address company issues and downfalls.

Morgan Stanley, a global investment banking and financial services company headquartered in Manhattan, offers its employees, clients and non-clients an interesting podcast that is available not only locally within the United States, but also globally, using ambient sound to effectively tell stories.

Ambient sound? That is a new term that hasn't been mentioned up to this point, yet is one of the most important tools to use in audio storytelling.

I like to describe it as the sound of the atmosphere. Think of a car door slamming, bird chirping, the sound of a crowd in a restaurant or subway, traffic noises or music playing. These atmospheric, background noises can add vibrancy to your audio. They can also establish or reinforce the mood of your storytelling.

Here is an example of the effective use of ambient sound. Imagine you are a new mother with a newborn baby recently diagnosed with whooping cough, a highly contagious respiratory infection that is characterized by a persistent cough with a distinct, high-pitched sound. You decide to do some research on the Internet looking for a podcast that discusses whooping cough and, sure enough, you find one. The narrator, a respiratory specialist, discusses the symptoms of whooping cough and the effects it has on children. While the doctor is explaining it, you hear in the background what sounds like a public area, perhaps a doctor's office, people talking, feet shuffling and a baby coughing in a distinct, high-pitched manner. This is an example of using ambient sound to tell a story. The sounds of a public area and hearing feet shuffle and a baby coughing as though it had whooping cough bring the story to life. Ambient sound helps to make the narration more engaging, even though the podcast is about a serious medical topic.

Morgan Stanley's podcast really does a great job of incorporating ambient sound into its shows. The company has several podcasts, but the one I found interesting is the *Morgan Stanley Ideas* podcast, which is hosted by Ashley Milne-Tyte, a journalist hired by Morgan Stanley. She has a British accent, which gives the podcast a global feel as well as a professional and credible voice. It uses Milne-Tyte for the majority of the *Ideas* podcasts. The series' theme is about the future, with titles that include "Inventing Flavors: A Taste of the Future," "When Software Drives the Car, Who Pays the Insurance?," "The Shift Toward Consumer Driven Energy," and "Re-imagining the Plastics Economy." Each episode highlights a specific topic through storytelling, and since Morgan Stanley is a financial services company, all of the topics tie in to some sort of financial product or service it offers, as well as provide general insight on economic trends, investments or stocks.

One particular episode that caught my attention was the one on inventing flavors. I'm a foodie, so I immediately thought this was going to be about a chef creating new and exciting dishes. I was pleasantly surprised to discover that the podcast explored the future of naturally grown and lab-designed flavors, and how this will impact our palates and wallets. You first learn about a plant breeder, Michael Mazourek, who naturally creates flavors by cross-breeding seeds. The podcast then moves to a lab in Portland and interviews Sarah Masoni, a flavor designer who apparently has a "million-dollar palate." In between, Morgan Stanley incorporates its food retail analyst, Vincent Sinsi, who discusses the new opportunities that are being created for consumers and food retailers investing in both farm and lab-made flavors which will eventually make their way to your supermarket shelves. Sinsi effectively analyzes the food retail industry by discussing sales and trends, and skillfully ties in naturally grown flavors on a farm and in a lab.

The podcast is professionally produced and provides its audience with rich, relevant and unique content that beautifully ties into Morgan Stanley's brand. It is unclear if the companies highlighted are actual clients or researched content, but I felt as though I was listening to a podcast version of *60 Minutes*. The use of ambient sound is wonderfully done throughout, making the podcast engaging as well as educational. On the landing page of each podcast, Morgan Stanley provides a detailed description of the podcast, which creates effective SEO.

By comparison, give a listen to American Airlines' *Tell Me Why* podcast and then to Morgan Stanley's *Ideas* podcast so that you can truly see the importance of using ambient sound. You will hear the difference between a highly produced (and most likely expensive) podcast and the less expensively produced podcast of American Airlines.

Morgan Stanley's *Ideas* is no more than a half-hour, and the podcasts that relate more directly to the company's products and services are no more than ten minutes long. Once again, these short podcasts effectively use storytelling and ambient sound. American Airlines' podcasts are also short and run about ten minutes.

Now that you know the importance of storytelling and the use of ambient sound, in the next section we'll discuss the ways to get started.

How to Begin

Creating a podcast for your company is not that different from creating one for yourself. As discussed earlier, you will need to know the motivation for starting the podcast. In business, this will be messaging. What is it that you would like the public, current clients, and potential clients to know? What are the demographics you currently have, and what are the ones you would like to attract? Companies and/or departments have budgets, so you will need to consider what is or will be allocated for podcasts. When considering budget, you will need to ask yourself if there is room to create a high production podcast or a less expensive one? Will you invite outside guests on the show, or will you invite company executives and management to discuss a variety of topics that highlight your goods and services? Questions like these are important to know before you begin.

Unlike a personal podcast, when creating a company podcast, you have to be sure that it adheres to your company's code of conduct and work rules. In addition, you have to make sure that the content is not offensive, controversial or divisive. Remember, you are always accountable to the employees and clients of your company.

Be sure to know your company's mission statement, products and services. Remember that you need to know what it is that you want to convey to potential listeners. For example, do you want to position the company executives as experts in their field? Do you want to create compelling storytelling that ties into your company's products and services, like Morgan Stanley, or highlight diversity and inclusion initiatives? Make a list of what you would like people to know about your company—for example, highlight products/services, charitable work, cutting edge initiatives, and anything else you deem important. Then you must decide (most likely with company decision makers) the format, frequency and production quality of these podcasts. The budget allocated to this initiative will determine the type of podcast you produce.

Getting Internal Buy-In

Getting internal buy-in may not be easy. Companies look to their bottom line and will not want to incur additional expenses if they think they will not get a good return on their investment. So how do you convince your company that creating a podcast makes good business sense? Start with a plan.

You do this by creating a simple business plan. When I wanted to pitch the idea for a communications department to my law firm, I created a compelling business plan to show decision makers. I outlined all the advantages to creating a communications department and highlighted what our competitors were doing in that area. I remembered my boss saying to me many years ago, "You know we don't advertise, right?" Traditionally, law firms were not allowed to advertise. Those rules have loosened up, but some lawyers still find the process off-putting. They want that all-powerful earned media. It is a powerful marketing tool in and of itself, and it is prestigious because it is saying you are important enough for the media to seek you out. It also equals low marketing expenses. So I focused on this aversion to advertising and preference for earned media when I was pitching the development of a communications team at the firm.

I bought a book called *Anatomy of a Business Plan* (Pinson, 2008), which was helpful for my pitch. I did not use all of the categories of the business plan because that was not necessary, nor will it be for your plan. After all, you are not starting a brick and mortar business but simply doing an internal pitch. Below are the categories I adopted from the book and applied to the world of podcasting:

Executive Summary: "The Executive Summary is the abstract of your business plan, ... specifies who you are, ... where your company is going, ... and how it will get there" (Pinson 22). For example, you can include what the podcast will be covering, its program format, frequency, topics, why it will be successful, a mission statement, leadership teams, employees, and location, if applicable. Do not forget your target market, i.e., your ideal audience.

After the summary, break your pitch down into the following:

- **Opportunity**: Describe the void the podcast will fill. Then show why a podcast will work and what solutions it will bring to your current customers or clients, as well as potential customers and clients.
- **Market Analysis**: Look at your competitors. Do they have a podcast? If so, what type of content are they creating? Is it working for them, and, if so, how can you make yours better? Look at the trends and themes being discussed.
- **The Podcast**: Describe in detail the topics you will cover in the podcast by creating an editorial calendar. Explain how the podcast will position the company executives as experts, and provide at least five samples of creative storytelling that tie into products and services. Also explain the benefits for your clients or customers and discuss the format and your expectations. Will you include only interviews with executives/management, or will you also invite outside guests to participate?
- **Funding Requirements**: Explain all the expenses that you will require to get the podcast up and running. Include the initial startup cost and then any monthly fees. Consider including whether or not you are going to hire a host and what cost that will entail. If your plan is to produce a high-quality podcast, then include the cost of podcasting equipment for in studio and equipment for being out in the field to capture ambient sound or conduct interviews off site. Also, determine if you will need to rent a studio. In other words, include all the expenses that will arise in creating this podcast from start to finish. It may help to create two versions of a budget: your dream budget with everything you could ask for, and a really slim budget that may be more attractive to decision makers who are unfamiliar with the power of podcasts.

As you have learned in previous chapters, there are various inexpensive podcasting platforms that produce high-quality sound and eliminate the need for expensive studios. Keep this in mind and weigh all of your options.

Podcasts and the Federal Communications Commission (FCC): The FCC is a U.S. federal agency in charge of regulating media communications, specifically radio, television, and phone industries. So you might be surprised to learn that podcasts are not yet regulated by the FCC. They are actually protected under the First Amendment, which states, "Congress shall make no law respecting an establishment of religion, or prohibiting the free exercise thereof; or abridging the freedom of speech, or of the press."

Tom Hutton, the deputy division chief of law in the Audio Division of the Media Bureau at the FCC, gave me a very lawyerly answer when I asked him if the FCC regulated podcasts: "The fact is that the FCC does not regulate podcasts as a matter of First Amendment law and our limited jurisdiction under the Communications Act of 1934, as amended." I have worked in the legal field for over twenty years, so I understood what he was saying. For those who are not in the legal field, the Communications Act of 1934 obviously doesn't cover podcasts or Internet radio. According to *Britannica*, "The 1934 act is built upon the Radio Act of 1927, which was a temporary measure when it was passed, intended to stabilize the burgeoning but chaotic radio industry of the mid-1920s. The 1934 act added communications via common carrier and television." So in a nutshell, the FCC does not regulate podcasts because they are not considered radio and are therefore outside of the agency's purview. (See *Insights*: Helen M. Maher.)

That said, the law is always evolving, and podcasts may one day come to be regulated by the FCC. Whether or not that day comes, FCC guidelines for other mediums can still be helpful when you are planning a company podcast. Issues surrounding things like native advertising are important to keep in mind, and if you include this knowledge in your business plan, you increase your chance of getting buy-in from decision makers (especially if any of them have a legal background).

Everyone has their own process of gathering information and creating their own plan for a pitch. What I've included here is simply a helpful guide. Just remember that the more detailed your plan, the better the chance you will get internal buy-in. Adhering to your company's conduct and polices is also extremely important. Another important factor is to make sure you create content that is not offensive, controversial or divisive, because you are always accountable to the employees and clients of your company.

Insights: Intellectual Property Laws: What Podcasters Should Know

Helen M. Maher

Helen M. Maher is a partner at Cadwalader, Wickersham & Taft LLP. Ranked by Benchmark as one of the top 250 female litigators in the United States and as a litigation star in New York, Helen has tried, argued, and litigated cases in federal and state courts throughout the country.

Helen Maher.

Podcasters should also be aware of certain key exceptions in copyright law that render otherwise copyrighted material useable. For instance, without seeking additional permission from the author, a podcast can include work that is in the public domain, which means either (1) the term of the copyright has expired; (2) the copyright owner did not follow copyright rules; or (3) the copyright owner has indicated the work has been given to the public domain. Additionally, the doctrine of "fair use" enables podcasters to use protected material for certain limited purposes including but not limited to parodying, news reporting, criticism, or teaching about the copyrighted material. (*See* Section 107 of the Copyright Act.)

Trademark law, like copyright law, prohibits the unauthorized use of certain protected materials (usually words, phrases, symbols, or designs). Trademark laws are violated when the protected mark is used in a way that is likely to cause "consumer confusion," or dilution by tarnishment or blurring. Tarnishment occurs when a protected mark is used to promote a seemingly offensive product or in a manner that disparages the protected mark. Blurring occurs when a mark is used to cause consumers to mistakenly associate an unprotected mark with a protected trademark. Podcasts can generally use trademarks for informational purposes or for mere reference, but risk infringing on the mark if it is used for commercial purposes.

Publicity laws prohibit the public use of someone's image, voice, or likeness from being used for commercial purposes. For example, if a podcast uses a celebrity's picture or likeness to advertise or promote the podcast, consent of the celebrity should be secured. Publicity rights are protected by state laws, so it's important to research them and know which ones apply to your situation.

Given the ever-changing laws, podcasters should consult with an attorney to be sure that the content of their podcasts are compliant with the relevant laws.

Insights: Using Podcasts to Build a Professional Reputation and Increase Business

Hillary Nappi

Hillary Nappi is an associate at Hach Rose Schirripa & Cheverie LLP who has been ranked as a Rising Star by Super Lawyers in New York. Hillary has litigated cases in many jurisdictions across the country. (April 2020)

Hillary Nappi.

You are a young lawyer trying to build your reputation and legal acumen while rising in the ranks at your law firm. You are feverishly working and billing, all while desiring the coveted office with a window and the title of partner.

There is a piece of information that no law school, book, or television show prepared you for. This information is crucial to your success, as it will enable you to build your book of business, bring in revenue for your firm and help you achieve your career goals.

The secret information is simple: in addition to being an advocate for your client, keeping up with current legal changes, networking and balancing your personal life, you also have to market and build a brand for yourself. A podcast can be an effective way to do just that.

As lawyers, we value efficiency. A targeted legal podcast can become your best marketing tool as it will showcase your area of expertise, help you form connections with clients and potential clients, and engage you in the larger conversation surrounding legal trends and cases.

So, how to get started? First, decide which aspect of your practice, or the legal profession, you would like to focus on. If you are a solo practitioner recovering from Big Law, you could interview others with similar career paths and discuss the changes you would like to see in the industry. If you are in a management position, you could interview lawyers of different generations and backgrounds about the conditions that help them do their best work.

However, perhaps the best way to leverage a podcast to create new business is to focus on your practice. The more niche, the better. Do you practice real estate law in Houston? Are you dedicated to fighting for the legal rights of elders? Are you a tax lawyer with a handful of high-net worth individuals? Even if you have a generalized, varied practice of complex commercial litigation, it will still help you to get specific: say you served as a prosecutor in Brooklyn—you could focus your podcast on decisions coming out of that court, inviting other experts in to discuss the implications.

If you are a solo practitioner, once you decide what your topics will be you can start getting the equipment, hiring a producer and lining up guests.

If you are in a larger firm, however, you will first need to clear your plans with the decision makers. Lawyers tend to be risk-adverse, and while podcasts are pretty well established in the media landscape at this point, some lawyers, especially those in older generations who have spent their careers in conservative Big Law firms, might still balk at the concept.

Create your pitch for your boss. This is a business idea, and the best business ideas are solutions to problems. Figure out a pain point or area of weakness for the firm. If they're known as a deal firm but want to bring in more litigation work, you could develop a podcast around, say, trends in antitrust law, or key cases coming out of Delaware. Explain the theme of your podcast as if you were talking to a jury—no big words, terms that everyone can understand. Come armed with data on all the other legal podcasts out there, the topics they cover, their listenership numbers, and lists of guests whom your boss admires or respects. Highlight the benefits to the firm and to your personal career development. Have a budget in place that includes production and publishing costs. Explain whom your target audience consists of and how you plan to collaborate (if at all) to be able to push out regular content.

If you aren't able to get buy-in from your firm on starting a podcast, or the whole process is just not for you, consider being a guest on another podcast. *Lawyer 2 Lawyer* is a popular, long-running podcast hosted by an attorney, J. Craig Williams, who discusses current events and cases from a legal perspective with guests in the industry. There are also dozens (and counting!) of more targeted legal podcasts that you could consider.

How do you get invited to be a guest on a legal podcast? If you are at a larger firm, you can enlist your marketing team. But there is also a lot you can do on your own. The first step is to find a podcast that is truly a good fit for you. If you practice criminal defense, listen to a few episodes of podcasts that cover the practice, such as *Criminal (In)justice*, *Reasonable Doubt*, and *Getting Off*. See which one you relate to, the one that makes you nod your head and think, "these people know what they're talking about."

It is also helpful to take tone into account: are you light-hearted, using a lot of humor and anecdotes in your life and practice? Or are you someone with more gravity, interested in serious debate or a thoughtful deconstruction of recent court decisions? Finding a host who matches your style will set you up for a successful interview.

Once you have chosen your target podcast(s), send a simple email, introducing yourself, complimenting the host on something specific you liked from a recent episode or their general style, and pitching them on a topic that you know would be of interest to their listeners (and at which you happen to be an expert, of course). Hosts are always looking for new guests who will resonate with their audience.

As a lawyer, you are constantly networking. This is no different. It is about showcasing your expertise but, more importantly, it is about building connections. If you are able to get your own podcast off the ground, every guest that comes on the show will be an opportunity for you to establish or strengthen a relationship, which can quickly lead to client work. And whether you are the host or a guest, every listener has the potential to become a client, too, as they are getting to know you in a way that feels both informal and intimate—even when you are speaking to hundreds or thousands of listeners at once. It doesn't get more efficient than that.

Insights: Best Ways to Monetize Your Podcast Guesting

Margy Feldhuhn *and* Jessica Rhodes

Margy Feldhuhn is CEO and co-owner of Interview Connections, a podcasting booking agency, with fellow co-owner and founder Jessica Rhodes. Feldhuhn and Rhodes are also co-hosts of Rock the Podcast *(adapted from an episode that aired on May 4, 2014).*

Being a guest on a podcast is one of the quickest and most effective ways to build more brand awareness. There are several different ways to monetize your podcast appearances.

When you are a guest on a podcast, hundreds—or thousands, or hundreds of thousands—of people are going to hear your interview. This can raise

Margy Feldhuhn (left) and Jessica Rhodes (right).

your credibility and brand awareness, which can be a great source of new business. But you have to approach it strategically to make the most of it.

One of the best ways to leverage your appearance is also the most overlooked: forming a bond with the podcast host directly. People often focus so much on the audience that they neglect the potential for a connection with the host. This is a big mistake. Remember, the reason you are being asked on the show is because the host considers you an expert in the field or subject area that the podcast covers. The host knows you're credible before you walk in the door. If you have a good connection during the interview, you will not only impress the listeners, but there's a good chance you will impress the host, too—and that can be extremely lucrative if you play it right.

We spend a lot of time talking about the potential here, because it really is a mindset shift for people. Many people go on a podcast thinking, "This is something I'm doing for the media exposure and to connect with listeners." The shift comes when you start to think of it first and foremost as a networking opportunity.

Just recently we were guests on a podcast, and at the end of the interview the host said, "I need to schedule a call with you two." We now have a consultation scheduled. Another time, the podcast host had a book coming out and he said after the interview that he would reach out to set up a date to talk to us about helping him promote it.

We have experienced this many times. Sometimes the host becomes a client. Other times, they become a strong source of referrals, sending potential clients our way. Hosts can also become affiliates for your course or programs.

They could also book you to speak at an event or conference. Being interviewed on a podcast is a terrific opportunity to build a professional relationship that can be fruitful in so many ways.

Following the actual interview, there are many other ways to leverage your appearance to get more business. Be sure to ask the host or producer for a link or copy of the podcast, as well as the air date if it's scheduled to run at later time. Then, send the episode out to prospective clients via your social media channels and newsletter or email lists. Your appearance on the show is an opportunity to get exposure to a new audience, but you don't want to overlook the fact that you now have a produced, featured, spotlight interview about your story and your expertise. This will help increase your positioning and credibility, and is a great way for current and prospective clients to learn more about you in a different, more intimate light. One major client of ours uses his podcasts in his newsletters and emails to prospective clients regularly as a big part of his communications and outreach strategy.

You also want to be sure and leverage your connection to the audience of the podcast you're on, and to do so strategically. In order to do that, you need to have some type of "nurture strategy" in place. It doesn't have to be overly complicated, but you need an easy way for listeners to connect with you and then to nurture them into potential clients.

For example: We use a text opt-in through a service called Call Loop. Most people listen to podcasts on their phones or another mobile device, so it's really easy for them to send a text in the moment, before they forget. Then we ask them to opt-in to join our Facebook group, which is where we really get to work on nurturing our leads. We're doing free training all the time on Facebook and work hard to engage our group.

If you also host your own podcast, then you have another great opportunity to nurture those leads. Ask the host to plug your show, or do so yourself during the interview. This sort of cross-promotion tends to be quite successful, because you are speaking to an audience that is clearly interested in your area of expertise. Converting them to listeners of your own show will get them one step closer to becoming clients.

There are a lot of other simple ways to monetize your guest appearances. One of our clients simply gives out his personal email address on the air and says, "Email me!" It works really well for him. He gets leads reaching out and he tracks them. Of course, if you take this approach, you have to make sure you're organized enough to keep track of these people and get them into your sales pipeline.

A crucial part of monetizing your time as a podcast guest is to give a compelling interview. This may seem really obvious, but if you want to monetize any type of content, the content needs to be good. So give a good interview. People will go to the ends of the earth to find you if your content is incredible and you solve the problem that they have.

To set yourself up for an excellent, compelling interview that will have clients knocking down your door, here are a few tips:

- **Research**. If you're just going on a podcast for the fun of it, then feel free to wing it. But if you're serious about monetizing podcast guesting, then you should be taking these interviews seriously. You should be preparing for them. You should research the show you're going on and see what the tone is, what topics they typically cover, and what their audience demographics are. Learn about the host's background, not just in regards to the topic at hand but any other points of connection as well. Like visiting someone's home, you want to put your best foot forward and be a gracious guest.
- **Prepare your content.** Great content is the number one way to monetize your appearance. We have listened to podcast interviews with guests who had great content, but their call to action was unclear. We got so much value from them that we took the trouble to Google them to find their website and figure out how to get in touch. If your content is really good and you're giving great stories and valuable tips and advice, those listeners are jotting down notes. They will find you! (But of course, it's best to cover your bases with a clear call to action.)
- **Practice**. Ask friends or family members to ask you questions relating to your interview. Record your answers and play them back for yourself and/or others who will give you honest, helpful feedback.
- **Tell a story**. We all have interesting anecdotes from our business and life. Think them through, and hone them to give the greatest impact. The more stories you have during your interview, the more people will remember you and the better you will connect with them. A compelling narrative gets stuck in our heads as much as catchy tune. The most effective stories are either emotionally resonant or funny—or both! Are you a single parent? Did you serve in the armed forces? Do you have a success story about a client that paints a picture of how your service improves people's lives? Have at least four or five of those (on-brand) stories in mind so that you're ready to deliver them in a natural way.
- **Be consistent.** Do a lot of these interviews. Even people who really appreciate your content and want to reach out to you in the moment often get distracted or otherwise forget or neglect to heed your call to action. Maybe they are driving while listening, for example, and by the time they park, they're on to a different episode, or their mind is somewhere else. Luckily, most podcast listeners tune in pretty voraciously. If you keep doing appearances, that's when you start to really stick in their minds. If you just go on one podcast one time and expect to monetize it in a significant way, you're kind of asking for lightning to strike twice in one spot. Once you start building that momentum, it gets much easier to monetize.
- **Be yourself.** It can feel like a lot of pressure being interviewed on air. But, once you've done your research on the host and show, and are prepared and have practiced your content with compelling stories and a call to action, now it's time to relax. Once you're in the studio, focus

on forming a genuine connection with the host and letting the listener get to know the real you. That's how powerful connections are made.

Monetizing your podcast doesn't have to be complicated, but you definitely want to have a strategy in place. You are putting yourself in front of a very targeted audience and a host who probably has a lot of valuable connections in your field. Nurture those connections. Be polite to the host, and always send a thank-you note. Have a clear place to send the listeners, who are now your prospective clients, and remember to do something with them once they get there! Above all, focus first on being a great guest and giving listeners content that they will value and appreciate.

Chapter Review

Businesses have been late to the game in using podcasts as a marketing tool. Now, they are slowly catching on. Podcasts build strong relationships with an audience, create brand awareness, and enable listeners to enjoy spending quality time with excellent content.

A professional podcast can increase traffic to your company's website and bring new business. It also presents you as an expert and has global reach. It is inexpensive to create, but remember that you will need a proper business plan to present to the decision makers of your company. Always be clear on why you want to create this podcast, who you are targeting, and what message you would like to convey. Include a realistic budget. Do your research on whether subscribing to a podcasting platform will do, or if you need to produce a higher budget podcast and rent a studio. Podcasts are not regulated, but that doesn't mean, as a business, you should produce offensive and unethical material. Remember, you are accountable to your stockholders and/or customers, so be sure that your podcast meets your company's code of conduct and adheres with all policy that effects clients and employees.

Work on the discussion questions and exercises below to help deepen your knowledge of the subject.

Exercises and Discussion Questions

a. Compare and contrast Morgan Stanley's *Ideas* podcast with American Airlines' *Tell Me Why* podcast. Discuss your first impressions of each podcast.

b. Keeping those two podcasts in mind, do you think that ambient sound makes a difference? Please explain your answer in detail, whether you agree or disagree.

c. An audio postcard is a short audio clip that uses only ambient sounds to tell a story. Produce a one-minute audio postcard to effectively tell a story.

Resources

Morgan Stanley's *Ideas* podcast: https://www.morganstanley.com/ideas/morgan-stanley-ideas-podcast

American Airlines' *Tell Me Why* podcast: https://soundcloud.com/american-airlines-internal-news

Federal Communications Commission: https://www.fcc.gov/

Hootsuite: https://hootsuite.com

HubSpot: https://www.hubspot.com

SproutSocial: https://sproutsocial.com

Conclusions: The Final Presentation

I hope you enjoyed reading this book as much as I enjoyed writing it. My goal was to arm you with all the information you will need to make educated and thoughtful decisions when it comes to creating your own show. Whether you are in the academic world, a business professional, or an individual looking for a comprehensive overview of all things podcasting, I hope *The Podcast Handbook: Create It, Market It, Make It Great* will remain a valuable reference for years to come.

For your final project, you must either create a podcast using the tools you have learned in this guide, or create a business plan to present to your company. Choose from the options below. Happy podcasting!

a. **Option 1**: By now you should know what content and format you would like your podcast to be. Go all out and create your first fully produced podcast. Using everything you have learned here, produce a 15-minute podcast.

- Write a paper in which you describe your podcast and the premier show. Be sure to include your research topic, potential guest(s), programming format, script, pitch letter and talking points. Also include your experience with an editing platform, sharing about your experience if you did the editing yourself or hired someone.
- Invite a guest. Prepare talking points and pre-questions.
- If you cannot get a guest, grab a friend and ask the person to play the role so that you can experience engaging in a question-and-answer environment.
- Use the tools that you learned in this book.
- Post the podcast on your social media platform(s).

b. **Option 2**: You are a communications specialist and you want to sell your company on creating a podcast. Using the information you learned in chapter 19, create a business plan for your company and describe the podcast you would like to produce for it.

- Be sure to include your research topic, potential guest(s), programming format, script, pitch letter and talking points.
- Be sure to include budget, equipment and platform choices.
- Use the tools that you learned to create a compelling plan.

Bibliography

Addy. (2018, July 18). *The difference between serial and episodic podcasts.* Simplecast. https://help.simplecast.com/en/articles/2715214-the-difference-between-serial-and-episodic-podcasts

Barnouw, E. (1966). *A Tower of Babel: A history of broadcasting in the United States.* New York: Oxford University Press.

Belt, D. (2016, September 15). Ravens' John Harbaugh picks at "BoogerGate" claims about brother. *Annapolis Patch*, https://patch.com/maryland/annapolis/ravens-john-harbaugh-picks-boogergate-claims-brother.

Boris, V. (2017, December 20). What makes storytelling so effective for learning? Harvard Business Publishing Corporate Learning, https://www.harvardbusiness.org/what-makes-storytelling-so-effective-for-learning/.

Companies turning more to podcasting to Brand. (2019, August 21). Podcast Business Journal. https://podcastbusinessjournal.com/companies-turning-more-to-podcasting-to-brand/

Corbett, R. (2016). *Do you need a "radio voice" to host a podcast?* Rachel Corbett's PodSchool. https://rachelcorbett.com.au/podcast-hosting-voice/

Creech, K.C. (1996). *Electronic media law and regulation.* Boston: Focal Press.

D'Anza, J. (2018, August 21). *Podcast production planning, skillsets, and time needed.* Learning Solutions. https://learningsolutionsmag.com/articles/podcast-production-planning-skillsets-and-time-needed

Duggal, R. (2018, May 29). The one marketing truism you cannot ignore: Perception is reality. *Forbes*, https://www.forbes.com/sites/forbescommunicationscouncil/2018/05/29/the-one-marketing-truism-you-cannot-ignore-perception-is-reality/?sh=2feff7f57030.

Edison Research and Triton Digital. (2019). *The infinite dial 2019.* Edison Research. http://www.edisonresearch.com/wp-content/uploads/2019/03/Infinite-Dial-2019-PDF-1.pdf

Fair, L. (2016, March 15). *FTC's Lord & Taylor case: In native advertising, clear disclosure is always in style.* Federal Trade Commission. https://www.ftc.gov/news-events/blogs/business-blog/2016/03/ftcs-lord-taylor-case-native-advertising-clear-disclosure

Gallagher, D. (1999, September 10). Snake River jump launched generations of daredevils. [Vancouver, WA] *Columbian*, p. B8.

Geyser, Werner. (2021, September 24). *How to podcast: A reliable guide to get you started with your podcast.* Influencer Marketing Hub. https://influencermarketinghub.com/how-to-podcast/

Hammersley, B. (2004, February 11). Audible revolution. *The Guardian.* https://www.theguardian.com/media/2004/feb/12/broadcasting.digitalmedia

Havsy, J. (1998, November 16). Other options during the lockout. *Journal News*, p. 36.

IAB. (2019, June 3). *IAB FY 2018 podcast ad revenue study.* IAB. https://www.iab.com/insights/third-annual-podcast-ad-revenue-study-by-iab-and-pwc-reports-significant-growth/

Ingraham, N. (2012, June 26). *Apple releases dedicated podcasts app for iPhone and iPad.* The Verge. https://www.theverge.com/2012/6/26/3118820/apple-podcasts-app-release

Last, S. (2017, June 12). *Why marketers shouldn't tune out podcast advertising.* Marketing Drive. https://www.marketingdive.com/news/why-marketers-shouldnt-tune-out-podcast-advertising/444356/

Lee, J. (n.d.). *18 life-changing tips for keeping a journal.* BuzzFeed. https://www.buzzfeed.com/jarrylee/life-changing-tips-for-keeping-a-journal

Leist, R. (2020, February 18). *The definition of SEO in 100 words or less.* Hubspot. https://blog.hubspot.com/marketing/what-is-seo

Lord & Taylor, LLC, No. C-4576, at 3–7 (F.T.C. May 20, 2016).

Maron, M. (2018, October 22). *Episode 961—John Cleese.* Listen Notes. https://www.listennotes.com/podcasts/wtf-with-marc/episode-961-john-cleese-EV0GIbMz4ST/

Mashayekhi, R. (2019, May 30). *Investment banks are pressing 'play' on podcasts.* Fortune. https://fortune.com/2019/05/30/investment-banks-are-pressing-play-on-podcasts/

Maud Purcel, L. C. (2018, October 18). *The health benefits of journaling.* PsychCentral. https://psychcentral.com/lib/the-health-benefits-of-journaling/

Messitte, N. (2018, May 15). *11 tips for mixing and sound-designing a fiction podcast.* iZotope. https://www.izotope.com/en/learn/11-tips-for-mixing-and-sound-designing-a-fiction-podcast.html

Moulton, S. (n.d.). *World history 1600–1900, history of radio.* Study. https://study.com/academy/lesson/history-of-the-radio.html

Nycz-Conner, J. (2008, February 8). *Dixie Consumer Products signs sponsorship deal with MommyCast.* BizJournals. https://www.bizjournals.com/washington/stories/2008/02/04/daily57.html.

The old time radio scripts page! (n.d.). Simply Scripts. https://www.simplyscripts.com/radio_all.html

Paul, F. (2008, January 31). *Amazon to buy Audible for $300 million.* Reuters. https://www.reuters.com/article/us-audible-amazon/amazon-to-buy-audible-for-300-million-idUSN3129158120080131

Pettit, H. (2019, October 10). Dead strange: Mysterious Egyptian coffin covered with "nonsense hieroglyphics" baffles archaeologists. *The Sun,* https://www.thesun.co.uk/tech/10104942/ancient-egyptian-coffin-hieroglypics-practical-joke/.

Pinson, L. (2008). *Anatomy of a business plan: The step-by-step guide to building a business and securing your company's future. Out of your mind and into the marketplace.* Tustin, CA: Out of Your Mind … and Into the Marketplace.

Prudente, T. (2019, April 8). Adnan Syed, of 'Serial' podcast, asks Maryland high court to reconsider decision refusing him a new trial. *Baltimore Sun.* https://www.baltimoresun.com/news/crime/bs-mdi-ci-adnan-syed-reconsideration-20190408-story.html

Quah, N. (2019, September 30). *We're entering the era of big podcasting.* Vulture. https://www.vulture.com/2019/09/podcasting-history-three-eras.html

Quah, N. (2019, October 1). *The 10 nonfiction podcasts that changed everything.* Vulture. https://www.vulture.com/article/best-nonfiction-podcasts-all-e.html

Quah, N. (2019, October 03). *The 10 essential fiction podcasts that shaped the genre.* Vulture. https://www.vulture.com/article/best-fiction-pocasts-all-time.html

Rodriguez-Zaba, D. (2019, June 20). *How to build a strong team culture in seven steps.* Forbes. https://www.forbes.com/sites/forbeschicagocouncil/2019/06/20/how-to-build-a-strong-team-culture-in-seven-steps/#2b894a3361a6

Saylor, M. J. (1999). *Evolution of radio broadcasting.* Saylor Academy. https://saylordotorg.github.io/text_understanding-media-and-culture-an-introduction-to-mass-communication/s10–01-evolution-of-radio-broadcastin.html

Skretvedt, R. (2018, November 15). *Radio broadcasting.* Encyclopedia Britannica. https://www.britannica.com/topic/radio

Slaney, R. (2018, August 14). Guardian podcasts—the very best of our audio journalism. *Guardian.* https://www.theguardian.com/media/2016/sep/14/podcasts

Statista. (2021, March 31). *Share of smartphone users that use an Apple iPhone in the United States from 2014 to 2021.* Statista. https://www.statista.com/statistics/236550/percentage-of-us-population-that-own-a-iphone-smartphone/

Stern, R. (2018, February 23). *Podcasting in Europe: Is an American trend crossing the Atlantic?* European Journalism Observatory. https://en.ejo.ch/specialist-journalism/podcasting-in-europe-is-an-american-trend-crossing-the-atlantic

Stidham, L. (2009, January 12). *Super moms juggle seven kids and a business with 'MommyCast'* Tubefilter. https://www.tubefilter.com/2009/01/12/super-moms-juggle-seven-kids-and-a-business-in-mommycast/

Sullivan, J. (2019, October 9). Marc Maron has shed his bitter self for a better self. *Boston Globe*. https://www.bostonglobe.com/arts/2019/10/09/marc-maron-has-shed-his-bitter-self-for-better-self/7fwvoW0KNGLTjmJCQ5zYBL/story.html

Swant, M. (2016, June 3). *ComScore says people prefer ads in podcasts over any other digital medium*. AdWeek. http://www.adweek.com/digital/comscore-says-people-prefer-ads-podcasts-over-any-other-digital-medium-171804/

Urban, J. (2016, June 17). *Millennial sports fans win: 3 stats that prove social sports is where the game is*. MediaPost. https://www.mediapost.com/publications/article/278343/millennial-sports-fans-win-3-stats-that-prove-soc.html

Whetmore, E. J. (1981). *The magic medium: An introduction to radio in America*. Belmont, CA: Wadsworth.

Whitner, G. (2021, April 7). *Podcast statistics (2021)—[Infographic]*. Music Oomph. https://musicoomph.com/podcast-statistics/

Yaffe-Bellany, D. (2019, August 20). Welcome to McDonald's. Would you like a podcast with that? *New York Times*. https://www.nytimes.com/2019/08/20/business/media/branded-podcasts.html

Index